Mastering NGINX for Site Reliability and Performance Optimization

Master Web Server Configuration, Load Balancing, Traffic Optimization with NGINX for Scalable and High-Performance Systems

Richa Garg

www.orangeava.com

First Published: May 2025

Published By: Orange Education Pvt Ltd, AVA®

Address: 9, Daryaganj, Delhi, 110002, India

275 New North Road Islington Suite 1314 London,
N1 7AA, United Kingdom

ISBN (PBK): 978-93-48107-17-6
ISBN (E-BOOK): 978-93-48107-81-7

Scan the QR code to explore our entire catalogue

www.orangeava.com

Dedicated To

My Beloved Mom,

Late Sunita Agarwal, My Guardian Angel

My Dad,

Rakesh Agarwal, For the Dream You Planted

About the Author

Richa Garg brings a wealth of hands-on experience and deep technical expertise in the field of **Site Reliability Engineering (SRE)**. With over nine years of industry experience, she has progressed from a college intern at **Dell Technologies** to a seasoned leader. She now leads a team that manages critical SRE operations for enterprise-grade applications.

Her journey is a testament to adaptability and technical excellence. As an SRE for Dell's **$70 billion e-commerce platform**, Richa played a pivotal role in transitioning **Dell.com** to a hybrid cloud infrastructure using **NGINX**. This resulted in significantly improved ecosystem availability and a marked reduction in production incidents.

Her technical skill set includes **CI/CD pipelines, automation**, and **advanced observability using Splunk**. She is also proficient in essential networking technologies such as **GTM, LTM, SSL, firewalls, DNS**, and **routing**. Richa has represented Dell at leading industry conferences and earned accolades for her impactful contributions to **migration strategies** and **digital transformation initiatives**.

Beyond her engineering achievements, Richa is a passionate **public speaking coach**. She has mentored over **100 students** in her home city—including schoolchildren, adults, and even aspiring politicians—helping them find their voice and express themselves with clarity and confidence.

In her free time, Richa enjoys music, painting, journaling, and dancing, finding balance and creativity both in and out of the tech world. She loves exploring the world, one place at a time, with her husband—her biggest cheerleader and companion through it all. While working on this book, she has also been navigating a deeply personal chapter in her life—one that has brought new perspective, quiet strength, and a renewed sense of purpose. Her writing draws from real-world experience, offering readers practical insights into building and maintaining large-scale, resilient systems.

About the Technical Reviewer

Neeraj Singh brings 15 years of experience in Data Engineering, Middleware, and Database Architecture and Administration. His expertise encompasses overseeing complex data engineering projects, designing middleware solutions, and managing databases across diverse environments while ensuring system reliability, scalability, and security. Neeraj has refined his skills in optimizing database performance and streamlining middleware processes, consistently delivering high-quality results. His strategic approach combines cutting-edge technologies and best practices to enhance data workflows, improve system interoperability, and support business intelligence initiatives. He has worked across industries such as global transportation and logistics, retail, food and beverage, recycling, and more.

Currently, Neeraj serves as a Technical Manager in the Data Engineering practice at Rackspace Technology, where he leads the implementation and optimization of automated data pipelines to ensure high-quality, reliable, and scalable data delivery. He plays a key role in implementing new technologies and streamlining workflows to enhance data efficiency, scalability, and reliability. Additionally, he manages resources, budgets, and timelines to ensure the successful completion of projects that align with business needs.

Acknowledgements

I would like to express my deepest gratitude to Dell Technologies, the company where my professional journey began. Joining as a fresher, Dell has shaped me into a seasoned engineer and gifted me with some of the finest learning experiences in the industry.

A heartfelt thanks to T. Sita, Murali M V, Kunal Mehta, and N. Venna for recognizing and encouraging my potential. I am especially grateful to Nagarajan Thiruvellore (fondly known as TP) and Scott Mosqueda for introducing me to the world of NGINX and entrusting me with opportunities to lead and grow in this domain.

I am thankful to my mentor Midhun Prasad R for helping me refine my technical skills and for his invaluable feedback and review of this book. His guidance has been instrumental. I also sincerely thank Anoop Kumar P for taking the time to read the manuscript and offer thoughtful suggestions, and Sanket Pandey for reading through the chapters and providing valuable insights. Their collective support has made this work far stronger than I could have achieved alone.

I would like to thank my amazing team and colleagues at Dell, for their constant collaboration, camaraderie, and support—working with them has been one of the most rewarding aspects of my journey.

To my rock, my husband Archit Bidawatka— I thank him for his endless support, belief, and strength. I extend my gratitude to my sister Meghna, my brother Shivansh, my brother-in-law Tanshiq, and my wonderful father-in-law and mother-in-law for believing in me and pushing me forward every step of the way.

I thank my friends for the timely encouragement and confidence that kept me going.

And finally, to you, the reader—thank you for choosing this book as your companion in learning NGINX. I hope it becomes a trusted and empowering resource throughout your journey.

Foreword

- Nagarajan T P

Senior Director, Dell Technologies

The Shift to Microservices and the Role of Nginx

Enterprise architecture has evolved dramatically–from monolithic systems (2000–2015) to agile, scalable microservices post-2015. While this shift brings flexibility and faster deployments, it also introduces significant complexity. In monoliths, even minor changes required full redeployment, risking cascading failures. Microservices address this by enabling independent, parallel development and deployment, accelerating innovation in today's competitive digital landscape.

Microservices align well with CI/CD, enabling rapid iteration and faster feedback. They support polyglot programming and multi-cloud setups, boosting resilience and reducing vendor lock-in. However, their distributed nature adds complexity in service discovery, routing, load balancing, and fault tolerance.

In this complex environment, Nginx serves as a key orchestrator, functioning as a load balancer, reverse proxy, and API gateway for large-scale systems. It standardizes traffic control, security, and observability across diverse tech stacks, simplifying operations and ensuring consistent policies. This streamlines disaster recovery, strengthens security with centralized controls, and supports multicloud strategies, enhancing performance, cost-efficiency, and continuity.

Richa's Expertise in Action

Richa, a pioneer in large-scale Nginx deployment in e-commerce, brings battle-tested expertise. From Dell to leading cloud-agnostic traffic migration adopted by top firms and recognized by CII, she's known for scalable, robust architecture–making her a rare industry asset.Your Guide to Scalable Nginx Deployments

Your Guide to Scalable Nginx Deployments

This book distills Richa's expertise into a practical, jargon-free guide to deploying Nginx at scale, offering real-world examples and actionable insights for both seasoned architects and newcomers in enterprise settings.

Preface

In the ever-evolving world of web infrastructure, performance, scalability, and reliability are non-negotiable. **NGINX**, a high-performance web server and reverse proxy, has emerged as the backbone of modern digital architecture. Welcome to *Mastering* NGINX *for Site Reliability and Performance Optimization* –a hands-on journey crafted from real-world experience and industry best practices.

This book comprises **12 practical chapters**, each designed as a standalone module to help readers deeply understand NGINX–from installation and configuration to advanced features such as canary testing, caching, performance tuning, and security. Whether you are an aspiring DevOps engineer, a developer looking to build scalable apps, or an SRE handling critical web infrastructure, this book is your go-to guide.

Packed with exercises, examples, and real-world scenarios, this book blends clarity with depth. Let us dive into the chapters that await you on this journey.

Chapter 1. Introduction to NGINX: This chapter helps you start your NGINX journey with a clear understanding of what NGINX is, why it matters, and how it compares with other technologies such as Apache. This chapter covers installation across various platforms, and introduces commands to manage the NGINX service effectively.

Chapter 2. Get Started with Nginx Configurations: This chapter focuses on the building blocks of an NGINX configuration file. Learn about directives, contexts (such as HTTP, stream, and events), variables, and how to validate syntax. With step-by-step examples and hands-on exercises, this chapter prepares you to write and interpret NGINX configs confidently.

Chapter 3. Load Balancing: This chapter explores how NGINX distributes traffic across multiple servers for optimized performance and fault tolerance. Understand upstreams, load-balancing methods such as round robin and session persistence, and how to configure each with clarity and control.

Chapter 4. Health Checks: This chapter dives into the significance of active and passive health checks in ensuring application availability. This chapter walks you through HTTP, UDP, and gRPC health checks with detailed examples and practical configurations.

Chapter 5. NGINX Plus API: This chapter discovers the power of NGINX's dynamic API and how it enables real-time configuration changes. Learn to secure the API, interact with maps, split-clients, and key-value pairs–laying the groundwork for advanced use cases such as canary deployments.

Chapter 6. Canary Testing with NGINX: This chapter delves in what canary testing, A/B testing, and blue-green deployments are–and how to implement them using NGINX. This chapter leverages maps, split-clients, and API integrations to demonstrate traffic routing between different upstreams with precision.

Chapter 7. NGINX as a Web Server: This chapter discovers how NGINX shines not just as a reverse proxy but also as a capable web server. Learn how to serve static content efficiently and implement compression for optimized performance.

Chapter 8. Caching in Nginx: This chapter understands how to cache both static and dynamic content to accelerate delivery and reduce backend load. Explore request/response caching, byte-range caching, purging, and tuning for efficient cache control.

Chapter 9. Advanced Activity Monitoring: This chapter details how to enable and use the NGINX dashboard to monitor real-time traffic and metrics. Dive into setting zones and using the NGINX API to collect custom metrics for deeper observability.

Chapter 10. Debugging and Troubleshooting NGINX: This chapter explores methods to effectively trace and debug NGINX errors. Learn how to configure access and error logs, correlate log data, and perform request tracing to troubleshoot issues in production systems.

Chapter 11. Performance Enhancements: This chapter fine-tunes NGINX for high performance. This chapter explains how to tune worker processes, enable keepalive connections, manage buffers, and apply OS-level tuning for optimal throughput and response time.

Chapter 12. Security with NGINX: This chapter secures your applications behind NGINX with built-in features such as rate limiting, IP whitelisting, and geo-restrictions. Learn to protect both HTTP and TCP traffic, and implement security best practices for robust application defense.

This book is more than just a reference—it is a roadmap shaped by real production experience. Whether you are deploying your first web server or scaling a global application, this guide will empower you to make the most of what NGINX has to offer.

Let's begin.

Get a Free eBook

We hope you are enjoying your recently purchased book! Your feedback is incredibly valuable to us, and to all other readers looking for great books.

If you found this book helpful or enjoyable, we would truly appreciate it, if you could take a moment to leave a short review with a 5 star rating on Amazon. It helps us grow, and lets other readers discover our books.

As a thank you, we would love to send you a free digital copy of this book, and a **30%** discount code on your next cart value on our official websites:

www.orangeava.com

www.orangeava.in (For Indian Subcontinent)

☑ **Here's how:**

Leave a review for the book on Amazon.

Take a screenshot of your review, and send an email to **info@orangeava.com** (it can be just the confirmation screen).

Once, we receive your screenshot, we will send you the digital file, within 24 hours.

Thank you so much for your support – it means a lot to us!

Downloading the code bundles and colored images

Please follow the links or scan the QR codes to download the ***Code Bundles and Images*** of the book:

https://github.com/ava-orange-education/Mastering-NGINX-for-Site-Reliability-and-Performance-Optimization

The code bundles and images of the book are also hosted on ***https://rebrand.ly/17234f***

In case there's an update to the code, it will be updated on the existing GitHub repository.

Errata

We take immense pride in our work at **Orange Education Pvt Ltd,** and follow best practices to ensure the accuracy of our content to provide an indulging reading experience to our subscribers. Our readers are our mirrors, and we use their inputs to reflect and improve upon human errors, if any, that may have occurred during the publishing processes involved. To let us maintain the quality and help us reach out to any readers who might be having difficulties due to any unforeseen errors, please write to us at :

errata@orangeava.com

Your support, suggestions, and feedback are highly appreciated.

DID YOU KNOW

Did you know that Orange Education Pvt Ltd offers eBook versions of every book published, with PDF and ePub files available? You can upgrade to the eBook version at **www.orangeava.com** and as a print book customer, you are entitled to a discount on the eBook copy. Get in touch with us at: **info@orangeava.com** for more details.

At **www.orangeava.com**, you can also read a collection of free technical articles, sign up for a range of free newsletters, and receive exclusive discounts and offers on Print Books and eBooks.

PIRACY

If you come across any illegal copies of our works in any form on the internet, we would be grateful if you would provide us with the location address or website name. Please contact us at **info@orangeava.com** with a link to the material.

ARE YOU INTERESTED IN AUTHORING WITH US?

If there is a topic that you have expertise in, and you are interested in either writing or contributing to a book, please write to us at **business@orangeava.com**. We are on a journey to help developers and tech professionals to gain insights on the present technological advancements and innovations happening across the globe and build a community that believes Knowledge is best acquired by sharing and learning with others. Please reach out to us to learn what our audience demands and how you can be part of this educational reform. We also welcome ideas from tech experts and help them build learning and development content for their domains.

REVIEWS

Please leave a review. Once you have read and used this book, why not leave a review on the site that you purchased it from? Potential readers can then see and use your unbiased opinion to make purchase decisions. We at Orange Education would love to know what you think about our products, and our authors can learn from your feedback. Thank you!

For more information about Orange Education, please visit **www.orangeava.com**.

Table of Contents

CHAPTER 1
Introduction to Nginx

Introduction

Picture this: It's the year 2001. You are seated at a large, boxy computer system, the kind that used to be the pride of every home or office. In front of you, the CPU box stands tall, and beside it, your broadband modem's lights blink on and off. You open Internet Explorer– a browser that once ruled the internet and type "*yahoo.com*" into the address bar. As you hit enter, you wait eagerly for each pixel of Yahoo's homepage to fade into view. After a good few seconds, it finally loads. The relief and excitement of seeing that familiar purple logo, even after a short wait, feels almost magical.

Fast forward to today. In the blink of an eye, a webpage appears on our sleek mobile screens or compact laptops. We are no longer talking about waiting few seconds; instead, we measure load times in milliseconds. The journey from seconds to milliseconds represents more than just a numerical reduction; it symbolizes the tireless innovation driving the internet forward.

We are at a crucial point where customers don't like waiting for websites to load. With so many options available today, even a short delay can make people look for faster alternatives, which could mean losing business. Amazon estimated that a **1-second delay in page load time could result in a loss of approximately 1.6 billion dollars in annual sales**. This calculation was based on a correlation between site speed and revenue, as delays can lead to reduced customer satisfaction, increased abandonment rates, and fewer conversions.

Platforms such as Instagram further indicates how our patience has gotten shorter. We get hooked on quick snappy videos in just seconds. In a world brimming with choices, lightning-fast load times for websites have become an essential, not just a nice-to-have.

Well, what factors has contributed to making websites fast, robust, efficient, and scalable?

Drumroll.... its web servers!

Behind the scenes, web servers are the backbone of the digital infrastructure, ensuring that websites and online services are accessible to users around the clock.

As the volume of online traffic continues to surge and user expectations for speed and reliability soar, the need for web servers that can handle these demands with ease becomes paramount. Organizations and individuals alike rely on web servers to deliver content quickly, securely, and without interruption, regardless of the scale of their operations.

This explains why the significance of robust, efficient, and scalable web servers cannot be overstated. Amidst the plethora of options available, one name stands out prominently: **Nginx**.

Structure

In this chapter, the following topics will be covered:

- Understanding Nginx
- Load Balancer
- Nginx versus Apache
- Nginx versus Nginx Plus
- Basic Linux Commands
- Installing Nginx Open-Source Version
- Running Nginx on Docker
- Restarting, Reloading, Starting, and Stopping of Nginx

Understanding Nginx

Nginx, pronounced as "*Engine*-X", represents a paradigm shift in web server technology. Originally developed by Igor Sysoev in 2004 to address the challenges provided by traditional solutions of handling high concurrency, today Nginx has rapidly emerged as one of the most popular and widely used web servers in the world. Its *lightweight architecture*, *unparalleled performance*, and *extensive feature* set have made it the go-to choice for powering some of the busiest websites on the internet, including Netflix, Airbnb, and Dropbox.

But what exactly is Nginx, and what sets it apart from other web servers?

Nginx is:

- A popular **open-source** web server and reverse proxy server known for its high performance, low memory usage, and efficient handling of concurrent connections.
- A widely used **Hypertext Transfer Protocol (HTTP) Server** used by large-scale websites and applications to handle a significant amount of web traffic efficiently.

- A **proxy server** for email (IMAP, POP3, and SMTP) and a **reverse proxy server** and **load balancer** for HTTP, TCP, and UDP services.

The three major component that makes Nginx so popular are:

- **Efficiency and Stability**: Nginx exhibits remarkable efficiency and stability, due to its ability to excel under high-load scenarios. Whether serving static content, handling dynamic requests as reverse proxy, or acting as a load balancer, Nginx is an ideal choice for applications that demand unparalleled performance and reliability.
- **Versatility and Extensibility:** Nginx has earned acclaim for its versatility and extensibility. With a modular architecture and a rich ecosystem of third-party modules and extensions, Nginx can be customized and tailored to suit a diverse range of use cases. From serving as reverse proxy, caching content, **and** securing connections with SSL/TLS, to even functioning as a full-fledged application server through modules such as **`ngx_http_fastcgi`**, Nginx offers a level of flexibility that is unmatched by its counterparts.
- **Microservices Architectures and Containerization:** Nginx has emerged as a critical component in modern infrastructure setups with the rise of microservices architectures and containerization. Its lightweight footprint and seamless integration with cloud technologies including Docker and Kubernetes, Nginx has become an indispensable tool for orchestrating complex application deployments and managing network traffic within distributed systems.

In this book, we embark on a journey to explore the intricacies of Nginx, from its fundamental concepts to advanced configurations. Whether you are a seasoned web administrator, a DevOps engineer, or a curious tech enthusiast, this book will serve as your comprehensive guide to mastering Nginx and harnessing its full potential.

Since the start of this chapter, we have been repeatedly using words such as web server, reverse proxy server, and load balancer. Are you confused about what is the difference between the three? Let me help you refresh your knowledge.

Webserver

A web server is a hardware or software that accepts an HTTP request from clients, commonly a web browser and responds with an HTTP response (refer to *Figure 1.1*). Widely used webservers are IIS, Apache, Node.js, and Nginx.

Figure 1.1: *Web Server*

Reverse Proxy Server

Reverse proxy server is a hardware or software that acts as an intermediary between client and web server. Client makes an HTTP request to reverse proxy server. The reverse proxy server sends the same HTTP request to the web server. Web Server sends an HTTP response to the reverse proxy server. The reverse proxy server sends that data as its HTTP response back to the client (refer to *Figure* 1.2). Widely used reverse proxy servers are Apache, HAProxy, and Nginx.

Figure 1.2: *Reverse Proxy*

Load Balancer

A load balancer is a device, software application, or service that distributes client traffic across multiple servers or resources. The primary purpose of a load balancer is to ensure that no single server or resource becomes overwhelmed with too much traffic. There are different algorithms to load balance traffic which we will discuss more in detail in *Chapter 3, Load Balancing* (refer to *Figure 1.3*).

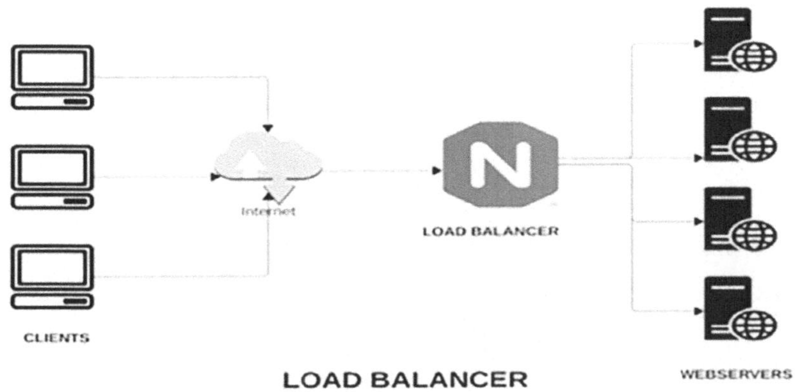

Figure 1.3: *Load Balancer*

Now that we have covered the fundamentals, let us deep dive into the unique Nginx architecture that makes Nginx so widely preferred over other available solutions in the market.

Nginx Architecture

Nginx's **Event-Driven**, **Asynchronous**, and **Non-blocking** architecture makes it high performing and widely trusted.

Let us understand this concept with a pizza shop analogy.

Imagine you own a pizza shop. You have

- Manager (master process)
- Staff (worker process)
- Head chef (cache manager) **and**
- Pre-prepared pizza ingredients (cache loader).

The job of the **manager** is to take customer order and manage the staff. Wherein the **staff** does the actual work of making the pizza.

The pizza shop prepares popular pizza's ingredients in advance and places them in a designated area (cache). When a customer orders a frequently requested pizza, the shop can quickly retrieve it from the pre-prepared cache, saving time compared to making it from scratch. (This analogy could be used to understand the task of a cache loader in Nginx.)

The cache manager would be the head chef responsible for monitoring and maintaining the cache (stock) of pre-prepared pizza ingredients. The cache manager ensures that the pizza shop efficiently uses its resources by having the right pizzas ready at the right time.

Now let us understand this in the context of Nginx.

Just like in a pizza shop we have a manager and multiple staffs; in Nginx we have one master process and multiple worker processes. The master process manages the worker processes. Imagine if the manager starts making pizzas for each customer, it will increase the waiting time for the customers substantially.

- When the Nginx Service is started, the master process is initialized. The master process performs privileged operations such as reading configuration, logging of requests, and binding to ports. It creates worker processes, cache loader and cache manager. It is also responsible for load balancing requests in a reverse proxy setup among worker processes.
- The worker processes do all the actual work! They handle network connections, read and write content to disk, do health checks, and handle client requests. It is also responsible for load balancing requests in a reverse proxy setup among the upstreams.
- The cache manager process runs periodically and checks entries in the disk where the cache is stored. It manages the content of the cache just like a Head Chef.
- When NGINX is restarted (or on initial startup during the setup), the cache loader scans the on-disk cache directory to identify any existing cached files and adds their metadata to memory. Once the metadata is in memory, NGINX can serve those previously cached files immediately—without waiting to re-request or recompute the content. Consider this just like pre-prepared pizza ingredients that are ready to be used to make the pizza.

Figure 1.4: *Master and Worker Process (Source: https://www.nginx.com/)*

When Nginx service is running, only the worker processes are busy. Each worker process is single-threaded and is responsible for executing new connections and processing them. The workers processes in turn communicate with each other using shared memory zones for shared cached data, session persistence data, and other shared resources. You will learn about this later in the book.

You can define the number of worker process as follows in the **nginx.conf** file, located in **/etc/nginx** path of your server.

```
worker_processes  auto;
OR
worker_processes  1;
OR
worker_processes  2;
OR
worker_processes  3;
```

Figure 1.5: *Number of worker process*

The number of worker process can be equal to or less than the CPU cores available.

How do you know how many worker processes are available in your nginx setup?

Go to your Linux terminal and type the following command:

```
grep -E 'processor core id' /proc/cpuinfo
```

You would observe something similar to *Figure 1.6*, which shows:

Figure 1.6: *CPU Processors*

The number of processors you see is the number of CPU cores you have. Here we have 2 CPU core in the system. So, we can set **`worker_process 1`**; or **`worker_process 2`**; or **`worker_process auto`**. It is suggested to always set it as **`worker_process auto`**; when you set the **`worker_process`** as auto, the nginx automatically adjusts the value to available CPU cores.

How do you validate the master process and worker process after your **Nginx** setup?

Type the following command in your terminal:

```
ps -ef -forest | grep nginx
```

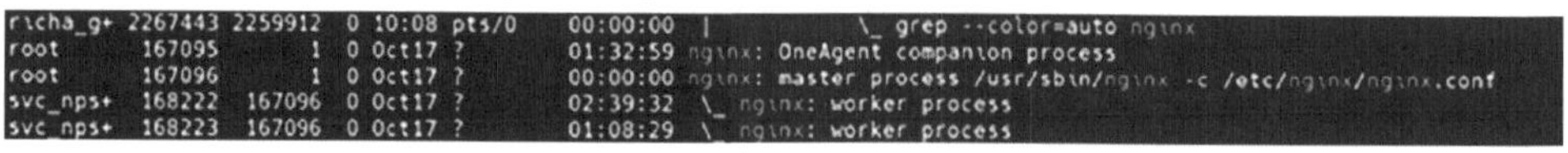

Figure 1.7: *Master and Worker Process*

In this example, you can see 1 master and 2 worker processes (refer to *Figure 1.7*).

Now that you know what master and worker processes are, we can now move to understand Nginx's **event-driven**, **asynchronous**, and **non-blocking** architecture.

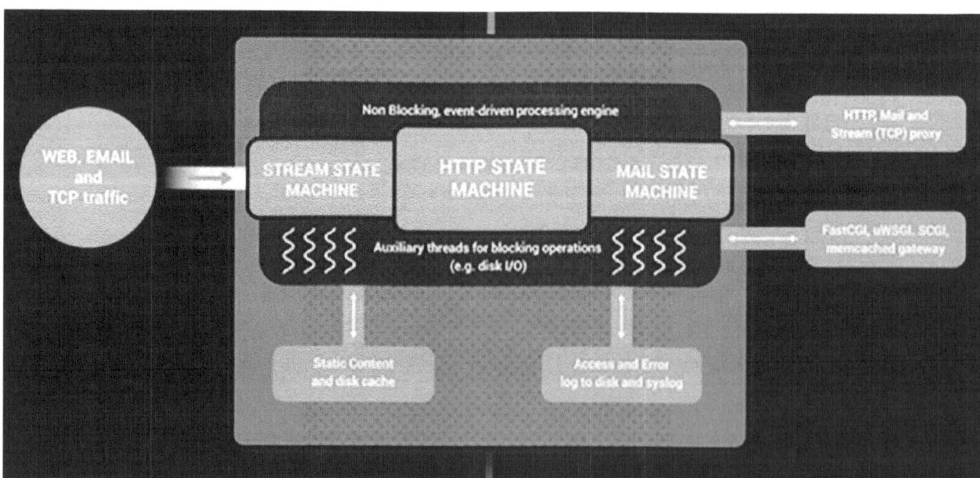

Figure 1.8: *Inside the NGINX Worker Process (Source: https://www.nginx.com/*

- **Event-Driven:** In an Event-driven architecture, instead of assigning a dedicated process or thread to each connection, NGINX employs a small number of worker processes that rely on an event loop. This loop uses system-level calls to execute I/O events and processes them as soon as they occur. This way Nginx is always ready to handle new concurrent connections efficiently without waiting.

Events can include things such as receiving a new connection, completing a read or write operation, reloading configuration, and so on. The event-driven model allows Nginx to respond quickly to various events without relying on a dedicated thread or process for each connection.

- **Asynchronous Processing:** Asynchronous processing is similar to the kitchen staff working on multiple pizza orders at the same time without waiting for each one to be fully ready before starting the next.

  Similarly, Nginx does not wait for one operation to complete before moving on to the next. For example, Nginx performs I/O operations, such as reading from or writing to a file, it does not block the execution of other tasks for example reloading configurations. Instead, it continues processing other events parallelly while waiting for I/O operations to complete.

  Hence, Nginx can handle a large number of concurrent connections efficiently, allowing it to utilize system resources more effectively.

- **Non-Blocking I/O:** It is similar to taking orders without stopping the entire pizza-making process. It allows the pizza shop to keep functioning smoothly even during busy times.

  Similarly, Nginx employs a non-blocking I/O model. This means that when an operation is requested such as reading data from a client, Nginx doesn't wait for the operation to complete before moving on to the next task. Instead, it continues to handle other events and requests.

  In summary, Nginx's event-driven, asynchronous, and non-blocking architecture allows it to efficiently handle a large number of concurrent connections with minimal resource consumption. These features are particularly beneficial in scenarios where high performance and scalability is required, such as Netflix.

Nginx Makes the Website More Secure

We host websites behind a reverse proxy to enhance their security. An e-commerce site such as Amazon might store sensitive data, such as personal information and payment details of the customers. This makes it crucial for both the web server and the reverse proxy server to be highly secure.

The following are a few ways Nginx makes the website more secure:

- **Restricts Access to Web Server Directly:** Reverse proxy is an intermediary between the client and the web server (*Figure 1.2*). With Nginx in place, web server's IP address is never exposed to the client. This makes it much harder for attackers to leverage a targeted attack, such as a DDoS attack. Nginx also has added security features such as IP blocking and Rate limiting, which we will learn in detail in the book later.

- **SSL Encryption:** A reverse proxy can be configured to decrypt all incoming requests before passing the request to the web server and encrypt all outgoing responses before sending it to the client. The encryption and decryption of requests are computationally expensive for the web server, hence also sharing the workload of the web server.
- **Rate Limiting:** Nginx provides rate limiting capabilities, allowing you to control the number of requests a client can make within a specified time (rate per minute or rate per second). This helps protect a website against various types of attacks, including brute-force attacks and DoS attacks.
- **Access Controls:** Nginx allows you to set up access controls to restrict or allow access to specific resources based on IP addresses, geographical locations, or other criteria. This helps in preventing unauthorized access to sensitive parts of the website.
- **Security Headers:** Nginx allows the configuration of security headers, such as Content Security Policy (CSP), Strict-Transport-Security (HSTS), and X-Content-Type-Options. These headers add an extra layer of security, preventing certain types of attacks. One such example of a security header is the Nginx directive **`server_token off`**. This directive hides the server info from the response headers in the browser. After enabling it, you will not be able to see a particular **`Server: nginx 1.21.1`** header as part of the response, thus hiding the origin details.
- **Request Filtering:** By being able to write regex specific location blocks and specific string matches, Nginx can be configured to filter incoming requests and configure unwanted paths with 404s. This would block requests with malicious payloads or patterns commonly associated with attacks.

Let us now go through the difference between the two most compared software available in the market today, that is, Nginx and Apache.

Nginx versus Apache

Apache is free, open-source web server software developed and maintained by the Apache Software Foundation. Apache is an alternative to Nginx. It is fast, reliable, and one of the most widely used web servers after Nginx.

Nginx has an event-driven architecture that handles multiple requests within a single thread, while Apache is process-driven, creating a thread per request.

According to recent data, Nginx currently holds a larger market share than Apache, with Nginx typically claiming around 33.9% of the web server market, and Apache holding around 27%.

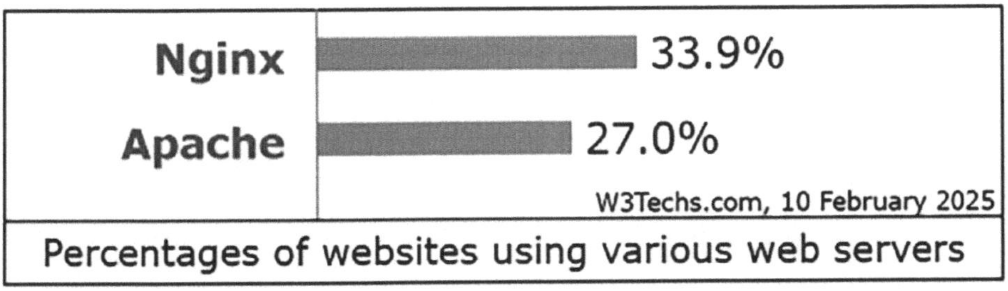

Figure 1.9: *Market Share of Nginx and Apache*

(Source: https://w3techs.com/technologies/comparison/ws-apache,ws-nginx)

Few key differences between Nginx and Apache are listed here to help you choose the right software for you.

Feature	**Nginx**	**Apache**
Architecture	Event-driven	Process-driven
Performance	High performance, efficient	Slightly slower
Concurrency	Handles large concurrent connections with low memory consumption	Efficient for moderate connections, can be configured for high performance
Configuration	Structured and declarative syntax	Traditional, human-readable directive-based syntax
Modules/ Extensibility	Modular architecture, simplicity	Extensive modules, versatile
Language	Written in C	Written in C and XML
Security	Better security	Less security compared to Nginx

Table 1.1: *Nginx versus Apache*

Nginx versus Nginx Plus

There are two primary versions of Nginx available today: the open-source Nginx and the commercial Nginx Plus. Although they both share a common foundation, each version targets different needs and use cases. Let us take a closer look at how they differ.

- **Nginx:** The open-source edition is the Nginx which is available free of cost with limited features.
- **Nginx Plus:** The Nginx Plus is a paid subscription that requires one to connect with the company F5. In addition to extra features, it also includes the professional services support to help you configure your application.

Listed are the detailed differences between the Nginx Open Source and the paid version Nginx Plus:

Feature	**Nginx Open Source**	**Nginx Plus**
Cost	Free and open source	Commercial license with paid subscription
Support	Community-supported	24/7 assistance with additional service cost
Load Balancing	Basic load balancing features	Advanced load balancing algorithms, health checks, session persistence, and more
Modules	Limited support for dynamic modules	Full support for dynamic modules
HTTP/2 and HTTP/3 Support	Yes	Yes
Nginx Plus Dashboard	No	Advanced real-time monitoring using Nginx dashboard (https://demo.nginx.com/)
Session Persistence	Limited or no built-in support	Advanced session persistence options
NGINX App Protect	Not included	Enhanced security against web application attacks with extra cost
Caching	Basic caching features	Advanced caching with cache purging and dynamic content caching
High Availability (HA)	Basic HA configurations	Enhanced HA features with active-active clustering and DNS load balancing
API Management	No Nginx Plus API available	Nginx Plus API available
Access Control and Security	Basic access controls and security features	Enhanced access controls and additional security features
WebSockets	Yes	Enhanced WebSockets support with improved performance

Table 1.2: *Nginx versus Nginx Plus*

We will explore how to install Nginx (open source) and Nginx Plus (paid version) on Ubuntu/Debian or Docker. The installation package and steps change from time to time with newer updates. Hence, it is recommended to get the latest updates on installation from the official documentation: https://docs.nginx.com/nginx/admin-guide/installing-nginx/

Before diving into the detailed Nginx installation guide, let us review some essential Linux commands that might be useful to you.

Basic Linux Commands

When working with Nginx on Linux, knowing a few core commands can make managing your server much easier. Here is a list of some basic commands and why they are useful:

Navigation and File Management

- `cd`: Change directories.

  Example: `cd /etc/nginx` moves you to the Nginx configuration folder.

- `ls`: List directory contents.

  Example: `ls -la` shows detailed information about files, including hidden ones.

- `cp` **and** `mv`: Copy and move files or directories.

  Example: `cp nginx.conf nginx.conf.bak` creates a backup of your configuration.

- `rm`: Remove files or directories.

  Example: `rm nginx.conf` removes nginx.conf file

  `rm -r conf.d` removes all the files inside conf.d directory

Viewing and Editing Files

- `cat`: Display the contents of a file.

  Example: `cat /etc/nginx/nginx.conf`

- `less`: View files one page at a time, useful for large logs or config files.

  Example: `less /var/log/nginx/error.log`

- `tail`: View the end of a file.

  Example: `tail -f /var/log/nginx/access.log` to watch acccss logs in real time.

- Text Editors (for example, vim, nano): Edit configuration files directly from the terminal.

  Example: `vim /etc/nginx/nginx.conf`

Process and Service Management

- `sudo`: Execute commands with superuser privileges.

  Example: `sudo systemctl restart nginx`

- `systemctl`: Manage system services.

  Example:

  - `sudo systemctl start nginx`
  - `sudo systemctl stop nginx`
  - `sudo systemctl restart nginx`
  - `sudo systemctl status nginx` to check Nginx's running status.

- `service`: An alternative for managing services on some Linux distributions.

  Example: `sudo service nginx status`

Network and Port Utilities

- `netstat or ss`: Check open ports and network connections.

  Example: `sudo netstat -tulpn | grep nginx` to see if Nginx is listening on the expected ports.

- `curl`: Test HTTP requests to your server.

  Example: `curl -I http://localhost` to view the HTTP headers returned by Nginx.

Searching and Monitoring

- `grep`: Search within files.

  Example: `grep 'error' /var/log/nginx/error.log` to find error messages.

- `ps` and `kill`: Monitor running processes and terminate them if necessary.

  Example: `ps aux | grep nginx` to view Nginx processes, and `sudo kill <PID>` to stop a problematic process.

These commands form the backbone of effective Nginx management on Linux, helping you navigate the file system, manage services, and troubleshoot issues with ease.

Installing Nginx Open Source Version

NGINX Open Source is available in two versions:

- **Mainline**: It is the latest stable version that includes the latest features and bug fixes.

  Use Case: Suitable for users who want to leverage the newest features and improvements. It is generally stable but may include experimental features.

- **Stable:** It may not have the latest feature but includes the critical bug fixes.

  Use Case: Recommended for production servers due to its focus on stability and reliability.

The package can be installed from:

- A default Ubuntu or Debian OS repository.
- The official repo at nginx.org.

Installing a Prebuilt Package from an OS Repository

Step 1: Update Package List

Before installing any new software, it is a good practice to update the package list in your machine to ensure you are installing the latest versions of packages. To update the package list, run the following command from the terminal:

***Figure 1.10:** Command to update Package List*

Step 2: Install Nginx

After latest package is installed, we can use the following command to install Nginx:

***Figure 1.11:** Command to Install Nginx*

Step 3: Check Nginx version

To verify if Nginx is installed and running, run the following command:

***Figure 1.12:** Command to Nginx Version*

This command will output the Nginx version, similar to the following figure, confirming that the `1.21.6` version of Nginx is installed.

```
nginx version: nginx/1.21.6
```

Figure 1.13: *Output of Nginx Version*

Step 4: Start Nginx

Once the installation is complete, sometimes we may need to start Nginx manually. In this case, the **`sudo nginx -v`** will not return any version.

```
sudo systemctl start nginx
```

Figure 1.14: *Command to Start Nginx Service*

Step 5: Check Nginx Status

Other way to check if Nginx is running is by using the following command:

```
sudo systemctl status nginx
```

Figure 1.15: *Command to Check Nginx Service Status*

If Nginx is running correctly, you should see an output indicating that the service is active.

Other way to test if Nginx is installed correctly is by running the following curl command in the terminal.

```
Curl -I 127.0.0.1
```

Figure 1.16: *Curl Command to Validate Nginx Setup*

The output will indicate the Nginx is able to load. The header **`Server: nginx`** further confirms it.

```
HTTP/1.1 308 Permanent Redirect
Server: nginx
Date: Fri, 24 Nov 2023 12:16:32 GMT
Content-Type: text/html
Content-Length: 164
Connection: keep-alive
Location: https://127.0.0.1/
```

Figure 1.17: *Output for Curl*

Installing a Prebuilt OS Package from the Official NGINX Repository

Please refer to https://docs.nginx.com/nginx/admin-guide/installing-nginx/ for the latest steps.

Step 1: Installing the prerequisites:

For Ubuntu,

```
sudo apt install curl gnupg2 ca-certificates lsb-release ubuntu-keyring
```

Figure 1.18: *Installing the Prerequisites in Ubuntu*

For Debian,

```
sudo apt install curl gnupg2 ca-certificates lsb-release debian-archive-keyring
```

Figure 1.19: *Installing the Prerequisites in Debian*

Step 2: Importing an official Nginx signing key so that apt could verify the packages authenticity. Fetch the key:

```
curl https://nginx.org/keys/nginx_signing.key | gpg --dearmor \
  | sudo tee /usr/share/keyrings/nginx-archive-keyring.gpg >/dev/null
```

Figure 1.20: *Installing Nginx Key*

Step 3: Verifying that the downloaded file contains the proper key.

```
gpg --dry-run --quiet --no-keyring --import --import-options import-show /usr/share/keyrings/nginx-archive-keyring.gpg
```

Figure 1.21: *Verify the Downloaded Key*

The output should contain the full fingerprint **573BFD6B3D8FBC641079A6ABABF5BD827 BD9BF62** as follows:

```
pub   rsa2048 2011-08-19 [SC] [expires: 2024-06-14]
      573BFD6B3D8FBC641079A6ABABF5BD827BD9BF62
uid                      nginx signing key <signing-key@nginx.com>
```

Figure 1.22: *Output of the Nginx Key*

If the fingerprint is different, remove the file.

Step 4: To set up the apt repository for stable nginx packages, run the following command:

For Ubuntu,

```
echo "deb [signed-by /usr/share/keyrings/nginx-archive-keyring.gpg] \
http://nginx.org/packages/ubuntu `lsb release -cs` nginx" \
   | sudo tee /etc/apt/sources.list.d/nginx.list
```

Figure 1.23: *Command to Set the Apt Repository for Stable Nginx Package in Ubuntu*

For Debian,

```
echo "deb [signed-by=/usr/share/keyrings/nginx-archive-keyring.gpg] \
http://nginx.org/packages/debian `lsb_release -cs` nginx" \
    | sudo tee /etc/apt/sources.list.d/nginx.list
```

Figure 1.24: *Command to Set the Apt Repository for Stable Nginx Package in Debian*

Step 5: If you would like to use mainline Nginx packages, run the following command instead:

For Ubuntu,

```
echo "deb [signed-by=/usr/share/keyrings/nginx-archive-keyring.gpg] \
http://nginx.org/packages/mainline/ubuntu `lsb_release -cs` nginx" \
    | sudo tee /etc/apt/sources.list.d/nginx.list
```

Figure 1.25: *Command to Set the Apt Repository for Mainline Nginx Package in Ubuntu*

For Debian,

```
echo "deb [signed-by=/usr/share/keyrings/nginx-archive-keyring.gpg] \
http://nginx.org/packages/mainline/debian `lsb_release -cs` nginx" \
    | sudo tee /etc/apt/sources.list.d/nginx.list
```

Figure 1.26: *Command to set the Apt Repository for Mainline Nginx Package in Debian*

Step 6: Setting up repository pinning to prioritize our packages over those provided by the distribution.

```
echo -e "Package: *\nPin: origin nginx.org\nPin: release o=nginx\nPin-Priority: 900\n" \
  | sudo tee /etc/apt/preferences.d/99nginx
```

Figure 1.27: *Pinning the Desired Repository*

After placing the package in the local repository, continue with the usual steps for updating and installing–just as you would when installing a prebuilt package from an operating system repository.

Installing Nginx Plus Version

To install Nginx Plus on Ubuntu/Debian, follow the succeeding steps. Note that we will need access to the Nginx Plus repository. We can typically obtain this through a subscription from Nginx, Inc., by contacting the F5 support.

Prerequisites for Installing Nginx Plus:

- NGINX Plus subscription (purchased or trial)
- A supported operating system

- Root privilege
- Your credentials for the MyF5 Customer Portal, provided by F5, Inc. through email
- Your NGINX Plus certificate and public key (**`nginx-repo.crt`** and **`nginx-repo.key`** files), provided by F5, Inc. through email.

Step 1: Obtaining Nginx Plus Repository Key:

```
sudo wget https://nginx.org/keys/nginx_signing.key
sudo apt-key add nginx_signing.key
```

Figure 1.28: *Command to Pull Nginx Plus Key*

Step 2: Adding the Nginx Plus Repository in the OS:

```
echo "deb https://pkgs.nginx.com/plus/ubuntu/ $(lsb_release -cs) nginx-plus" | sudo tee -a /etc/apt/sources.list.d/nginx-plus.list
```

Figure 1.29: *Adding Nginx Plus Repo*

Step 3: Updating the package list with the latest package:

```
sudo apt-get update
```

Figure 1.30: *Command to Update Package List*

Step 4: Installing Nginx Plus:

```
sudo apt install nginx-plus
```

Figure 1.31: *Command to Install Nginx Plus*

Step 5: Starting Nginx:

```
sudo systemctl start nginx
```

Figure 1.32: *Command to Start Nginx Service*

Step 6: Checking Nginx version

Check Nginx version to see if Nginx is installed and running:

```
sudo nginx -v
```

Figure 1.33: *Command to Check Nginx Version*

This command will output the Nginx version, as shown here:

```
nginx version: nginx/1.21.6
```

Figure 1.34: *Output for Nginx Version*

Step 7: If Nginx is running correctly, you should see an output indicating that the service is active:

```
Curl -I 127.0.0.1
```

Figure 1.35: *Curl Command to Validate Setup*

```
HTTP/1.1 308 Permanent Redirect
Server: nginx
Date: Fri, 24 Nov 2023 12:16:32 GMT
Content-Type: text/html
Content-Length: 164
Connection: keep-alive
Location: https://127.0.0.1/
```

Figure 1.36: *Output for the Curl*

Running Nginx on Docker

Docker is a **containerization platform** that enables developers and system administrators to package, distribute, and run applications in lightweight, portable containers. Dockers are heavily used in tech companies nowadays and running Nginx Open Source in a Docker container is a common practice. The steps to run Nginx in a Docker container are listed as follows:

Prerequisites

Docker installed on your Windows or Linux system.

Step 1: Pulling the Nginx Docker Image:

```
docker pull nginx
```

Figure 1.37: *Pull the Nginx Image*

Step 2: Running Nginx Container:

```
docker run -d -p 80:80 --name mynginx nginx
```

Figure 1.38: *Running the Nginx Container*

This command does the following:

a. **`-d`**: Run the container in the background

b. **`-p 80:80`**: Map port 80 from the container to port 80 on the host

c. **`--name mynginx`**: Assign a custom name "**`mynginx`**" to the container

d. **`nginx`**: The name of the Nginx image

Step 3: Access the Nginx Container:

Open a web browser and type **http://localhost.** Or, if you are using a specific IP address, type **`http://your_server_ip_address`** to access the Nginx Container.

You should see the default Nginx welcome page.

Figure 1.39: *Nginx Home Page*

Additional Docker Commands that may be needed to set the Nginx:

1. **Stop the Container**

   ```
   docker stop mynginx
   ```
2. **Start the Container**

   ```
   docker start mynginx
   ```
3. **Remove the Container**

   ```
   docker rm mynginx
   ```
4. **Remove the Nginx Image**

   ```
   docker rmi nginx
   ```

Please note that these are basic steps, and you may need to reconfigure them depending on your specific use case, such as handling SSL certificates, using a reverse proxy, or configuring more advanced Nginx settings. Always refer to the official Nginx Docker Hub page for the latest information and best practices.

Note: *After installing Nginx using any of the methods described above, you will see default files in /etc/nginx/—including conf.d, nginx.conf, and mime.types. This /etc/ nginx directory will serve as your main workspace for all Nginx configuration tasks.*

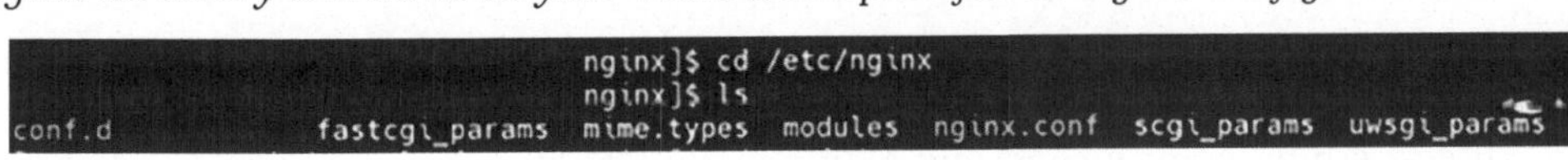

Figure 1.40: *Nginx Workspace*

Restarting, Reloading, Starting, and Stopping of Nginx

As Nginx Administrator, you will frequently update and create Nginx configurations. The following commands will be your primary tools. Nginx operates as a service on your server, so it always remains active in the background.

1. **Start Nginx Service:** The command is used to start the Nginx.

   ```
   sudo systemctl start nginx
   ```

2. **Stop Nginx Service:** This command is used to stop the Nginx.

   ```
   sudo systemctl start nginx
   ```

3. **Restart Nginx Service:** This command is used to restart the Nginx. The restart command will shut down the already running Nginx Service and restart it again. We should restart Nginx only when making significant configuration updates, such as changing ports or interfaces. This command forces shut down of all worker processes.

   ```
   sudo systemctl restart nginx
   ```

4. **Reload Nginx Service:** This command is used to reload the Nginx. This is the most important command that you will be using for your daily workflow. The reload command keeps the old Nginx server configuration running as it reloads updated new configuration files. This command is graceful and does not kill old connections. If Nginx notices a syntax error in any of the new loaded configuration files, the reload is aborted and the server keeps running based on old config files.

   ```
   sudo nginx -s reload
   ```

   Note: *Please note that reloading is safer than restarting Nginx. Each time you do a change in Nginx configuration; you will need to run the following command to implement the change.*

5. **To view the Nginx Service Status:** The command to check the status is:

   ```
   sudo systemctl status nginx
   ```

   If the Nginx service is running or active, you will see a green **`active (running)`** status in the third line (*Figure 1.41*).

   If Nginx service is not running, it will display as inactive.

   If something went wrong and Nginx could not load, you will see a red status failed, with some information about the failure.

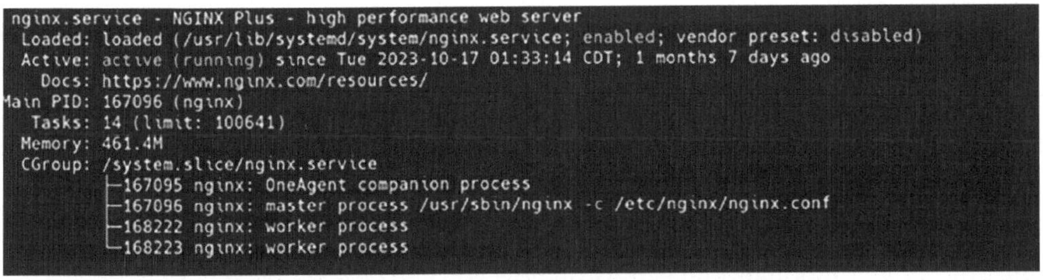

Figure 1.41: *Master and Worker Process Information*

Since we are already discussing Nginx commands, let us talk about two more commonly used **nginx** command **nginx -t** and **nginx -T**:

- **nginx -t:** The **nginx -t** command is used to test the syntax of the Nginx configuration file without reloading the Nginx service. It reports any errors it finds. This is useful command to run before reloading the Nginx to ensure that your configuration syntax is correct.

The following figure shows a screenshot of the error output when the **nginx -t** command fails:

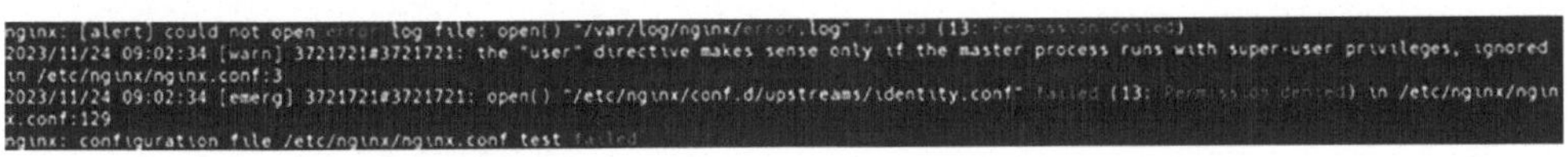

Figure 1.42: *Error Output Example in the Terminal*

The following figure shows a screenshot of the output that you see when the **nginx -t** command is successful:

Figure 1.43: *Successful Syntax Output in the Terminal*

- **nginx -T:** Nginx configurations can be well structured using different file structures. For instance, you can separate two different app configurations into two separate **.conf files** to increase readability and manageability. All files are then included in the main **nginx.conf** file using the **include** directive. **nginx -T** combines all the files and prints the entire Nginx configuration to the terminal. This can be helpful for debugging, verifying changes, or quickly reviewing all directives in effect.

Conclusion

This chapter explained the fundamentals of Nginx and its architecture. We understood key terminologies such as web server, reverse proxy, load balancer, event driven, and so on, which will be frequently used in subsequent chapters.

Now that you have installed Nginx in your desired platform, we will learn about the Nginx directives, modules and syntax on how you can write and execute your very first Nginx configuration in the next chapter.

CHAPTER 2
Get Started with Nginx Configurations

Introduction

In this chapter, we will dive into the heart of Nginx configuration–where the magic happens! As we learnt, Nginx is renowned not only as a high-performance web server but also as a powerful proxy server and load balancer. It operates according to its configuration. Whether we are hosting a simple website or managing a complex infrastructure, configuring Nginx correctly is crucial for optimal performance and security.

At its core, Nginx configurations are a set of instructions written in plain text files. These files allow administrators to fine-tune how the server handles incoming HTTP requests and outgoing responses. This flexibility enables Nginx to serve static files, manage dynamic content, reverse proxy requests to application servers, handle load balancing, and much more.

As we work with Nginx, we will be interacting with its configuration files on a regular basis. In this chapter, we will guide you through their structure and explain you how each directive impacts Nginx's behavior.

Structure

In this chapter, the following topics will be covered:

- Understanding **`nginx.conf`** File
- Algorithm to Choose Location Block to Process Request
- Nginx Directives
- Nginx Modules
- Nginx Variables
- Example Configuration

Let us start with the most important file, that is, **nginx.conf**. We can also refer it to as the master file.

Understanding nginx.conf File

The **nginx.conf** file is the main configuration file for the Nginx web server. The **nginx.conf** file contains all the directives and settings that govern how Nginx should operate. It includes all the server configurations, proxy settings, logging configurations, and more.

Every bit of the configuration setting defined in any other file is ultimately included in the **nginx.conf** file. During nginx compilation, every configuration setting, even those defined in separate files, ultimately becomes part of the **nginx.conf**. We typically structure it into different files to increase readability and better management.

Every NGINX configuration file is organized into distinct contexts, each designed to serve a specific purpose. At the highest level, the configuration is divided into several major contexts, including:

- main
- events
- http
- server
- location

Let us explore each of the aforementioned contexts one by one.

main context

This is the starting point of the Nginx configuration, also known as the global section. This means it lies outside the http, events, server, and location context (we will use the terms "**context**" and "**block**" interchangeably).

The main context is used to configure details such as:

- The system user or group that would be required to run the worker processes:

  ```
  user  nginx;
  ```

- The number of worker processes (remember how it depends on the CPU Core that we learned in the previous chapter):

  ```
  worker_processes auto;
  ```

- The file to save the main Nginx process's ID:

  ```
  pid  /var/run/nginx.pid;
  ```

- Setting the default error file for the entire application. This setting can be overridden if defined in server or location contexts:

  ```
  error_log  /var/log/nginx/error.log;
  ```

- Other additional directives such as **`worker_rlimit_nofile`**, **`load_module`** as per the requirement:

  ```
  worker_rlimit_nofile 17000;
  load_module modules/ngx_http_js_module.so;
  ```

The following is the **sample configuration**, consolidating all the preceding elements discussed:

```
load_module modules/ndk_http_module.so;
load_module modules/ngx_http_lua_module.so;
load_module modules/ngx_http_js_module.so;

user nginx;

worker_processes auto;

error_log  /var/log/nginx/error.log ;
pid        /var/run/nginx.pid;

worker_rlimit_nofile 16192;
```

***Figure 2.1**: Main Context*

event context

In the event context, we define how Nginx handles connections at a general level. The **`worker_connections`** directive is used to define the same. There can only be a single event context defined within the entire Nginx configuration.

Sample Configuration:

```
#main context
load_module modules/ndk_http_module.so;
load_module modules/ngx_http_lua_module.so;
load_module modules/ngx_http_js_module.so;

user nginx;

worker_processes auto;

error_log  /var/log/nginx/error.log ;
pid        /var/run/nginx.pid;

worker_rlimit_nofile 16192;

#events context
events {
    worker_connections  8096;
}
```

***Figure 2.2**: Event Context*

`http` context

The "**`http`**" **`context`** is a top-level configuration block where we define settings and behaviors specific to web (HTTP/HTTPS) traffic. It is typically written at **`/etc/nginx/nginx.conf`** file after the event context. It will contain everything that is needed to operate as an HTTP web server or reverse proxy. It encapsulates all the other directives, that is, server blocks, location blocks, include, `log_format`, caching rules, compression techniques, and so on.

Sample Configuration:

```
#http context
http {

    include /etc/nginx/mime.types;

    log_format main '"$time_local" client=$remote_addr '
              'method=$request_method request="$request" '
              'request_length=$request_length '
              'status=$status bytes_sent=$bytes_sent '
              'body_bytes_sent=$body_bytes_sent '
              'upstream_addr=$upstream_addr '
              'upstream_status=$upstream_status '
              'request_time=$request_time '
              'upstream_response_time=$upstream_response_time '
              'upstream_connect_time=$upstream_connect_time '
              'upstream_header_time=$upstream_header_time '
              'body=$request_body' ;

    include /etc/nginx/conf.d/configuration.conf;

 server {
      listen 8080;
       access_log off;

       location = / {
            return 301 /dashboard.html;
       }
       location /api {
            api write=on;
       }
       location /dashboard.html {
            root /usr/share/nginx/html;
       }
    }
}
```

Figure 2.3: *http Context*

server context

The "**server**" context is always defined *inside* the "**http**" context. This context is important for configuring how would the Nginx server handle different aspects of incoming requests. We can define multiple server blocks allowing Nginx to serve multiple websites or applications on the same server. Each server block is differentiated by the unique **server_name**. The DNS name or the hostname is the value for the **server_name**.

What is DNS or hostname?

DNS name, often called a **hostname**, is the human-readable address that helps users reach websites or online resources without memorizing numeric IP addresses. These are names mapped to unique IP addresses. All these DNS IP mappings are mapped in a global DNS system.

For example, instead of typing an address like 93.184.216.34 to access a website, you can type www.example.com. Some example of DNS names are www.amazon.com, www.google.com.

Sample Configuration for the server context

```
#http context
http {

    include /etc/nginx/mime.types;
    log_format main '"$time_local" client=$remote_addr '
                    'method=$request_method request="$request" '
                    'request_length=$request_length '
                    'status=$status bytes_sent=$bytes_sent '
                    'body_bytes_sent=$body_bytes_sent '
                    'upstream_addr=$upstream_addr '
                    'upstream_status=$upstream_status '
                    'request_time=$request_time '
                    'upstream_response_time=$upstream_response_time '
                    'upstream_connect_time=$upstream_connect_time '
                    'upstream_header_time=$upstream_header_time '
                    'body=$request_body' ;

    include /etc/nginx/conf.d/configuration.conf;

#server context
 server {
       listen 80;
       server_name www.test.com;
 }
 server {
       listen 80;
       server_name www.test1.com;
 }
 server {
       listen 443;
       server_name www.test2.com;
 }
}
```

***Figure 2.4**: http Context*

location context

Location blocks are defined within the server contexts and just like server blocks, we can have multiple location blocks. Each location is defined to handle a certain type of client request, and each location is selected by matching a specific URI path or string pattern or regular expressions defined in that location block.

The location block also allows us to specify how Nginx proxies request to the backend servers, serve static files, or implement specific behavior.

Sample configuration of few location contexts defined inside a server context

```
server {
    listen       80 default_server;
    listen 443 default_server;
    server_name  localhost;

    #Dell certificate and key
    ssl_certificate /etc/nginx/dellcert/dcqonpCert.pem;
    ssl_certificate_key /etc/nginx/dellcert/dcqonpKey.pem;

    #location context
    location / {
        root   /usr/share/nginx/html;
        index  index.html index.htm;
    }

    location /nginx_status {
          stub_status;
          allow 127.0.0.1;
          deny all;
    }

    error_page   500 502 503 504  /50x.html;
    location = /50x.html {
        root   /usr/share/nginx/html;
    }
```

Figure 2.5: *location Context*

Algorithm to Choose Location Block to Process Request

As previously stated, Nginx can have multiple location block, each of which can handle certain traffic patterns. So, each time a client request lands in the Nginx server, Nginx begins the process of determining which location blocks should be used to handle the request. There is an algorithm that Nginx follows and understanding this process is a crucial requirement in being able to configure Nginx reliably and accurately.

A **regex** (short for **regular expression**) is a sequence of characters that defines a search pattern. It is used to match, locate, and manage text by specifying patterns of characters. Regular expressions are widely used in programming, text processing, and configuration tools (such as, NGINX) to perform powerful pattern matching and text manipulation tasks.

Before we jump into the algorithm, let us first get ourselves familiar with few important regex symbols and what do they represent.

Symbol	Description
=	Exact match
~	Case sensitive Regex match
^	Denotes the start of the match
$	End of the staring match
~*	Case In-sensitive Regex match
~ ^	Structured and declarative syntax. ^ indicates the start of the string match

Table 2.1: *Regex Symbols*

Nginx utilizes PCRE regular expressions, and you can test your regex patterns using various online tools, such as regex101(https://regex101.com/).

Understanding the Algorithm

When a client makes an HTTP request, Nginx matches the request URL of the HTTP request against the defined location blocks in the order of their appearance. The matching is performed against a normalized URI. For example, http://example.com/index.html and http://EXAMPLE.COM//index.html can be normalized to a single, canonical form, such as http://example.com/index.html.

Following is the order of execution when an HTTP request lands on a Nginx Servers.

Take a Sample URL: https://www.test.com/understanding/nginx/chapter/2

The location block search that would match the preceding URL closest starts after https://www.test.com, where HOST or DNS is www. example.com.

Exact Match

Nginx first looks for any possibility of a location block with an exact match sequence of characters. For exact match, the string defined in the location context should be exactly same as the incoming request, **including the case of the string**.

The exact match location block is preceded with = symbol. If an exact match between the request URI and the location directive happens, Nginx stops all the further location block search and executes the one that matched.

Example:

```
server {
    listen 443 ssl;
    server_name www.test.com;

    #ssl cert and key

    #location context
    #exact match
    location = /understanding/nginx/chapter/2 {
        return 301 https://www.test2.com;
    }
}
```

Figure 2.6*: Exact Match*

Prefix Match or String Match

If there is no exact match location block that matched the request, Nginx looks for the second preferred location block, that is, a string match. Basically, it will try to find a location block that starts with string /understanding. It can be either /understanding or /understanding/nginx or /understanding/nginx/chapter or /understanding/nginx/chapter/2. The location that matched the longest string is selected and ***stored in the memory***.

Example:

```
server {
    listen 443 ssl;
    server_name www.test.com;

    #ssl cert and key

    #location context
    #prefix match
    location ~ ^/understanding/nginx/chapter/2 {
        return 301 https://www.test1.com;
    }

    location ~ ^/understanding/nginx/chapter {
        return 301 https://www.test2.com;
    }


    location ~ ^/understanding/nginx {
        return 301 https://www.test3.com;
    }
}
```

Figure 2.7*: string Match*

In the preceding example, all the three location blocks match the incoming request URI /understanding/nginx/chapter/2. But the longest string match, that is, location **`~^/understanding/nginx/chapter/2`** is selected and ***stored in the memory***.

Regex Match

If a location defined with a string matches, it is not immediately processed. Rather, the location is stored in memory. The algorithm then proceeds to look for a potential regex match. *This is because the regex is always given priority over string match.*

If a location is matched with a regex pattern that matches the incoming URI, the processing stops. The regex match is sequential process and hence even though there are more location blocks with better regex match, the first match is taken into consideration.

Example:

```
server {
    listen 443 ssl;
    server_name www.test.com;

    #ssl cert and key

    #location context
    #prefix match
    location ~ ^/understanding/nginx/chapter/2 {
        return 301 https://www.test1.com;
    }

    location ~ ^/understanding/nginx/chapter {
        return 301 https://www.test2.com;
    }


    location ~ ^/understanding/nginx {
        return 301 https://www.test3.com;
    }

    #regex match
    location ~* "^/understanding.*" {
        return 301 https://www.test4.com;
    }

    location ~* "^/understanding/nginx.*" {
        return 301 https://www.test5.com;
    }

}
```

***Figure 2.8**: Regex Match*

For the URL `https://www.test.com/understanding/nginx/chapter/2`, even though the location block with string match is present, the regex location **`~* "^/understanding.*"`** is executed. The second regex location **`~* "^/understanding/nginx.*"`** will NOT even considered as the first matched will be given a priority.

It is very important to understand the algorithm properly to configure Nginx. From simpler to complex websites, the rule writing is the most important step.

We have explored the various contexts involved in crafting an Nginx configuration. In the next section, we will learn about Nginx directives. It is essential to understand that an Nginx configuration, at its core, is a collection of directives–each one signifying how the server processes incoming requests and delivers content.

Nginx Directives

If you are familiar with any programming language such as JAVA, C or C++, you must have come across the term keyword.

Keywords are reserved words that have predefined meaning to the compiler. These are part of the syntax and cannot be used as user defined identifiers or custom words in the program.

Nginx directives are reserved keywords that holds a special meaning and does a special job. The configuration is configured using these directives. For example, to enable compression of requests in Nginx, we use the directive gzip in the http context. So, if we write

```
gzip on;
```

It will signify that the nginx will compress the incoming requests.

This one is just one example. There are 100s of them. Let us now dive into the most important directives one by one that can be configured.

- **`user`**

Syntax	`user user [group];`
Default	`user nobody nobody;`
Context	`main`
Example	user nginx;

Table 2.2: *user*

'**`user`**' directive is used to identify the user group with which Nginx process runs.

In the preceding example, the **`user`** directive specifies that Nginx worker processes should run with the user and group privileges of '**`nginx`**'. By specifying user, we limit privileges of the web server process which helps us in minimizing the potential impact of security vulnerabilities.

It is important to note that when defining the user directive, the specified user should have the necessary permissions to access the required files and directories for serving the web content.

- **`worker_processes`**

Syntax	`worker_processes number | auto;`
Default	`worker_processes 1;`
Context	`main`
Example	`worker_processes 4;`

Table 2.3: *worker_processes*

The **`worker_processes`** directive in Nginx is used to configure the number of worker processes that the Nginx server should spawn at the start of Nginx service. Worker processes are responsible for handling incoming connections, processing requests, and serving content. Each worker process runs independently and handles its own set of connections.

'**`number`**' is an integer value representing the desired number of worker processes. The recommended value for this directive is usually the number of CPU cores on the server. We have already discussed in the previous chapter how to decide on what number to set.

In the above example, **`worker_processes 4`** means Nginx is configured to run with 4 worker processes.

Note: *Having too few worker processes may limit the server's ability to handle concurrent connections efficiently, while having too many worker processes may lead to increased resource consumption. It is always better to set the* **`worker_processes`** *to auto.*

- **`worker_connections`**

Syntax	`worker_connections number;`
Default	`worker_connections 512;`
Context	`events`
Example	`worker_connections 1024;`

Table 2.4: *worker_connections*

The **`worker_connections`** directive in Nginx is used to configure the maximum number of simultaneous connections that each worker process can handle.

The total number of simultaneous connections that Nginx can handle is calculated as the product of **worker_processes** and **worker_connections**.

For example,

```
worker processes =4
worker_connections 1024;
```

The total number of connections would be 4 * 1024 = 4096.

This means Nginx can handle 4096 simultaneous connections.

You can further limit this value with **worker_rlimit_nofile** to reduce over consumption of the system resources.

- **worker_rlimit_nofile**

Syntax	`worker_rlimit_nofile number;`
Default	–
Context	`main`
Example	`Worker_rlimit_nofile 8192;`

Table 2.5: *worker_rlimit_nofile*

The **worker_rlimit_nofile** directive in Nginx is used to set the maximum number of file descriptors that each worker process can open.

File descriptors in Unix-like systems are **references** to files or sockets that the operating system uses to manage I/O operations. Every open file, network connection, or other I/O resource is represented by a unique file descriptor number.

Few examples of where file descriptors are used in Nginx configuration include:

1. Each active connection to a client will use 1 file descriptor.
2. Using **proxy_pass** will open a socket to the **host:port** handling these requests.
3. Each worker connection open 2 file descriptors, that is, 1 for upstream and 1 for downstream.
4. Static files being served by nginx will use 1 file descriptor.

Note: *The number of file descriptors* (**worker_rlimit_nofile**) *indirectly affects the ability of each worker process to handle connections* (**worker_connections**).

Each open connection typically requires an associated file descriptor. Therefore, the total number of file descriptors available to worker processes affects the overall capacity to handle connections.

While setting **worker_rlimit_nofile** parameter, OS's file descriptor values should be first checked which will give us the per user hard and soft file limits respectively.

Ulimit, Hard Limit, and Soft Limit in Linux System

The **soft limits** are the limits which are allocated for actual processing of application or users.

Hard limits are an upper bound to the values of soft limits. Soft limit is less than or equal to hard limit.

To check the hard limit value, use the following command:

```
ulimit -Hn
```

To check the soft limit value, use the following command:

```
ulimit -Sn
```

***Figure 2.9**: Soft Limit Value*

We will learn how to alter the hard and soft limit in a later chapter about *Performance Enhancements* in Nginx.

The **`access_log`** directive in Nginx is used to capture the history of client requests and server responses in the access log files.

- **`access_log`**

Syntax	`access_log path [format [buffer=size] [gzip[=level]] [flush=time] [if=condition]];` `access_log off;`
Default	`access_log logs/access.log combined;`
Context	`http, server, location, if in location, limit_except`

Example	`access_log /var/log/nginx/log_request.log mainformat;`
	`access_log /var/log/nginx/log_request.log mainformat buffer=64K;`
	`access_log /var/log/nginx/log_request.log mainformat gzip=8;`
	`access_log /var/log/nginx/log_request.log mainformat if=$loggable;`

***Table 2.6**: access_logs*

The nginx log file location is generally saved in directory path **`/var/log/nginx/(YourLogFileName.log)`**. For each request the information that will be logged are defined using log format directive in the **`nginx.conf`** file.

In the preceding examples from the table, the log file's save path is **`/var/log/nginx/log_request.log`**. The format at which each log will be logged is '**`mainformat`**'.

- For the example,
  `access_log  /var/log/nginx/log_request.log mainformat buffer=64K;`

  buffer keyword sets the log buffer to 64K. If the buffer is enabled, Nginx writes to log will be buffered.

- For the example,
  `access_log /var/log/nginx/log_request.log mainformat gzip=8;`

  `gzip` keyword enables compression for log file rotation. The value can be set from 1 to 9, where 1 is lowest and 9 is the highest level of compression.

- For the example,
  `access_log  /var/log/nginx/log_request.log mainformat if=$loggable;`
  `if=$loggable` `allows conditional logging.`

  In the following Nginx map, **`$status`** is the nginx variable that stores the response code of the client request. If the request code is 2xx or 3xx, the value of **`$loggable`** is 0. For any other response code, the value of **`$loggable`** is 1.

```
map $status $loggable {
  ~^[23]  0;
  default 1;
}
```

Figure 2.10: *$status*

When **`$loggable=0`**, **`access_log  /var/log/nginx/log_request.log mainformat if=0;`** Hence, **`nginx`** will not write the log in the **`log_request.log`** file for that request.

For requests with 4x and 5x status code, **`$loggable=1`**. **`access_log  /var/log/nginx/log_request.log mainformat if=1;`** Hence, **`nginx`** will write the specific log in the **`log_request`** log file for that request.

This is how conditional logging is done in Nginx.

- **`log_format`**

Syntax	`log_format name [escape=default|json|none] string ...;`
Default	`log_format combined "...";`
Context	`http`

Example	log_format mainformat '"$time_local" client=$remote_addr ' 'method=$request_method request="$request" ' 'request_length=$request_length ' 'status=$status bytes_sent=$bytes_sent ' 'upstream_addr=$upstream_addr ' 'upstream_status=$upstream_status ' 'request_time=$request_time ' 'upstream_response_time=$upstream_response_time ' 'upstream_connect_time=$upstream_connect_time ' 'upstream_header_time=$upstream_header_time ' 'body=$request_body';

Table 2.7: *log_format*

The **`log_format`** directive in Nginx is used to define a custom log format for access logs. This directive allows you to specify the format in which Nginx records information about client requests and server responses in the access logs.

The '**`mainformat'`** in the preceding example is a custom or user defined name given to the log format. This will be further used in the **`access_log`** directive as:

```
access_log  /var/log/nginx/log_request.log mainformat;
```

We can define more than one **`log_format` with different custom** name depending on what all information we want to log.

For the previously defined log format '**`mainformat`**' in the table's example, the log entry for GET https://www.test.com/understanding/nginx/chapter/2 will be logged as:

```
[11/Feb/2025:04:57:23 -0600] client=143.189.129.145 method=GET request=
/understanding/nginx/chapter/2 request_length=4054 status="200" bytes_
sent=605 228 upstream_addr="10.43.204.51:443" upstream_status="200"
request_time="0.007" upstream_response_time="0.007" upstream_connect_
time="0.000" upstream_header_time="0.007" body=-
```

- **`include`**

Syntax	include file | mask;
Default	–
Context	any
Example	include /etc/nginx/mime.types; include /etc/nginx/hello*.conf

Table 2.8: *include*

In Nginx, we can structure the configuration files by segmenting into many multiple files. It can be then included in the main Nginx configuration file, that is, **nginx.conf**. This is achieved by using the *include* directive. This directive helps in organizing and modularizing the configuration, making it easier to manage and maintain.

- **listen**

Syntax	listen address[:port] [default_server] [ssl] [http2] [reuseport];
Default	listen *:80 | *:8000;
Context	Server
Example	listen 80; listen 80 default_server; listen 80 reuseport; listen 443 ssl; listen 127.0.0.1:8000; listen [::]:80; listen [::]:443;

***Table 2.9**: listen*

The listen directive in Nginx is used to specify the IP address and port on which the server should accept incoming connections. If no address is mentioned, the incoming request is accepted for all available IP addresses.

```
listen 80;
```

All the non-secured (http) incoming request with any IP address is accepted on port 80.

```
listen 80 default_server;
```

The **default_server** marks this specific server block as a default server block. This means, if any incoming http request does not match any other server block, the client will fall back to the default server block and the locations in the default server block is executed.

```
listen 80 reuseport;
```

reuseport option allows multiple sockets to bind to the same address and port combination, facilitating parallel processing of incoming connections. It is particularly useful for load balancing and improving the performance of web servers by distributing incoming connections among multiple worker processes.

```
listen 443 ssl;
```

ssl parameter is added to the listen directive to specify that the server should only accept secure connections. Additionally, SSL certificate and key files for the server are needed to be specified as they would be needed to encrypt or decrypt data.

```
listen 192.168.2.100:8080;
```

Here the incoming request with IP 192.168.2.100 is listened on port 8080.

```
listen [::]:80;
listen [::]:443;
```

Here the incoming request is listened on both IPv4 and IPv6 on the default HTTP and HTTPS ports.

- **server_name**

Syntax	server_name [string][regex][_][IP]
Default	-
Context	server
Example	server_name www.test.com test.com; server_name *.test.com; server_name 127.0.0.1; server_name _;

Table 2.10: *server_name*

The **server_name** directive in Nginx tells Nginx which domain names (or IP addresses) a particular server block should respond to. This is crucial for hosting multiple sites on the same NGINX instance (known as virtual hosting).

For example, **server_name www.test.com test.com;** tells Nginx that this block handles requests for both **www.test.com** and **test.com.**

You can also define a regex or a wildcard pattern in the **server_name** directive.

For example, **server_name *.test.com;** tells Nginx to cover all subdomains such as test1.test.com or sample.test.com.

Big websites usually use regex to generalize the domain name in the server block.

In the following screenshot, the server block for Amazon can be defined as:

```
server_name ^.+\.amazon\.(com|in)$;
```

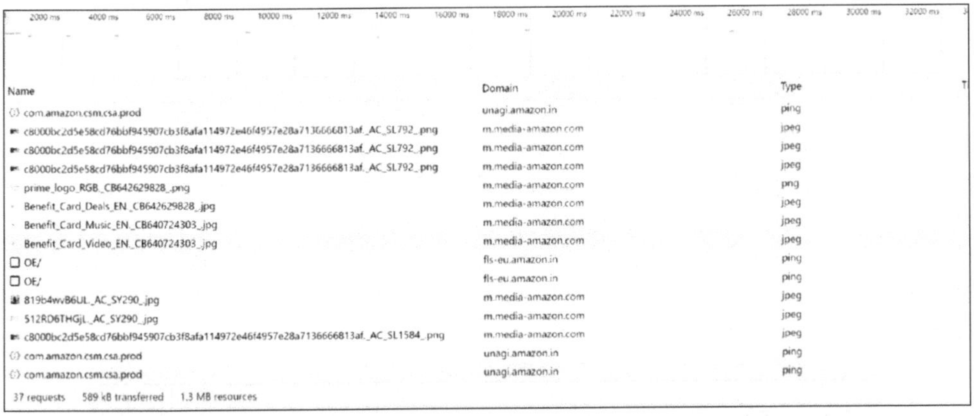

***Figure 2.11**: Screenshot from amazon.in Showing Different DNS Names*

```
server_name 127.0.0.1;
```

In this example, all the localhosts will be accepted in this server block.

```
server_name _;
```

This depicts that any request with all server names by default can be accepted in the specified server block.

- **`proxy_pass`**

Syntax	`proxy_pass [URL][backend server];`
Default	–
Context	`location, if in location, limit_except`

Example	`proxy_pass https://backend_server/url;`
	`proxy_pass https:// backend_server;`
	`proxy_pass https://backend_server$1;`

***Table 2.11**: proxy_pass*

The **`proxy_pass`** directive instructs Nginx where a particular incoming client request should be sent to. The server where the request is sent to is called a proxied or upstream or a backend server.

An optional URI path should be defined that depicts how the request is sent to the upstream server. This directive is commonly used in reverse proxy configurations.

The **`proxy_pass`** statement mandatorily includes:

- **`$scheme`** (an Nginx variable to denote the protocol: http or https),
- The complete URL or the backend server upstream name,
- An Nginx variable containing a part of the incoming URL, represented by back referencing.

Example 1: Example of **proxy_pass** directive with a URL

```
    location /url/ {
    proxy_pass http://www.test.com/link/;
}
```

***Figure 2.12**: proxy_pass to a URL*

Example 2: Example of **proxy_pass** directive with only upstream (backend/proxied) server

```
    location /url/ {
    proxy_pass http://backend_server;
}

upstream backend_server {
    server server1.com:443;
    server server2.com:443;
}
```

***Figure 2.13**: proxy_pass to an Upstream Server*

Example 3: Example of **proxy_pass** directive with back referenced variable

```
upstream backend_server {
    server server1.com:443;
    server server2.com:443;
}

 location ~* "~(001|002|003)" {
   proxy_pass http://backend_server/test/$1;
 }
```

***Figure 2.14**: proxy_pass with a Variable*

Back Referencing

Back Referencing in Nginx leverages regex capture groups to extract portions of a URL (or other text) and reuse them in our configuration. This allows for **dynamic** rewrites, redirects, or routing rules based on the specific pattern of an incoming request.

In the example shown in *Figure* 2.14, whatever is captured within the **()**, that is, **(001|002|003)** is called a captured group. The value of the captured group is then used in **proxy_pass**, along with the upstream name, to construct a certain URL pattern. This URL is sent to the backend server in such a way that the backend server can understand and process.

In the preceding example, $1 would be 001, 002, or 003. The URL that is formed while sending the request to the backend server server1.com is http://server1.com/test/001, http://server1.com/test/002, or http://server1.com/test/003. This process is called back referencing.

The following table lists some widely used regex patterns with their description:

Regex Pattern	Description	Example Match
`\w+`	Matches one or more-word characters	`"hello123"`
`\b\w+\b`	Matches a single word (alphanumeric characters)	`"Hello"`
`\d+`	Matches one or more digits	`"456"`
`\D+`	Matches one or more non-digit characters	`"abcXYZ"`
`\s+`	Matches one or more whitespace characters	`" \t"`
`\S+`	Matches one or more non-whitespace characters	`"abc123"`
`\b\w+\b`	Matches whole words	`"regex"`
`\b[A-Za-z0-9._%+-]+@[A-Za-z0-9.-]+\.[A-Za-z]{2,}\b`	Matches email addresses	`"user@test.com"`
`\b(?:\d{1,3}\.){3}\d{1,3}\b`	Matches IPv4 addresses	`"192.168.1.1"`
`\b[A-Z][a-z]*\b`	Matches capitalized words	`"Apple"`
`\b\d{2}-\d{2}-\d{4}\b`	Matches a date in MM-DD-YYYY format	`"01-23-2023"`

***Table 2.12**: Regex Patterns*

- **`return`**

Syntax	`return code [text];`
	`return code URL;`
	`return URL;`

Default	–
Context	`server, location, if`
Example	`return 301 https://newsite.example.com$request_uri;`

***Table 2.13**: return*

The **`return`** directive in Nginx provides a straightforward way to send an HTTP response that immediately redirects the client. When you use this directive, NGINX stops further processing and sends back a status code along with the new URL. This method is perfect for cases where a simple redirection is all that's needed.

In the preceding example, return 301 sends an HTTP 301 status code (which indicates a permanent move) along with the new URL constructed by appending the original request URI to your new domain.

You can also return a custom message like return 503 "**We'll be back soon!**";

- **`rewrite`**

Syntax	`rewrite regex replacement [flag];`
Default	–
Context	`server, location, if`
Example	`rewrite ^/oldpath/(.*)$ /newpath/$1 permanent;`

Table 2.14: *rewrite*

The **`rewrite`** directive, in contrast, offers a more powerful solution by allowing you to modify the request URI before it's processed further. Using regular expressions, you can capture and transform parts of the original URI, enabling dynamic URL rewriting that adjusts to various patterns.

For the preceding example, **`rewrite ^/oldpath/(.*)$ /newpath/$1 permanent;`**

In this configuration:

- The regular expression **`^/oldpath/(.*)$`** captures the trailing part of the URL.
- The replacement URL **`/newpath/$1`** reconstructs the URL using the captured segment.
- The flag '**`permanent`**' ensures that the client receives a 301 redirect status.

Common Flags:

- **`last`**: stop rewriting and search for a new location matching the new changed URI by the rewrite.
- **`break`**: stop rewriting and searching for other location and continues with the current one.
- **`redirect`**: returns a temporary redirect with the 302 code.
- **`permanent`**: returns a permanent redirect with the 301 code.

return 301 Versus return 302 Versus return 308

```
return 301 https://example.com$request_uri;
```

Tells browsers and search engines: "*This resource has moved permanently.*"

The new URL is cached and the search engines update their index to the new URL.

We use it when we have permanently changed URLs (e.g., **`http`** → **`https`**, **`/old`** → **`/new`**)

```
return 302 https://example.com/temp/$request_uri;
```

Tells browsers: "*This is a temporary move – don't cache this as permanent.*" Search engines may keep the original URL indexed.

We use it when we are doing A/B testing and we are showing users content from a temporary location.

```
return 308 https://example.com$new_uri;
```

The return status code 308 is much like 301, but preserves HTTP method and body (important for POST requests).

The key reason to use 308 is because 301 may convert **`POST`** to **`GET`**, but 308 does not.

We may think of 308 as the modern, method-safe 301.

- **`upstream`**

Syntax	`upstream name { ... }`
Default	–
Context	`http`

Example	`upstream backend_server {`
	`    server server1.com:443;`
	`    server server2.com:443;`
	`}`

Table 2.15: *upstream*

The upstream block in Nginx is used to define a group of backend servers where an incoming request can be proxied to. It is commonly used for load balancing the incoming traffic to multiple servers to improve the overall performance, availability, and reliability of a web application.

- **`server`**

Syntax	`server address [parameters];`
Default	–
Context	`upstream`
Example	`server server1.com:443;` `server server2.com:443;`

Table 2.16: *server*

As explained in the preceding upstream directive, we define the backend servers in the upstream directive where the request should be proxied to. Each backend server is defined using the server directive.

The server directive in Nginx includes domain name or IP address of the backend server, with an optional port. If a port is not specified, by default the 80 port is used.

The following parameters can be defined for advanced setups of each backend server when configuring an upstream group for load balancing requests, setting active health checks, and do similar tasks.

weight

This parameter assigns relative "*importance*" to each server. By default, Nginx distributes requests in a round-robin fashion among all servers in the upstream block. When we specify a weight value, NGINX sends a higher proportion of requests to the server with the larger weight. By default, the weight is 1.

```
upstream backend_server {
    server server1.com:443 weight=1;
    server server2.com:443 weight=3;
}
```

***Figure 2.15**: upstream server with weights*

If **server1** has **weight=1** and **server2** has **weight=2**, NGINX sends 3 out of 4 requests to **server2**, and 1 out of 4 requests to server1.

max_fails

This parameter sets the number of unsuccessful count that Nginx attempts to communicate with the backend server before considering it to be in a failed state.

```
upstream backend_server {
    server server1.com:443 max_fails=2;
    server server2.com:443;
    server server3.com:443;
}
```

***Figure 2.16**: upstream server with max_fails*

In the preceding example, **max_fails=2** for **server1.com** will mark the server as "**down**" after it encounters 2 consecutive request failures. Once a server is marked down,

Nginx temporarily stops sending traffic to it until the defined **fail_timeout** period has elapsed, after which it retries the server to see if it is back online.

Note: *Setting* **max_fails=0** *effectively disables this check. In other words, no matter how many times a server fails, Nginx will never mark it as "down" due to failed attempts. This disables the active health check of the server.*

fail_timeout

After the server is marked down, the **fail_timeout** parameter defines the time period during which a specified number of unsuccessful attempts must happen for a backend server to be considered in a down state.

```
upstream backend_server {
    server server1.com:443 max_fails=2 fail_timeout=10s;
    server server2.com:443;
    server server3.com:443;
}
```

Figure 2.17: *upstream server with fail_timeout*

In the preceding example, the server1.com remains marked "**down**" for 10 seconds. During this interval, Nginx stops sending new requests to the server. Once the 10 seconds passes, Nginx tests the server again to see if it has recovered and should be marked up to take the requests again.

backup

This parameter marks a server as a **backup**. Requests will be sent to the backup server only if all non-backup servers are unavailable.

```
upstream backend_server {
    server server1.com:443 max_fails=2 fail_timeout=10s;
    server server2.com:443;
    server server3.com:443 backup;
}
```

Figure 2.18: *upstream server with backup*

In the preceding example, the incoming requests will be sent to **server1.com** and **server2.com** only. If both **server1.com** and **server2.com** are unavailable, Nginx will start routing traffic to **server3.com**.

resolve

This parameter tells NGINX to dynamically re-resolve DNS for the specified server during runtime. This is crucial when we have upstream hosts whose IPs change frequently, such as in containerized environments.

```
upstream backend_server {
    server server1.com:443;
    server server2.com:443 resolve; #DNS resolved during runtime
}
```

Figure 2.19: *upstream server with resolve*

For the resolve parameter to work, it is important to define the resolver directive.

resolver

The resolver directive specifies which DNS server(s) Nginx should query when it needs to resolve hostnames and backend servers dynamically. It is always defined in the http block of the Nginx configuration.

```
http {
    resolver 8.8.8.8;

    server {
        listen 80;
        server_name www.test.com;

        location /resolved {
            proxy_pass http://backend_server;
        }
    }
    upstream backend_server {
        server backend1.test.com resolve;
        server backend2.test.com;
}
}
```

Figure 2.20: *upstream server with resolver*

In the preceding example, **`resolver 8.8.8.8;`** instructs NGINX to send all its DNS queries to Google's public DNS server at **`8.8.8.8`**.

`slow_start`

This parameter gradually increases the volume of traffic sent to a previously offline or newly added upstream server or when unhealthy server becomes healthy. This feature often give the server time to "**`warm up`**" caches, load data, or reach optimal performance levels. Default value is zero, that is, slow start is disabled.

```
upstream backend_server {
    server server1.com:443 max_fails=2 fail_timeout=10s slow_start=5s;
    server server2.com:443;
    server server3.com:443;
    server server4.com:443;
}
```

***Figure 2.21**: upstream server with slow_start*

In the preceding example, **`slow_start=5s`** will gradually increase the traffic sent to server1.com over a **5-second** period.

`down`

This parameter marks the backend server as permanently unavailable.

```
upstream backend_server {
    server server1.com:443 max_fails=2 fail_timeout=10s;
    server server2.com:443 backup;
    server server3.com:443 down;
}
```

***Figure 2.22**: upstream server with down parameter*

In the preceding example, the **`server3.com`** marked with keyword down is offline and unavailable to route requests.

`drain`

Draining an upstream server is a way to gracefully marking the server as unavailable. When we mark a server as drained:

- Nginx stops sending new traffic to that server.
- Once all existing connections close naturally, allowing to shut the server down without disrupting active users and their sessions.

down Versus drain

Marking a server as "**down**" immediately removes it from load balancing and terminates active connections, treating the server as completely unavailable. By contrast, marking a server as "**draining**" stops new traffic from going to that server *but allows existing connections to continue until they naturally complete.*

- **client_body_buffer_size**

Syntax	client_body_buffer_size size;
Default	client_body_buffer_size 8k|16k;
Context	http, server, location
Example	client_body_buffer_size 10K;

Table 2.17: *client_body_buffer_size*

This directive configures the maximum size of the buffer used for storing the request body from the client. If the request body exceeds this size, it will be written to a temporary file.

In the preceding example, the buffer size is set to 10 KB, meaning that if the client sends a request body larger than this size, it will be written to a temporary file.

- **client_header_buffer_size**

Syntax	client_header_buffer_size size;
Default	client_header_buffer_size 1k;
Context	http, server
Example	client_header_buffer_size 1k;

Table 2.18: *client_header_buffer_size*

This directive configures the maximum size of the buffer used for storing headers from the client (request headers). If the headers exceed this size, Nginx will return a **400 Bad Request** response to the client.

In the preceding example, client header buffer size is set to 1 KB. If the headers from the client exceed this size, Nginx will reject the request with a **400 Bad Request** response. You may need to increase this buffer value to resolve the 400 error.

By defining a limit to the accepted client header size, the website is safeguarded from potential **Host Header Injection or Header Poisoning attacks**.

- **large_client_header_buffers**

Syntax	large_client_header_buffers number size;
Default	large_client_header_buffers 4 8k;

Context	`http, server`
Example	`large_client_header_buffers 2 1k;`

***Table 2.19**: large_client_header_buffers*

This directive sets the maximum number and size of buffers used for processing large client headers. It is useful when dealing with large cookies or numerous headers.

In the preceding example, **`large_client_header_buffers`** is set to 2 1k, which means there will be a maximum of 2 buffers, each with a size of 1 KB.

client_header_buffer_size Versus large_client_header_buffers

In Nginx, both **`client_header_buffer_size`** and **`large_client_header_buffers`** control how HTTP request headers are buffered, but they serve different roles.

Let us understand this with an example.

```
client_header_buffer_size 1k;
large_client_header_buffers 4 8k;
```

***Figure 2.23**: client_header_buffer_size vs. large_client_header_buffers*

`client_header_buffer_size` sets the size of the initial buffer to 1KB. If the initial request line (for example, the **`GET/POST`** line) or headers fit within this buffer, NGINX won't need additional buffers.

If it exceeds 1 KB (like a big cookie), NGINX uses 4 buffers of 8 KB each to handle that data.

In short, **`client_header_buffer_size`** is for smaller or typical headers, while **`large_client_header_buffers`** accommodates bigger headers that don't fit into the initial buffer.

- **`proxy_buffers`**

Syntax	`proxy_buffers number size;`
Default	`proxy_buffers 8 4k|8k;`
Context	`http, server, location`
Example	`proxy_buffers 4 8k;`

***Table 2.20**: proxy_buffers*

This directive sets the number and size of buffers used for reading a response from the proxied server.

In the preceding example, **proxy_buffers** is set to 4 8k, indicating that there are 4 buffers each of size 8 kilobytes.

- **proxy_buffer_size**

Syntax	proxy_buffer_size size;
Default	proxy_buffer_size 4k|8k;
Context	http, server, location
Example	proxy_buffer_size 4k;

Table 2.21: *proxy_buffer_size*

This directive sets the size of the buffer that receives the response from the proxied server. Default is 4k.

If response headers are large (for example, multiple or very long header lines), we need to increase this value to avoid 400 bad request error that would throw "**header too large**" errors.

In the preceding example, **proxy_buffer_size** is set to 4k, specifying the size of the buffer that receives the response from the proxied server.

- **proxy_busy_buffers_size**

Syntax	proxy_busy_buffers_size size;
Default	proxy_busy_buffers_size 8k|16k;
Context	http, server, location
Example	proxy_busy_buffers_size 16k;

Table 2.22: *proxy_busy_buffers_size*

This directive sets the maximum size of temporary memory that is used when reading responses from the proxied server. If the response size exceeds this limit, it is saved to a temporary file.

In the preceding example, **proxy_busy_buffers_size** is set to 16k configuring the maximum size of temporary memory that is used when reading responses from the proxied server.

proxy_buffer_size Versus proxy_busy_buffer_size

proxy_buffer_size focuses on the initial buffer used to store the proxied response headers, while **proxy_busy_buffers_size** dictates the maximum total size of buffers in the "**busy**" state–that is, buffers that have been read from the proxied server but not yet fully sent to the client.

- **`client_max_body_size`**

Syntax	`client_max_body_size size;`
Default	`client_max_body_size 1m;`
Context	`http, server, location`
Example	`client_max_body_size 20M;`

Table 2.23: *client_max_body_size*

This directive is used to limit the size of the client request body. It defines the maximum allowed size of the HTTP request body from the client.

This is very useful in security aspects of the website. It prevents clients from making requests with large payloads that may consume significant server resources or sometimes be malicious.

If the size of the request exceeds the configured value, the status code 413 with **`'Request Entity Too Large'`** error is returned to the client.

Note: *Setting size to 0 disables checking of the client request body size, which is never suggested.*

- **`proxy_connect_timeout`**

Syntax	`proxy_connect_timeout time;`
Default	`proxy_connect_timeout 60s;`
Context	`http, server, location`
Example	`proxy_connect_timeout 120s;`

Table 2.24: *proxy_connect_timeout*

This directive sets how long Nginx waits to establish a connection with an upstream server before timing out. This timeout specifically targets the initial TCP handshake phase between Nginx and the backend.

In the preceding example, it is set to 120 seconds, that is, 2 minutes. This means that Nginx will wait up to 2 minutes for a connection to be established with the backend server.

- **`proxy_send_timeout`**

Syntax	`proxy_send_timeout time;`
Default	`proxy_send_timeout 60s;`
Context	`http, server, location`
Example	`proxy_send_timeout 120s`

Table 2.25: *proxy_send_timeout*

This directive defines the timeout for sending the client request to the proxied server.

In the preceding example, it is set to 120 seconds. If Nginx doesn't finish sending the request to the backend server within this time frame, the connection will be closed.

- **`proxy_read_timeout`**

Syntax	`proxy_read_timeout time;`
Default	`proxy_read_timeout 60s;`
Context	`http, server, location`
Example	`proxy_read_timeout 120s;`

***Table 2.26**: proxy_read_timeout*

This directive sets a timeout for reading a response from the proxied server.

In the preceding example, the **`proxy_read_timeout`** is set to 120 seconds. If the backend server takes more than 2 minutes to respond, the connection will be closed.

- **`send_timeout`**

Syntax	`send_timeout time;`
Default	`send_timeout 60s;`
Context	`http, server, location`
Example	`send_timeout 120s;`

***Table 2.27**: send_timeout*

This directive defines the maximum time allowed for transmitting a response to the client once Nginx has started sending data. If during the specified time period the client stops reading data or is otherwise slow or idle, Nginx will end the connection.

In the preceding example, if the client doesn't read any data for 120 seconds after Nginx starts sending the response, Nginx ends the connection.

`proxy_send_timeout` Versus `send_timeout`

`proxy_send_timeout` is how long Nginx will wait for an upstream server to read data from Nginx (**`Nginx`** → **`Upstream server`**, for example, app).

`send_timeout` is about how long Nginx will wait for a client to continue reading data from Nginx (**`Nginx`** → **`Client`**, for example, browser).

- **`proxy_http_version`**

Syntax	`proxy_http_version 1.0 | 1.1;`
Default	`proxy_http_version 1.0;`

Context	`http, server, location`
Example	`proxy_http_version 1.1;`

***Table 2.28**: proxy_http_version*

The **`proxy_http_version`** directive in Nginx is used to set the HTTP version that Nginx should use when communicating with a proxied server.

In the preceding example, it is set to 1.1, indicating that Nginx should use HTTP/1.1 when proxying requests to the backend server.

Setting it to 1.1 is generally recommended for better performance because it enables features such as persistent connections (keep-alive), and NTLM authentication and supports chunked transfer encoding.

- **`keepalive`**

Syntax	`keepalive connections;`
Default	–
Context	`upstream`
Example	`keepalive 15;`

***Table 2.29**: keepalive*

This directive is configured within an upstream block. It configures how many idle (persistent) connections to maintain open with each backend server. This allows Nginx to reuse existing TCP connections for subsequent requests, reducing overhead from repeatedly establishing new connection.

In the preceding example, **`keepalive 15`** means that Nginx will keep maximum number of 15 idle open connections to the backend server for reuse.

If there are more connections than this number, Nginx may close some of the idle connections to maintain the specified limit.

Relationship Between keepalive and proxy_http_version

For Nginx to keep connection alive, we need to set **`proxy_http_version`** to 1.1 or above. This setting is a mandate to enable the use of persistent connections using keepalive directive.

These settings can work together to optimize the connection management between Nginx and upstream servers, improving performance by reducing the latency associated with establishing new connections for each request.

- **proxy_set_header**

Syntax	proxy_set_header field value;
Default	proxy_set_header Host $proxy_host; proxy_set_header Connection close;
Context	http, server, location
Example	proxy_set_header Host $host; proxy_set_header X-Real-IP $remote_addr; proxy_set_header HOST www.example.com;

Table 2.30: *proxy_set_header*

This directive customizes or overrides the HTTP request headers that Nginx sends to an upstream server

In the preceding example, **`proxy_set_header Host $host;`** ensures the upstream sees the original Host header (for example, **`mydomain.com`**) instead of the upstream server's hostname.

`proxy_set_header X-Real-IP $remote_addr;` passes the client's real IP address to the upstream in a custom header X-Real-IP, which can further help with logging or other IP-based logic.

`proxy_set_header HOST www.example.com;` overrides the HOST header to **`www.example.com`** for all requests to the upstream server, even if the incoming request is https://www.mydomain.com/helloworld.

- **add_header**

Syntax	add_header name value [always];
Default	–
Context	http, server, location, if in location
Example	add_header RuleName redirect always;

Table 2.31: *add_header*

This directive adds custom header to the response returned to the client. It is also typically used for adding security-related headers (X-Frame-Options, Content-Security-Policy), for providing additional information to the client and for troubleshooting errors.

`[always]` parameter is an optional parameter but highly recommended.

It ensures that the header is added even if there is a header with the same name in the response or even if the header value is empty.

Note: *When working Nginx as a reverse proxy, it is recommended to rely on* **add_header** *directive to observe which values end up stored in various variables—whether it is a back-referenced variable or any other custom variable. By assigning a specific header, you can then open your browser's Inspect Element tool to verify the variable value, making it easy to confirm that your configuration and variable assignments are working as intended.*

proxy_set_header Versus add_header

The use case between these two is a common point of confusion.

Use **add_header** for headers that you want to include in the response generated by Nginx for the client.

Use **proxy_add_header** for headers that you want to include in the request sent to the proxied server or in the response received from the proxied server.

- **merge_slash**

Syntax	merge_slashes on | off;
Default	merge_slashes on;
Context	http, server

Table 2.32: *Merge_slash*

This directive enables or disables compression of two or more adjacent slashes in a URI into a single slash. The removal of extra slashes is essential for the correct location block matching with prefix string and regular expression.

For example, the incoming URL is https://www.example.com/hello//world and merge_slashes is off, the URL will not match the following location block.

```
location /hello / {
    ...
}
```

Hence, using **merge_slasshes** on; will ensure the URL gets converted to "**/hello/world**".

We have only highlighted the most commonly used Nginx directives here; however, please note that more than 500 exist in total, including both the core directives and those provided by official and third-party modules. You can find the complete list on the official NGINX website. Additional directives related to load balancing, Nginx dashboards, and maps will be explored in later chapters.

Nginx Modules

Just as in object-oriented programming–whether in C, C++, or Java–you can import a Math module to access functions such as pow or sum, Nginx also uses a modular architecture to extend its capabilities. Its functionality is neatly divided into specialized modules as:

- HTTP modules
- Stream modules
- Mail modules

Each module is designed to handle a specific type of network protocol or task. This design lets administrators activate only the features they need, much like selectively importing a library to solve a particular problem in your code.

http Modules

Role: Handles HTTP and HTTPS traffic.

Use Cases:

- Serving static files
- Acting as a reverse proxy or load balancer for web applications
- Providing caching, compression, and other HTTP-specific features

The following table lists all the HTTP modules along with example configurations for each:

Module	Description	Example

`ngx_http_core_module`	Core HTTP functionality, including server and location block configuration.	`http {`
		`server {`
		`listen 80;`
		`server_name example.com; location`
		`/ {`
		`root /var/www/html;`
		`index index.html;`
		`} } }`

`ngx_http_access_module`	Allows or denies access to specific client addresses or ranges.	`location /admin/ {` `allow 192.168.1.0/24; deny all; }`
`ngx_http_api_module`	Provides an API for other modules to interact with the NGINX configuration.	Used internally by other modules; not typically configured directly by users.

ngx_http_auth_basic_module	Implements HTTP Basic Authentication.	`location /secure/ {`
		`auth_basic "Restricted Area";`
		`auth_basic_user_file /etc/nginx/.htpasswd;`
		`}`

ngx_http_geo_module	Enables variables based on client addresses or request values.	`geo $country {`
		`default "US";`
		`192.168.1.0/24 "Local";`
		`}`

ngx_http_gzip_module	Enables response compression using the gzip algorithm.	`gzip on;` `gzip_types text/plain text/css application/json;`

ngx_http_gzip_static_module	Serves pre-compressed static files, reducing CPU load.	`location /static/ {`
		`gzip_static on;`
		`}`

ngx_http_headers_module	Allows modification of HTTP response headers.	`add_header X-Custom-Header "MyValue";`

ngx_http_js_module	Embeds JavaScript in the configuration for more dynamic behavior.	`js_import myscript.js;`
		`server {`
		`js_content my_js_function;`
		`}`

ngx_http_keyval_module	Provides a key-value store for variables.	`keyval_zone zone=myzone:10m; server {`
		`keyval_lookup myzone key $arg_key;`
		`}`

ngx_http_limit_conn_module	Limits the number of simultaneous connections per IP address.	`limit_conn_zone $binary_remote_addr zone=addr:10m;`
		`location / {`
		`limit_conn addr 10;`
		`}`

ngx_http_limit_req_module	Limits the rate of incoming requests.	`limit_req_zone $binary_remote_addr zone=one:10m rate=1r/s; location /api/ {`
		`limit_req zone=one burst=5;`
		`}`

ngx_http_log_module	Enables logging of HTTP requests and errors.	`access_log /var/log/nginx/access.log; error_log /var/log/nginx/error.log warn;`

ngx_http_map_module	Creates new variables based on values of other variables.	`map $http_user_agent $mobile {`
		`default 0;`
		`"~Mobile" 1;`
		`}`

<table>
<tr><td>ngx_http_mirror_module</td><td>Mirrors requests to another server for testing or logging purposes.</td><td><code>location / {
mirror /mirror;
}
location = /mirror {
internal;
proxy_pass http://mirror.example.com;
}</code></td></tr>
<tr><td>ngx_http_rewrite_module</td><td>Provides powerful URL rewriting capabilities.</td><td><code>rewrite ^/oldpath/(.*)$ /newpath/$1 permanent;</code></td></tr>
<tr><td>ngx_http_split_clients_module</td><td>Splits clients into groups using various methods.</td><td><code>split_clients "$remote_addr" $variant {
50% "A";
50% "B";
}</code></td></tr>
<tr><td>ngx_http_ssl_module</td><td>Enables SSL/TLS support for secure HTTPS connections.</td><td><code>server {
listen 443 ssl;
ssl_certificate /path/to/cert.pem;
ssl_certificate_key /path/to/key.pem;
}</code></td></tr>
<tr><td>ngx_http_status_module</td><td>Provides a simple HTML status page for monitoring server health.</td><td><code>location /status {
stub_status on;
access_log off;
}</code></td></tr>
<tr><td>ngx_http_upstream_module</td><td>Manages communication with upstream servers, including load balancing.</td><td><code>upstream backend {
server backend1.example.com; server backend2.example.com;
}</code></td></tr>
</table>

Table 2.33: *HTTP Modules with Examples*

Mail Modules

Role: Acts as a proxy for email protocols such as SMTP, IMAP, and POP3.

Use Cases:

- Running mail services behind Nginx for advanced load balancing or SSL termination
- Consolidating multiple mail servers under one domain

Module	Description	Example

ngx_mail_core_module	Core functionality for the mail proxy server.	mail {
		server {
		listen 25;
		protocol smtp; proxy_pass_error_message on;
		}
		}
		#Core mail functionality configuration

ngx_mail_auth_http_module	Allows authentication through an HTTP server.	mail {
		server {
		listen 25;
		protocol smtp;
		auth_http 127.0.0.1:9000/cgi-bin/auth;
		}
		}
		#Pass authentication requests to an HTTP service

ngx_mail_proxy_module	Implements the mail proxy functionality.	mail {
		server {
		listen 25;
		protocol smtp;
		xclient off;
		}
		}
		#Enable proxying for mail traffic proxy on;

***Table 2.34**: Mail Modules*

Stream Modules

Role: Handles TCP and UDP traffic.

Use Cases:

- Load balancing or proxying non-HTTP protocols (for example, database connections, custom TCP/UDP services)
- SSL/TLS offloading for applications that do not use HTTP

Module	Description	Example

ngx_stream_core_module	Core functionality for the stream proxy server.	stream {
		server {
		listen 12345;
		proxy_pass backend;
		} }

ngx_stream_access_module	Allows or denies access to specific client addresses or ranges.	`stream { server { listen 12345; allow 192.168.1.0/24; deny all; proxy_pass backend; } }`
ngx_stream_geo_module	Enables variables based on client addresses or request values.	`stream { geo $client_group { default 0; 192.168.1.0/24 1; } }`
ngx_stream_geoip_module	Integrates with GeoIP databases for obtaining geo-location information.	`stream { geoip_country /usr/share/GeoIP/GeoIP.dat; server { listen 12345; proxy_pass backend; } }`
ngx_stream_js_module	Embeds JavaScript code into the NGINX configuration for dynamic behavior.	`stream { js_import myscript.js; server { listen 12345; js_content my_function; } }`
ngx_stream_keyval_module	Provides a key-value store for managing variables.	`stream { keyval_zone myzone:10m; }`
ngx_stream_limit_conn_module	Limits the number of concurrent connections per client (IP address).	`stream { limit_conn_zone $binary_remote_addr zone=addr:10m; server { listen 12345; limit_conn addr 5; proxy_pass backend; } }`
ngx_stream_log_module	Enables logging of stream requests.	`stream { server { listen 12345; access_log /var/log/nginx/stream_access.log; proxy_pass backend; } }`
ngx_stream_map_module	Creates variables based on values of other variables.	`stream { map $remote_addr $group { default "A"; 192.168.1.0/24 "B"; } }`

ngx_stream_proxy_module	Implements generic TCP/UDP stream proxy functionality.	stream {
		upstream backend {
		server backend1.example.com:12345;
		server backend2.example.com:12345; }
		server {
		listen 12345;
		proxy_pass backend;
		} }

ngx_stream_realip_module	Replaces the client IP address with the one provided in the X-Real-IP or X-Forwarded-For header.	stream {
		server {
		listen 12345 proxy_protocol;
		real_ip_header proxy_protocol; set_real_ip_from 192.168.0.0/16;
		proxy_pass backend;
		} }

ngx_stream_set_module	Sets variables to specified values.	stream {
		server {
		listen 12345;
		set $foo "bar";
		proxy_pass backend;
		} }

ngx_stream_split_clients_module	Splits clients into groups using various methods, useful for A/B testing or traffic segmentation.	stream { split_clients "$remote_addr" $group { 50% "groupA"; 50% "groupB"; } }

ngx_stream_ssl_module	Enables SSL/TLS support for securing TCP/UDP streams.	stream {
		server {
		listen 443 ssl; ssl_certificate /path/to/cert.pem; ssl_certificate_key /path/to/key.pem; proxy_pass backend;
		} }

ngx_stream_upstream_module	Manages communication with upstream servers in a stream context, including load balancing and failover.	stream {
		upstream backend {
		server backend1.example.com:12345;
		server backend2.example.com:12345;
		}
		server {
		listen 12345;
		proxy_pass backend;
		} }

Table 2.35: *Stream Modules*

Nginx Variables

There are two types of variables in Nginx:

- Nginx in-built variables
- Nginx custom variables

Nginx In-Built Variables

Nginx variables are placeholders that allow us to store and reuse data within your configuration. They are typically prefixed with a dollar sign (**$**) and can represent various aspects of a current request or server state. Variables are useful for tasks such as rewriting URLs, conditional processing, and logging custom information.

The following table outlines some of the most common Nginx variables along with their descriptions:

Variable	**Description**
`$scheme`	The request scheme (HTTP or HTTPS).
`$host`	The value of the Host header in the request.
`$request_uri`	The full original request URI, including arguments like query parameters.
`$uri`	The request URI without the arguments.
`$document_root`	The root directory where the Nginx server is serving files.
`$remote_addr`	The client's IP address.
`$is_args`	Signify '**?**' in the URL
`$args`	The request arguments after the ? parameter
`$server_name`	The name of the server block handling the request.
`$request_method`	The request method (e.g., GET, POST, PUT, DELETE).
`$http_user_agent`	The user-agent string from the client's request (browser, postman).
`$http_referer`	The referrer (referrer) header from the client's request.
`$http_cookie`	The value of the Cookie header from the client's request.
`$sent_http_content_type`	The Content-Type header of the response sent to the client.
`$status`	The HTTP status code of the response sent to the client.
`$proxy_host`	The name of the upstream that served the request.
`$proxy_add_x_forwarded_for`	The X-Forwarded-For header value from the client request.

Variable	Description
$upstream_addr	The IP address and port of the upstream server to which a request was sent.
$time_local	Local time of the server when the request was processed (Common Log Format).
$remote_addr	Client's IP address.
$request	Full original request URI, including arguments.
$request_length	Length of the client request.
$bytes_sent	Number of bytes sent to the client.
$body_bytes_sent	Number of body bytes sent to the client.
$upstream_status	HTTP status code received from the upstream server.
$request_time	Total time taken to process the request, in seconds with millisecond resolution.
$upstream_response_time	Time taken for the upstream server to respond to the request.
$upstream_connect_time	Time spent establishing a connection with the upstream server.
$upstream_header_time	Time spent receiving the response headers from the upstream server.
$request_body	Request body.

***Table 2.36**: Nginx Variables*

Nginx Custom Variable

You can create custom variables using the set directive. Custom variables are user-defined and can be used to store and manipulate values within the configuration. Here is an example of how to create and use a custom variable:

```
set $custom_variable "HelloWorld!";
```

In this example, a custom variable named **$custom_variable** is created the value "**HelloWorld!**" is assigned to it.

Custom variables are useful when you need to store intermediate values, dynamically generate content, or simplify complex configurations. They have a limited scope and are only available within the block in which they are defined. If you want to make a variable available in multiple locations or blocks, you may need to use a different approach, such as the map directive.

Conclusion

In this chapter, we have delved into the intricacies of Nginx configuration, uncovering the powerful features that make it a preferred choice for high-performance web serving and reverse proxying. We explored the key components such as location blocks, directives, and modules and learned how they work together to manage complex web traffic scenarios.

This understanding is critical when configuring modules such as rate limiting or caching, where precision and efficiency directly impact server performance.

We will continue to learn more about the directives as we explore other aspects such as load balancing, rate limiting, and health checks in dedicated chapters. In the next chapter, we will learn about load balancing.

Example Configuration

Let us now write a sample Nginx configuration using the contexts, directives, and modules we have discussed.

Write Nginx configuration to accept incoming traffic for http://www.test.com/understanding/nginx/chapter/2 and route the traffic to https://www.test.com/understanding/nginx/chapter/2, where the backend is www.backend1.com and www.backend2.com, distributing the load equally on both the servers.

Solution:

```
nginx.conf

user nginx;

worker_processes auto;

error_log  /var/log/nginx/error.log ;
pid        /var/run/nginx.pid;

worker_rlimit_nofile 16192;

#events context
events {
    worker_connections  8096;
}

#http context
http {
```

```
    include /etc/nginx/mime.types;
    log_format main ‹"$time_local" client=$remote_addr ‹
                ‹method=$request_method request="$request" ‹
                ‹request_length=$request_length ‹
                ‹status=$status bytes_sent=$bytes_sent ‹
                ‹body_bytes_sent=$body_bytes_sent ‹
                ‹upstream_addr=$upstream_addr ‹
                ‹upstream_status=$upstream_status ‹
                ‹request_time=$request_time ‹
                ‹upstream_response_time=$upstream_response_time ‹
                ‹upstream_connect_time=$upstream_connect_time ‹
                ‹upstream_header_time=$upstream_header_time ‹
                ‹body=$request_body› ;

    keepalive_timeout  65;

    gzip  on;
    client_body_buffer_size 80M;
    client_header_buffer_size 1M;
    client_max_body_size 1M;
    large_client_header_buffers 2 1M;

    proxy_http_version 1.1;

    proxy_connect_timeout 60s;
    proxy_send_timeout 60s;
    proxy_read_timeout 60s;
    send_timeout 60s;

    proxy_buffer_size 512k;
    proxy_buffers 6 512k;
    proxy_busy_buffers_size 512k;

    include /etc/nginx/conf.d/configuration.conf;

}

configuration.conf

server {
    listen 80;
    server_name www.test.com;

    access_log /var/log/nginx/access.log main;

   location / {
    proxy_set_header Connection "";
```

```
        proxy_set_header HOST $host;
        proxy_pass_header Server;
        return 301 https://$host$request_uri;
    }
    }
    server {
        listen 443;
        server_name www.test.com;

        access_log /var/log/nginx/access.log main;

        #Certificate and key
        ssl_certificate /etc/nginx/cert/cert.pem;
        ssl_certificate_key /etc/nginx/cert/key.pem;

       location / {
        proxy_set_header Connection "";
        proxy_set_header HOST $host;
        proxy_pass_header Server;
        proxy_pass https://backend

       }
    }

    upstream backend {
        server www.backend1.com:443;
        server www.backend2.com:443;
        keepalive 15;
    }
```

The above Nginx configuration sets up a reverse proxy for the domain www.test.com, with a focus on scalability, request handling, and detailed logging.

- **Global Setup (`nginx.conf`)**
    - Uses **`worker_processes`** auto to scale with available CPU cores.
    - Sets **`worker_rlimit_nofile`** and **`worker_connections`** for high concurrency.
    - Defines a detailed **`log_format (main)`** for tracking client IPs, request metadata, response statuses, and upstream timings.
    - Enables Gzip compression and configures generous buffer sizes to handle large requests efficiently.
    - Sets timeouts (**`proxy_connect_timeout`**, **`proxy_read_timeout`**, etc.) to 60 seconds to prevent hanging connections.
    - Includes the secondary config file: **`/etc/nginx/conf.d/configuration.conf`**.

- **HTTP Server Block (Port 80)**
    - Listens on www.test.com.
    - Redirects all HTTP traffic to HTTPS using a 301 permanent redirect to ensure secure communication.
    - Logs access using the custom main format.
- **HTTPS Server Block (Port 443)**
    - Configured with SSL certificates (`cert.pem` and `key.pem`).
    - Proxies all requests to the backend, preserving the original host and server headers.
    - Uses `proxy_pass` https://backend, sending traffic securely to backend services.
- **Upstream Configuration**
    - Defines a load-balanced group named backend with:
        - Two backend servers (`www.backend1.com:443`, `www.backend2.com:443`).
        - `keepalive 15` to maintain persistent connections for performance.

Chapter 3
Load Balancing

Introduction

Let us return to the pizza shop example from the first chapter. Imagine it is a bustling day—a day when orders are continuously flooding in. As each new pizza order arrives, the manager surveys the entire kitchen. The manager does not simply distribute orders arbitrarily. Rather, he meticulously checks on every chef: gauging their current workload, assessing their pace, and understanding their capacity to handle more orders. The chef with the most available bandwidth without compromising the quality of the pizza is the one chosen to take on the incoming order.

In the very same essence of a manager in a pizza shop, load balancer ensures that each backend resource is neither overwhelmed nor underutilized by continuously monitoring the health, status, and capacity of backend resources. It evaluates which server is primed to accept a new client request, directing traffic efficiently and evenly. Its primary purpose is to ensure that no single server or resource becomes overwhelmed with too much traffic.

As we learned in the first chapter, a load balancer is a device, software application, or service that distributes client traffic across multiple backend servers or resources. To maintain optimal performance and reliability, load balancers employ various algorithms to distribute the incoming requests efficiently. The beauty of the load balancers is that we can set up health checks and proactively act if any application server goes down.

Load balancing across multiple application instances is a commonly used technique for modern, high-traffic websites, such as e-commerce giants including Amazon, Dell, Netflix, and many more.

To summarize, load balancers:

- Distributes client requests or network load efficiently across multiple backend servers.
- Ensures high availability and reliability by sending requests only to servers that are online.
- Provides the flexibility to add or subtract servers as per the demand.

- Helps in optimizing resource utilization, maximizing throughput, reducing latency hence improving performance, scalability, and reliability of web applications.

Structure

In this chapter, the following topics will be covered:

- Benefits of Load Balancing
- Types of Load Balancers
- Types of Network Traffic
- HTTP Load Balancing
- Nginx Configuration to Proxy HTTP Traffic
- Load Balancing Algorithms
- Session Persistence
- Limiting the Number of Connections
- Configuring Load Balancing for UDP and TCP Connections

Benefits of Load Balancing

Well, we can easily say that load balancer acts as the "*traffic police*" sitting in front of our application servers. In addition to redirecting and controlling traffic to the application server, it acts as a shield to protect the servers since the client won't have direct connection to them. Some key advantages of having load balancers in the network are listed as follows:

- **Enhanced Performance:** The load balancers ensure even distribution of the traffic load across the application servers. This prevents any single server getting overwhelmed or overused. The request will be sent to the server only that is capable of handling the traffic. This way it keeps a check on all the server resources being utilized effectively hence improving performance.
- **Enhanced Scalability:** Load balancers perform continuous health checks on the pool of servers to ensure that only the healthy servers receive incoming traffic. By routinely pinging each server or sending test requests, they verify that the servers are functioning correctly. If a server fails to meet the required standards due to network glitches—the load balancer temporarily removes it from the rotation. Similarly, to add the servers to the pool, we can simply add the server, and the load balancer will send traffic to the server only if it is healthy and ready to serve the request.
- **Disaster Recovery:** With the help of proper health checks, load balancers can detect if a server is not responding or is experiencing issues. In such cases,

the load balancer can redirect traffic to healthy servers, ensuring continuous service availability and minimizing downtime. This comes very handy when we try to do routine data centre maintenance activities or when there is any network outages.

- **High Availability:** Load balancing setups often include multiple application servers across multiple data centre. If one server fails or one data centre is down, the load balancer redirects traffic to the remaining healthy servers or the other data centre, ensuring that users experience no impact. Do you ever see Dell.com going down? Well, that doesn't mean they do not have network glitches. It simple mean they have a solid network architecture with load balancers doing their job right.
- **Optimized Resource Utilization:** Load balancers can handle several tasks that is traditionally done by application servers. For example, they can perform client server certificate validation, thereby freeing up server resources or also enable gzip encryption and decryption to optimize overall server resource utilization.
- **Absorbing Network Disturbances:** For distributed systems with multiple data centres, load balancers can dynamically adjust network disturbances. One classic example would be a datacentre network outage.
- **Routing Traffic to Nearest Geo Locations:** The load balancers have capability to read client IP and hence routing traffic to nearest datacentres, thereby reducing the overall response time of the request.
- **Enhanced Security:** Load balancers can help mitigate DDoS attacks by configuring rate limiting and blocking specific suspected Ips.
- **Enhanced Monitoring:** Load balancers often provide centralized management interfaces, making it easier to configure, monitor, and manage the overall traffic. For Nginx Plus, we have Nginx Dashboards that gives us an overview of all the 2xx, 3xx, 4xx, and 5xx along with healthy and unhealthy servers.

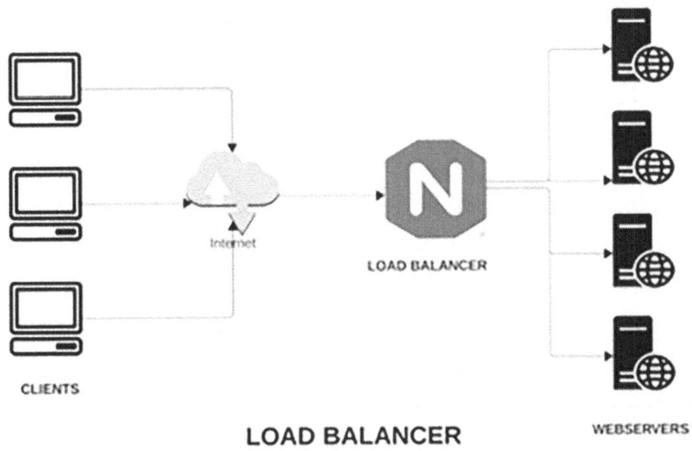

Figure 3.1: *Load Balancer*

In summary, load balancing is a crucial component for enhancing the performance, reliability, and scalability of applications and services in distributed computing environments.

Types of Load Balancers

Load balancers are two types: hardware load balancer and software load balancer.

- **Hardware Load Balancers:** A hardware-based load balancer is a physical hardware device that can securely load balance and redirect traffic to different application servers. Example: F5 BIGIP, Cisco ACE.

  Hardware load balancers require an initial investment and continuous maintenance. In scenarios when the traffic volume increases suddenly beyond its current capacity, we may need to add additional hardware that may not be easy to do.

- **Software Load Balancers:** A software-based load balancer is a software that operate on server hardware or virtual machines. They are often more flexible and can be deployed in a variety of environments. Example: Nginx, HAProxy, Apache.

  In contrast, software-based load balancers are much more flexible. They can scale up or down easily and are more compatible with modern cloud computing environments. They also cost less to set up, manage, and use over time.

Types of Network Traffic

There are three distinct types of network traffic:

- Hypertext Transfer Protocol (HTTP)
- Transmission Control Protocol (TCP)
- User Datagram Protocol (UDP)

HTTP

- **Application Layer (7th layer in an OSI Model) Protocol:** Specifically designed for transmitting web content, such as HTML documents, between clients and servers.
- **Built on TCP:** Relies on TCP for reliable data transfer, inheriting its connection-oriented characteristics.
- **Stateless Communication:** Each HTTP request is independent, making it scalable for the web.

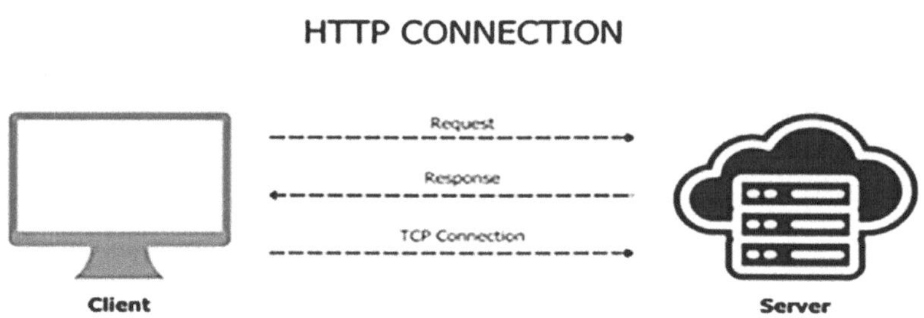

***Figure 3.2**: Hypertext Transfer Protocol (HTTP)*

TCP

- **Connection-Oriented:** Establishes a connection through a handshake process before data transmission.
- **Reliable Delivery:** Ensures data packets are delivered accurately and in sequence through error-checking and retransmission mechanisms.
- **Overhead:** Involves higher overhead due to connection management, making it suitable for applications where data integrity is critical (for example, file transfers, emails).

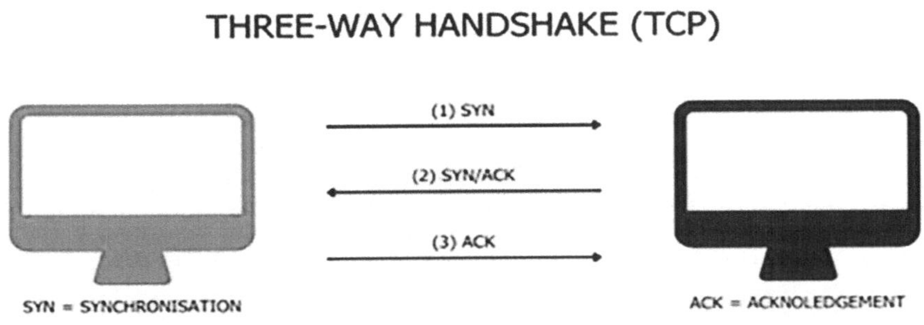

Figure 3.3: *Transmission Control Protocol (TCP)*

UDP

- **Connectionless:** Sends data packets without establishing a dedicated connection, reducing setup time.
- **Fast and Lightweight:** Minimal overhead allows for rapid transmission, making it ideal for time-sensitive applications.
- **No Guarantee:** Does not guarantee packet delivery or order, which is acceptable in scenarios including live streaming, online gaming, or VoIP where speed is prioritized over perfect reliability.

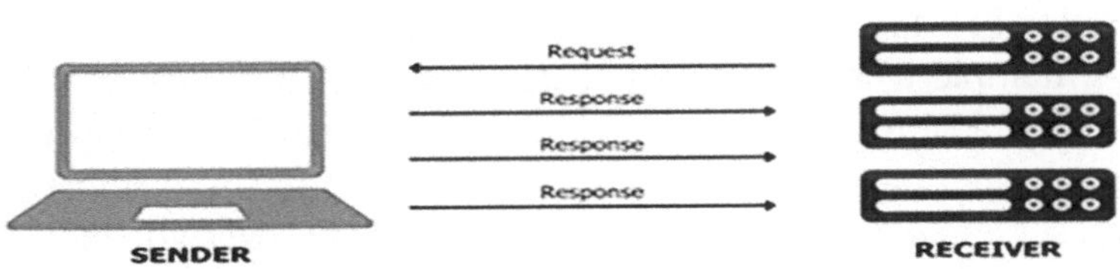

Figure 3.4: *User Datagram Protocol (UDP)*

HTTP versus TCP versus UDP Load Balancing:

Features	HTTP Load Balancing	TCP Load Balancing	UDP Load Balancing
Layer	Application Layer (Layer 7)	Transport Layer (Layer 4)	Transport Layer (Layer 4)
Protocol	HTTP	Transmission Control Protocol (TCP)	User Datagram Protocol (UDP)
Characteristics	Distributes client traffic based URL, and request headers information.	Distributes traffic based on TCP connection information (IP addresses and port numbers).	Distributes traffic based on UDP connection information (IP addresses and port numbers).
Use Case	Commonly used for balancing traffic to web servers, application servers, and other HTTP services.	Works well for load balancing non-HTTP applications, such as databases, email servers, and custom TCP-based services.	Often used for real-time applications, multimedia streaming, and certain gaming protocols.

Table 3.1: *HTTP versus UDP versus TCP*

HTTP Load Balancing

HTTP load balancing is commonly used in the context of web applications, where requests are routed based on the HTTP protocol. As HTTP operates over TCP, it inherits the TCP's connection-oriented, reliable nature, allowing load balancers to distribute traffic efficiently across multiple web servers.

An example of HTTP load balancing is seen in a popular online shopping website that employs multiple web servers to manage customer requests. In this scenario, a load balancer acts as a "*traffic police*" by distributing incoming traffic—whether users are browsing product pages, adding items to their cart, or proceeding to checkout—across several servers. This ensures that no single server is overwhelmed, preserving a seamless user experience even during peak traffic periods, such as Black Friday sales.

Nginx Configuration to Proxy HTTP Traffic

The key directives required to set load balancer for HTTP traffic are:

- `upstream`
- `server`

upstream

The **upstream** directive is used to define a pool or group of backend servers that will handle the HTTP traffic. It acts as an alias for multiple servers, allowing the load balancer to distribute incoming requests among them. Within the upstream block, you can configure various parameters such as load balancing methods, health checks, and timeouts to optimize traffic distribution.

We have discussed the detailed directive description in *Chapter 2, Get Started with Nginx Configurations (Section: Nginx Directive).*

server

Within the upstream block, the server directive is used to specify the individual backend servers. Each server directive defines the address and port where the request needs to be forwarded. This group of servers is called server pool.

Additionally, we can include parameters such as weight (to influence traffic distribution), **max_fails**, and **fail_timeout** to fine-tune how the load balancer interacts with each server. Together, these directives enable the load balancer to efficiently manage and distribute HTTP traffic, ensuring high availability and responsiveness even during traffic spikes.

For example, the following configuration defines a server group named **application_backend** and consists of three application server.

```
http {
    upstream application_backend {
        server server1.example.com:443;
        server server2.example.com:443;
    }
}
```

***Figure* 3.5:** *application_backend*

To pass requests to the upstream **application_backend**, the name of the group is specified in the **proxy_pass** directive specified in the location block, shown as follows:

```
http{
server {
    location / {
        proxy_pass http://application_backend;
    }
}
upstream application_backend {
    server server1.example.com:443;
    server server2.example.com:443;
    }
}
```

Figure 3.6: *proxy_pass*

This configuration demonstrates how the basic HTTP request load balancing is set up in Nginx. With this foundation, we can fine-tune Nginx to implement different load balancing algorithms based on the specific requirements of the application. In general, there are several types of load balancing algorithms available. Let us explore each one and see how we can configure them in Nginx.

Load Balancing Algorithms

Load balancing algorithms distribute incoming network traffic or workload across multiple servers or resources to ensure optimal performance, availability, and reliability.

Round-Robin

Round-robin load balancing is one of the most commonly used load balancing algorithms. Client requests are distributed sequentially to each application servers in circular rotation.

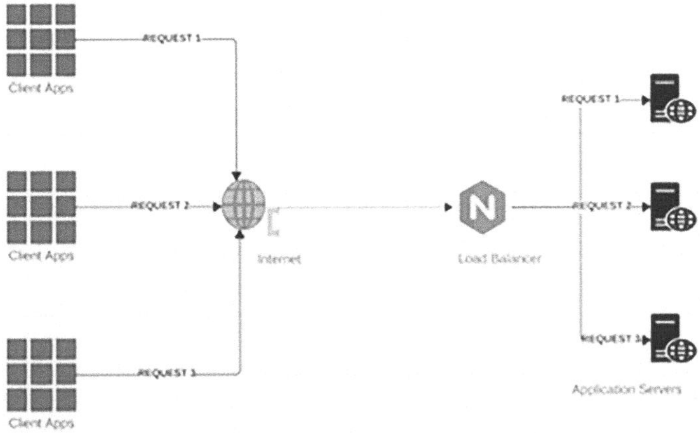

***Figure 3.7**: Round-Robin Load Balancing*

For example, if you have three application servers and three client requests:

1. The first client request is sent to the first application server.
2. The second client request is sent to the second application server.
3. The third client request to the third application server and so on.

The load balancer continues passing requests to servers based on this order. This ensures that the server load is distributed evenly to handle high traffic.

Round-robin load balancing is most appropriate for predictable client request that are being spread across web servers with equal processing capabilities and resources (such as CPU, RAM, and Network bandwidth).

- **Advantage:** It is simple and easy to implement with even distribution of requests.
- **Disadvantage:** Does not consider application server load.

Nginx configuration to implement Round-Robin: While configuring the upstream, by default the load balancing algorithm is round-robin.

```
upstream applicationName {
    # no keyword required. By default it is round robin
    server server1.example.com:443;
    server server2.example.com:443;
}
```

***Figure 3.8**: Nginx Configuration to Implement Round-Robin*

Weighted Round-Robin Load Balancing Method

Weighted Round-Robin is an extension of the basic Round-Robin load balancing algorithm. The disadvantage of a basic round-robin is resolved with weighted round-robin.

In weighted Round-Robin, each application server is assigned a weight that represents its capacity to handle traffic. The weight determines the proportion of requests each server receives. Servers with higher weights receive more client traffic, while those with lower weights receive less.

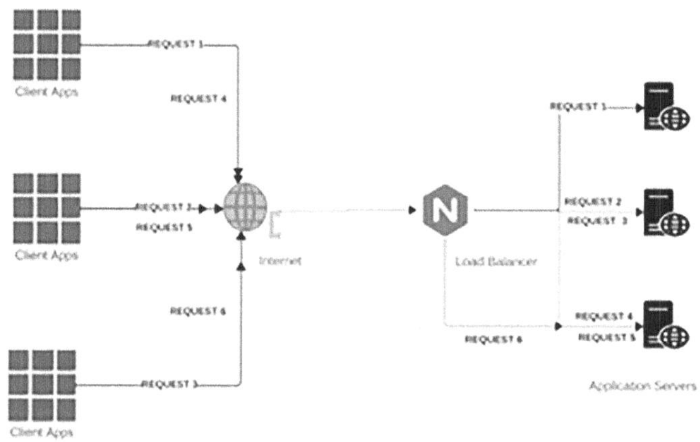

***Figure* 3.9**: *Weighted Round-Robin*

For example, if you have three application servers and six client requests, where on an average:

1. First application server can handle 5 requests per second
2. Second application server can handle 10 requests per second
3. Third application server can handle 15 requests per second

The six client requests are distributed as follows:

1. One request is sent to first application server
2. Two requests are sent to second application server
3. Three requests are sent to third application server

- **Advantages:** This algorithm offers more control over load distribution by considering server capabilities.
- **Disadvantages:** The weights are typically static and do not adapt to dynamic changes in server loads.

Nginx configuration to implement weighted Round-Robin: The "**weight**" parameter is added after the server address and port in the upstream directive. We learned about the **weight** parameter in details in *Chapter 2, Get Started with Nginx Configurations*, in "*server*" directive section.

```
upstream applicationName {
    server server1.example.com:443 weight=5;
    server server2.example.com:443 weight=10;
    server server2.example.com:443 weight=15;
}
```

***Figure 3.10**: weight Parameter*

IP Hash

IP Hash load balancing is a method of distributing client traffic across a group of application servers based on the source IP address of the client. This algorithm generates a unique hash key based on the client's IP address and then that requests from the same client IP address are consistently directed to the same server, providing a form of ***session persistence***. This method is most appropriate when it is vital that a client always return to the same server for each successive connection.

- **Advantages:** Provides session persistence for a specific client.
- **Disadvantages:** If the distribution of client IP addresses is not uniform, some servers may be more heavily loaded than others. Also, adding or removing servers may require redistributing the IP hash mappings, potentially causing network disruptions.

Nginx configuration to implement ip_hash: The **ip_hash** keyword or nginx directive is defined to instruct Nginx to use **ip hash** load balancing algorithm. We define the **ip_hash** within the upstream block.

- **ip_hash**

Syntax	ip_hash;
Default	–
Context	upstream

***Table 3.2**: ip hash*

```
upstream applicationName {
    ip_hash;
    server server1.example.com:443;
    server server2.example.com:443;
}
```

Figure 3.11: *ip_hash*

Least Connection

Least connection is a dynamic load balancing algorithm where client requests are distributed to those application server that has the least number of active connections. The server with the fewest active connections at a given time is chosen to handle the next incoming request. This technique is most appropriate for incoming requests that have varying connection times and a set of application servers that are relatively similar in terms of processing power and available resources. Hence, no server will be overwhelmed with the requests.

- **Advantages:** This algorithm balances the load based on the current application server load, adapting to dynamic changes.
- **Disadvantages:** While it considers the current number of connections, it doesn't consider the overall capacity or capability of each server.

Nginx configuration to implement least connection: The **`least_conn`** keyword or nginx directive is defined to instruct Nginx to use least connection load balancing algorithm. We define **`least_conn`** within the upstream block.

- **`least_conn`**

Syntax	`least_conn;`
Default	–
Context	`upstream`

Table 3.3: *least_conn*

```
upstream applicationName {
    least_conn;
    server server1.example.com:443;
    server server2.example.com:443;
}
```

Figure 3.12: *least_conn*

Generic Hash

For generic hash load balancing algorithm, the application server chosen to which a request is sent is based on a user-defined key which can be a text or a string, variable, or a combination of both. For example, the key may be pair of source IP address and port, or a URI for some case.

- **Advantages:** It can be tailored to specific requirements, making it suitable for a wide range of applications.
- **Disadvantages:** Depending on the chosen hashing criteria and implementation, it may introduce complexity compared to simpler load balancing algorithms which may lead to load imbalance.

Nginx configuration: The **`hash`** keyword or nginx directive is defined to indicate Nginx to use Generic hash load balancing algorithm.

- **`hash key`**

Syntax	`hash key [consistent];`
Default	–
Context	`upstream`

Table 3.4: *hash key*

```
upstream applicationName {
    hash $request_uri consistent;
   server server1.example.com:443;
   server server2.example.com:443;
}
```

Figure 3.13: *hash key*

We can use other variables such as **`$http_cookie`**, **`$arg_parameter`**, or any other relevant request attribute to create a hash based on our application's requirements. Requests are distributed across all backend servers based on the user-defined hashed key value.

The optional "**`consistent`**" parameter ensures that only a few keys will be remapped to different servers when a server is added to or removed from the server pool. This helps to achieve a higher cache hit ratio for caching servers.

[Ketama (Key-Tagged Hashing for Memcached) is a consistent hashing algorithm commonly used for distributed caching systems, specifically with Memcached. Consistent hashing is a technique that aims to minimize the rehashing required when the number of servers in a distributed system changes. Ketama uses a specific variation of consistent hashing known as "key tagging."]

Random

Random load balancing algorithm distributes incoming requests randomly across a group of servers. Unlike more sophisticated load balancing algorithms, random load balancing doesn't consider the current state or load of application servers. Instead, each incoming request is assigned to a server randomly.

While Random Load Balancing is easy to implement, it may not be the best choice for all scenarios, particularly in production environments with varying workloads or heterogeneous server capacities.

- **Advantages**: It is simple and easy to implement.
- **Disadvantages:** It lacks intelligence in load distribution and may not ensure an even distribution.

Nginx configuration

Syntax	`random [two [method]];`
Default	–
Context	`upstream`

***Table 3.5**: random*

```
upstream applicationName {
  random;
  server server1.example.com:443;
  server server2.example.com:443;
  server server3.example.com:443;
  server server4.example.com:443;
}
```

***Figure 3.14**: random*

The optional "**`two`**" parameter instructs nginx to randomly select two servers from the server pool and then choose a server using the specified "**`method`**". The default "**`method`**" parameter is **`least_conn`** algorithm which passes a request to a server with the least number of active connections.

```
upstream applicationName {
  random two;
  server server1.example.com:443;
  server server2.example.com:443;
  server server3.example.com:443;
  server server4.example.com:443;
}
```

***Figure 3.15**: random two*

You may also add additional parameters to the random directive, such as:

1. **`least_time=header`** passes a request to a server with the least **`$upstream_header_time`**, that is, time to receive the response header.
2. **`least_time=last_byte`** passes a request to the server with least **`$upstream_response_time`**, that is, time to receive the full response.

```
upstream applicationName {
    random two least_time=last_byte;
    server server1.example.com:443;
    server server2.example.com:443;
    server server3.example.com:443;
    server server4.example.com:443;
}
```

***Figure 3.16**: least_time=last_byte*

This concludes our discussion on HTTP load balancing methods in Nginx.

Now, let us delve into the more detailed aspect of load balancing, that is, session persistence which ensures that a user's requests consistently reach the same backend server for a seamless, stateful experience.

Session Persistence

Session persistence also known as sticky sessions or session affinity is a feature in load balancing that ensures a client's requests in a particular session are consistently directed to the same application server in a server pool where the first request was sent.

For example, you are logged into amazon ecommerce website. You load the website in your browser and search for a mobile phone. You add the product to the cart and then forget about it. When you come back to the website, let us say after an hour, you are still logged in! And the mobile phone is still added to the cart. You can now proceed and purchase the phone without having to login again, searching for the same phone and adding to the cart all over again. How does this happen? Well, your complete transaction on the website from login to checkout is called a client session. Here your login credential that you have entered is retained and remembered and made sure that you have a consistent experience whenever you browse the website. This process of retaining a client session is called session persistence.

In Nginx, session persistence can be achieved using various methods. For session persistence with Nginx Open Source, we can use hash or **`ip_hash`** load balancing algorithm.

Nginx Plus supports three additional session persistence methods. The methods are set with three sticky directive - **`sticky route`**, **`sticky cookie`**, and **`sticky_learn`**.

Here, we will cover the Nginx Plus session persistence options using **`stick route`**, **`sticky cookie`**, *and* **`sticky_learn`**.

Sticky cookie

When the sticky cookie method is used, information about the selected server is passed in an HTTP cookie generated by Nginx. For the first request, the load balancing algorithm selects any one server from the server pool of the upstream block. The same client's next request contains the cookie value which Nginx identifies and sends the other subsequent requests to the same upstream server.

- **`sticky cookie`**

Syntax	`sticky cookie name [expires=time] [domain=domain] [httponly] [samesite=strict|lax|none|$variable] [secure] [path=path];`
Default	–
Context	`upstream`

***Table 3.6**: Sticky cookie*

1. **`expires=time`**: Sets the time for which a browser should keep the cookie.
2. **`domain=domain`**: Defines the domain for which the cookie is set. This parameter value can also be Nginx variables
3. **`httponly`**: Adds the **`httpOnly`** attribute to the cookie.
4. **`samesite=strict | lax | none | $variable`**: Adds the "**`samesite`**" attribute to the cookie with one of the following values: *Strict*, *Lax*, *None*, or using *variables*.
    a. **`strict`**: The cookie is transmitted only if the request originates from the same site that set the cookie.
    b. **`lax`**: The cookie is retained on most cross-site requests.
    c. **`none`**: The cookie is sent in all contexts, including cross-site requests. When using this option, the cookie must be marked as secure, ensuring it is transmitted only over HTTPS, which helps mitigate some risks.
    d. **`$variable`**: This allows dynamic or variable-based assignment of the **`samesite`** attribute.
5. **`secure`**: Adds the secure attribute to the cookie.
6. **`path=path`**: Defines the path for which the cookie is set.

For example,

```
upstream application_backend {
    server server1.example.com:443;
    server server2.example.com:443;
    sticky cookie srv_id expires=1h domain=.example.com path=/;
}
```

***Figure* 3.17**: *cookie command*

In the example,

1. The **`srv_id`** parameter is the HTTP cookie named **`srv_id`**.
2. The optional expires parameter sets the time for the browser to keep the cookie for 1 hour.
3. The optional domain parameter defines the domain **`*.example.com`** for which the cookie is set.
4. The optional path parameter defines the path `/` for which the cookie is set which means for all the path with **`*.example.com`**, the cookie should be set.

Sticky route

When the sticky route technique is used, it involves ensuring that requests from the same client are consistently directed to the same backend server based on a route identifier, often carried in the URL. The route information is taken from either a cookie or the request URI.

- **`sticky route`**

Syntax	`sticky route $variable ...;`
Default	–
Context	`upstream`

***Table* 3.7**: *sticky route*

For example,

```
map $cookie_jsessionid $route_cookie {
    ~.+\.(?P<route>\w+)$ $route;
}

map $request_uri $route_uri {
    ~jsessionid=.+\.(?P<route>\w+)$ $route;
}

upstream backend {
    server backend1.example.com route=a;
    server backend2.example.com route=b;

    sticky route $route_cookie $route_uri;
}
```

Figure 3.18: *route command*

In the preceding example,

1. The **`$route_cookie`** and **`$route_uri`** parameter sets the name of the cookie using a Nginx map (we will read about maps in a coming chapter).
2. The **`$route_cookie`** value would be the value of **`jsessionid`** HTTP cookie. If **`$route_cookie`** is empty, **`$route_uri`** value is checked whose value is picked from **`$request_uri`**. (Remember **`$request_uri`** is nginx variable that hold the complete request url with query parameters)

Sticky learn

When the sticky learn technique is used, Nginx '**`learns`**' the session and creates HTTP cookie for the session. This cookie will be read from all the subsequent requests and the request is passed to the same backend selected server. If the server cannot process the request, the new server is selected with the load balancing method that is set.

- **`sticky learn`**

Syntax	`sticky learn create=$variable lookup=$variable zone=name:-size [timeout=time] [header] [sync];`
Default	–
Context	`upstream`

Table 3.8: *learn*

1. **`create=$variable`**: Specifies that if the client doesn't already have a sticky session identifier, Nginx should create one using the value of the provided variable.
2. **`lookup=$variable`**: Instructs Nginx to check incoming requests for an existing sticky session identifier using the given variable.
3. **`zone=name:size`**: Defines a shared memory zone (with the given name and size) where Nginx stores session persistence data. This shared zone allows the mapping between session identifiers and backend servers to be maintained across different worker processes.
4. **`[timeout=time]`**: An optional parameter that sets a timeout value, which can control how long a session or its associated data is considered valid.
5. **`[header]`**: An optional parameter indicates that session information might also be transmitted via an HTTP header, rather than solely through cookies. This can be useful in environments where cookies may drop.
6. **`[sync]`**: An optional parameter enables synchronization of session data across multiple Nginx worker processes. This ensures consistency of session information even if requests are handled by different worker processes.

The 'learned' sessions are stored in a shared memory zone defined by zone parameter. One megabyte zone can store about 4000 sessions on the 64-bit platform. The sessions can be read within the time defined. By default, timeout is set to 10 minutes.

For example,

```
upstream application_backend {
    server server1.example.com:443;
    server server2.example.com:443;

   sticky learn
          create=$upstream_cookie_examplecookie
          lookup=$cookie_examplecookie
          zone=client_sessions:1m;
}
```

***Figure 3.19**: learn command*

In the preceding example,

1. **'`create`'** creates the cookie name **'`examplecookie`'**.
2. **`lookup`** looks for the cookie in the subsequent calls.
3. zone is a shared memory zone assigned with the name **`client_sessions`** for a duration of 1 minute.

Limiting the Number of Connections

The **max_conns** directive in Nginx is used to limit the number of simultaneous connections a client can establish with the backend server. This feature helps prevent any single client or group of clients from overloading the server, ensuring fair resource allocation and improving server stability. Once a client exceeds this maximum number, further connection attempts are either queued, delayed, or rejected, based on the configuration. This directive is especially useful for managing traffic spikes and preventing DOS (Denial of Service) attacks. By controlling the number of concurrent connections, Nginx helps maintain a balanced and smooth experience for all users.

We can limit the number of simultaneous active connections to an upstream server by specifying the maximum number that a server can be allowed to process using the **max_conns** parameter.

If the **max_conns** limit is reached, the request is placed in a queue for the wait. For the queuing to initiate, we must specify the "**queue**" parameter with a timeout value.

```
upstream applicationName {
    server server1.example.com:443 max_conns=3;
    server server2.example.com:443;
    queue 100 timeout=60;
}
```

***Figure 3.20**: max_conns*

In the preceding example,

1. **server1.example.com** can accept only 3 simultaneous active connection.
2. **server2.example.com** has no limit since nothing is mentioned. Default value is 0.
3. **queue** parameter states it can hold 100 request in the queue for a duration of 60 seconds.

Configuring Load Balancing for UDP and TCP Connections

In Nginx, the "**stream**" context is used to handle TCP and UDP traffic, allowing us to set up load balancing, proxying, and other features for protocols that operate at the transport layer. Unlike the HTTP context, which is designed for web traffic, the stream context manages raw binary streams, making it ideal for applications such as database connections, VoIP, and custom TCP/UDP services. Within this context, we can define the upstream server groups, configure load balancing strategies, and set various parameters just like HTTP traffic. This flexibility ensures that Nginx can efficiently manage a wide range of network protocols and deliver robust performance across different types of services.

In addition to the events, http, main, server, and location contexts that we learned in the previous chapter, there is one more context, that is, stream context that handles the TCP and UDP traffic.

- `stream`

Syntax	`stream { ... }`
Default	–
Context	`main`

***Table 3.9**: stream*

The stream directive is used to configure TCP and UDP stream processing. It allows Nginx to act as a TCP and UDP proxy, enabling functionalities such as load balancing, SSL termination, and connection handling for non-HTTP traffic.

Note: *Configuring configurations for* TCP *and* UDP *are exactly same as we do for* HTTP *connections. The load balancing algorithms are exactly valid for* TCP *and* UDP *including the upstream setup for each case.*

Th only difference is that HTTP *request is written inside an http {} context and* TCP/UDP *is written under stream {} context.*

Here are the steps to write the configurations for TCP/UDP:

1. Instead of http being the main context, here we will define stream as the main context.

```
stream {
    server {
        #write server configurations
    }
    upstream {
        #write upstream configurations
    }

}
```

***Figure 3.21**: stream*

2. Inside the stream block, we define the server block with listen directive to listen on the IP address and Port.

By default, it is TCP connections.

To configure for UDP datagram, mention "**udp**" keyword in the listen directive line. The call will be redirected by listening on the specific IP address.

```
stream {
    # ...
    server {
        listen  127.0.0.1:8080 udp;
    }
}
```

Figure 3.22: *udp keyword*

3. To proxy the call to the backend, we use the **proxy_pass** directive in the similar fashion as we do for the HTTP connections. **All the load balancing algorithms applies here as well.**

```
stream {
    upstream streambackend {

        server server1.example.com:443 weight=5;
        server server2.example.com:443 max_fails=2 fail_timeout=30;
        server server3.example.com:443 max_conns=3;
    }

    upstream dnsserver {
        least_conn;
        server 192.168.136.130:53;
        server 192.168.136.131:53;
        server 192.168.136.132:53;
    }

    server {
        listen          12345;
        proxy_pass      streambackend;
        proxy_timeout 3s;
        proxy_connect_timeout 1s;
    }

    server {
        listen      53 udp;
        proxy_pass dns_servers;
    }
}
```

Figure 3.23: *proxy_pass directive*

Conclusion

This chapter gives you a practical look at how Nginx's load balancing capabilities can be tailored to fit different application needs. By experimenting with Round-Robin, Least Connections, IP Hash, and sticky sessions, you will gain insights into optimizing server resource utilization and maintaining session persistence for stateful applications. In the next chapter, we will explore the importance of Health Checks in Nginx.

Example Configuration

1. Write an Nginx Configuration to redirect the url from http://www.example.com/chapter3/learn to https://www.example.com/chapter3/learn and load balance the traffic in round-robin fashion for `server1.example.com`, `server2.example.com`, and `server3.example.com`.

   `nginx.conf`

   ```
   user nginx;

   worker_processes auto;

   error_log  /var/log/nginx/error.log ;
   pid        /var/run/nginx.pid;

   worker_rlimit_nofile 16192;

   events {
       worker_connections  8096;
   }

   http {

       include /etc/nginx/mime.types;

       log_format main '"$time_local" client=$remote_addr '
                  'method=$request_method request="$request" '
                  'request_length=$request_length '
                  'status=$status bytes_sent=$bytes_sent '
                  'body_bytes_sent=$body_bytes_sent '
                  'upstream_addr=$upstream_addr '
                  'upstream_status=$upstream_status '
                  'request_time=$request_time '
                  'upstream_response_time=$upstream_response_time '
                  'upstream_connect_time=$upstream_connect_time '
                  'upstream_header_time=$upstream_header_time '
   ```

```
                'body=$request_body' ;

    server_tokens off;

    gzip  off;
    client_body_buffer_size 10M;
    client_header_buffer_size 1M;
    large_client_header_buffers 2 1M;

    proxy_connect_timeout 120;
    proxy_send_timeout 120;
    proxy_read_timeout 120;
    send_timeout 120;

    proxy_http_version 1.1;

   include /etc/nginx/conf.d/example.conf;

}
```

example.conf

```
server {

  listen 80;

  server_name www.example.com;

  access_log /var/log/nginx/example.log main;

   location / {
    proxy_set_header Connection "";
    proxy_set_header HOST $host;
    return 301 https://$host$request_uri;
}
  }
server {

  listen 443;

  server_name www.example.com;

  access_log /var/log/nginx/example.log main;

   location / {
    proxy_set_header Connection "";
    proxy_set_header HOST $host;
    proxy_pass https://example_backend
```

```
}
  }

upstream  example_backend {
    server server1.example.com:443;
    server server2.example.com:443;
    server server3.example.com:443;
    #by default it is round robin
}
```

2. Write an Nginx Configuration to redirect the url from http://www.example.com/chapter3/learn to https://www.example.com/chapter3/learn and load balance the traffic in least connection method for `server1.example.com`, `server2.example.com`, and `server3.example.com`.

   Solution:

   `nginx.conf` will be same as Solution 1
   `example.conf`

```
server {

  listen 80;

  server_name www.example.com;

  access_log /var/log/nginx/example.log main;

   location / {
    proxy_set_header Connection "";
    proxy_set_header HOST $host;
    return 301 https://$host$request_uri;
}
  }
server {

  listen 443;

  server_name www.example.com;

  access_log /var/log/nginx/example.log main;

   location / {
    proxy_set_header Connection "";
    proxy_set_header HOST $host;
    proxy_pass https://example_backend
}
  }
```

```
upstream  example_backend {
    least_conn;
    server server1.example.com:443;
    server server2.example.com:443;
    server server3.example.com:443;
    #by default it is round robin
}
```

Sample Question

3. Write an Nginx Configuration to redirect the url from http://www.example.com/chapter3/learn to https://www.example.com/chapter3/learn and load balance the traffic in a round-robin fashion enabling session persistence using a sticky cookie.

   Solution:

   `nginx.conf` will be same as Solution 1

```
server {

  listen 80;

  server_name www.example.com;

  access_log /var/log/nginx/example.log main;

   location / {
    proxy_set_header Connection "";
    proxy_set_header HOST $host;
    return 301 https://$host$request_uri;
}
  }
server {

  listen 443;

  server_name www.example.com;

  access_log /var/log/nginx/example.log main;

   location / {
    proxy_set_header Connection "";
    proxy_set_header HOST $host;
    proxy_pass https://example_backend
}
  }
```

```
upstream  example_backend {
    server server1.example.com:443;
    server server2.example.com:443;
    server server3.example.com:443;
    sticky cookie mycookie expires=1h domain=.example.com path=/;
}
```

Chapter 4
Health Checks

Introduction

One of the most important aspects of a load balancer in a complex network architecture is continuously checking the status of backend servers with periodic health checks. Health checks ensure that the load balancer routes traffic only to servers that are available and performing well, thereby maintaining high availability and optimal performance for the application.

Similar to how regular health check-ups monitor a person's well-being and detect potential health issues early, health checks in computer networking include a range of proactive tests and measurements, such as ping tests, latency tests, and bandwidth tests, to assess the overall health and performance of a system or network.

Additionally, health checks can also be used to detect and diagnose potential issues before they become critical problems, allowing for proactive maintenance and troubleshooting.

Let us dive into the Nginx health check components.

Structure

In this chapter, the following topics will be covered:

- HTTP Health Check
- TCP Health Check
- UDP Health Check
- gRPC Health Check

HTTP Health Check

In Nginx, health checks are managed by the HTTP Health Check module and **`health_check`** directive. This module allows us to define parameters for the health check, including the interval, timeouts, and thresholds for determining when the server should be considered healthy or unhealthy. It can continually test the upstream servers, avoid the servers that have failed, and gracefully add the recovered servers into the load-balanced group. There are two types of health checks:

- Passive Health Checks
- Active Health Checks

Passive Health Checks

Passive health checks in Nginx are a type of health check that relies on the **actual client traffic** to determine the health of backend servers. They do not actively send health-check-specific URIs to the upstream servers. Instead, they consider a server healthy if it successfully handles client requests.

Passive health check features are available in both Nginx Open Source and Commercial Paid version of the software.

How Passive Health Checks Work

By default, passive health checks are enabled. We can further customize their frequency and the number of failures that occur before a server is marked unhealthy. Passive health relies on the **actual client traffic** to determine the health of backend servers.

Let us assume the client request https://www.example.com/learn/nginx that is proxied to the **`example_backend`** (*Figure* 4.1). The client request's response will be the parameter to decide the passive health check state.

If the client request returns with a 200, the passive health check is healthy. If the client request returns a 4xx or 5xx, that will be a counter to evaluate the passive health check to be unhealthy.

Nginx Configuration

```
upstream example_backend {
    server server1.example.com:443 max_fails=3 fail_timeout=10s;
    server server2.example.com:443;
}
```

Figure 4.1: *Passive Health Check Configuration*

The two customization parameters to alter the frequency and number of failures are **`max_fails`** and **`fail_timeout`**.

1. **`fail_timeout`**: The **`fail_timeout`** directive specifies the time period for which a server is considered "**`unhealthy`**" after it has failed a health check. If the server continues to fail health checks after this time period, Nginx considers it "**`failed`**" and stops sending traffic to it.

The default value is 10 sec.

2. **max_fails**: The **max_fails** directive specifies the maximum number of consecutive health check failures allowed for an upstream server before Nginx considers it "**failed**" and stops sending traffic to it. If the health check of the server stops failing before this number of consecutive failures is reached, the counter is reset, and the server is marked "**healthy**."

   The default value is 1.

To disable the passive health checks, set the **max_fails=0**.

Server Slow Start

The marked down server when is recovered or marked up can be overwhelmed by connections which may lead to a hung state of the server or even mark it again as unhealthy again. Slow start directive allows an upstream server to gradually recover its weight from zero to its nominal value after it has been recovered or became available.

```
upstream example_backend {
    server server1.example.com:443 max_fails=3 fail_timeout=10s slow_start=30s;
    server server2.example.com:443;
}
```

Figure 4.2: *Slow start*

Note that if there is only a single server in a group, the **slow_start** *parameter is ignored.*

In the preceding example (*Figure* 4.2), **max_fails=3** means that if the server fails three consecutive health checks, it will be considered "**failed**" and traffic will no longer be sent to it. After a failed server has been down for 10 seconds (as specified by **fail_timeout=10s**), Nginx will attempt to send traffic to it again. If the server responds successfully to the health checks, it will be considered "**healthy**" again and traffic will be sent to it.

Note that passive health checks are effective only when the upstream group is defined to have multiple members. When only one upstream server is defined, it is never marked unavailable.

Advantages of Passive Health Checks

NGINX runs passive health checks on load-balanced traffic by default. Here are few advantages listed for passive health checks:

- **Basic Monitoring**: Passive health checks monitor servers by observing real client traffic.

- **Automatic Setup**: Passive health checks come pre-installed in Nginx Open Source. It is also part of the commercial version.
- **Customizable**: Can be customized using **`max_fails`** and **`failed_timeout`** params.
- **Smart Restart (NGINX Plus)**: The upstream server is given ample time to gradually ramp up to accept the incoming requests.

In a nutshell, passive health checks are a low-key but effective way to make sure your servers are happy and healthy.

Active Health Checks

Active health checks in Nginx are a type of health check that sends specific health check requests to the backend servers periodically. If a server does not respond within a specified timeout period or with a desired response code, Nginx marks it as unhealthy and stops sending traffic to it.

Active health checks are available only in Commercial Paid version of the software.

How Active Health Checks Work

Nginx Plus sends a periodic HTTP request to the application server (upstream server) to ensure it responds with an expected response code and content. Active health checks enable continuous monitoring of the health of application and server. It provides a direct measurement of the availability of the application.

Nginx Configuration

To configure active health checks in Nginx, we use the **`health_check`** directive inside the location block.

- **`health_check`**

Syntax	`health_check [parameters];`
Default	–
Context	`location`

***Table 4.1**: health_check*

```
server {
    location / {
        proxy_pass http://example_backend;
        health_check;
    }
}
```

***Figure 4.3**: health_check*

shared memory zone

```
upstream example_backend {
        zone example_backend 64k;
        server server1.example.com:443 max_fails=3 fail_timeout=30s slow_start=30s;
        server server2.example.com:443;
        server server3.example.com:443;
    }
```

Figure 4.4: *zone example_backend*

We define a shared memory zone with the "**`zone`**" directive in the upstream block. In the preceding example, the zone is named "**`example_backend`**".

The zone stores the configuration of the upstream group and is accessible by all the worker processes. This enables the worker processes to use the same set of health check counters to keep track of responses from the servers in the group.

`health_check` directive parameters

```
server {
  location /
  {
    proxy_pass://example_backend;
    health_check uri=/health mandatory interval=10 passes=3 fails=3 jitter=5 port=8080 keepalive_time=60s;
  }
}
```

Figure 4.5: *health_check directive*

The optional parameter with the **`health_check`** directive can be any of the following:

- **`interval=time`**

  Sets the time interval between two consecutive health checks.

  The default value is 5 seconds.

- **`jitter=time`**

  Sets the time within which each health check will be randomly delayed.

  By default, there is no delay.

- **`fails=number`**

  Sets the number of consecutive failed health checks that should be considered to a particular server before which a server is considered unhealthy.

  The default value is 1.

- **`passes=number`**

  Sets the number of consecutive successful health checks that should be considered to a particular server before a server is considered healthy.

The default value is 1.

- `uri=uri`

  The HTTP requests or URI sent as a health check requests to the upstream servers. The default URI is "`/`".

- `mandatory [persistent]`

  Sets the initial "**`checking`**" state for a server until the first health check is completed. Client requests are not passed to servers in the "**`checking`**" state. The persistent parameter sets the initial "**`up`**" state for a server after reload if the server was considered healthy before reload.

  By default, if the parameter is not specified, the state is set as healthy.

- `match=name`

  Refers to the "**`match`**" block that a response should pass for a health check to pass. By default, the response should have status code 2xx or 3xx.

- `port=number`

  Defines the HTTP port to be used when connecting to a server to perform a health check. By default, equals the server port.

- `keepalive_time=time`

  Enables keepalive connections for health checks and specifies the time during which requests can be processed through one keepalive connection.

  By default, keepalive connections are disabled.

Using "`match`" directive to define custom health checks:

Syntax	`match name { ... }`
Default	–
Context	`http`

***Table 4.2**: match*

The **`match`** directive is used to define custom health checks. We can set custom conditions in such a way that the response must satisfy for the server to pass the health check. The conditions are defined in a **`match`** block, which is referenced in the **`match`** parameter of the **`health_check`** directive.

The status, header, and response body can be tested in the response.

Defining match block

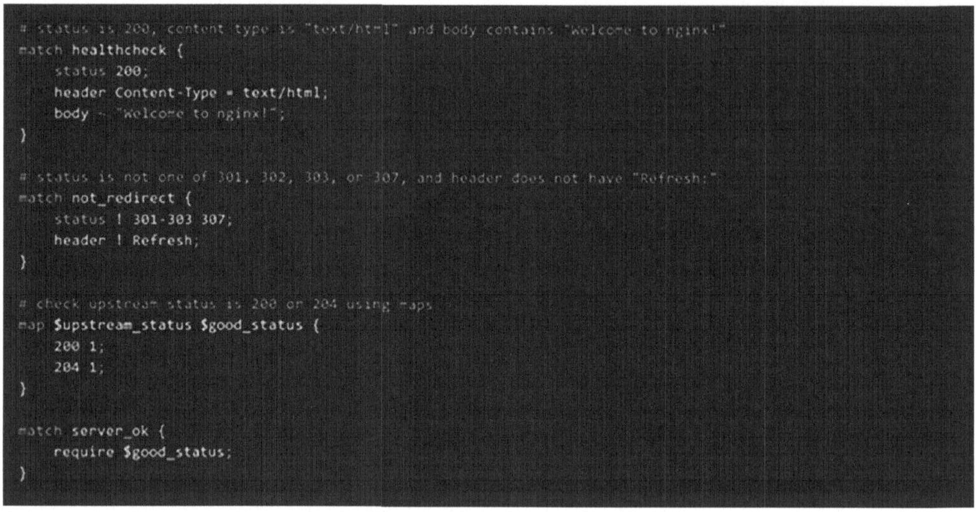

```
# status is 200, content type is "text/html" and body contains "Welcome to nginx!"
match healthcheck {
    status 200;
    header Content-Type = text/html;
    body ~ "Welcome to nginx!";
}

# status is not one of 301, 302, 303, or 307, and header does not have "Refresh:"
match not_redirect {
    status ! 301-303 307;
    header ! Refresh;
}

# check upstream status is 200 or 204 using maps
map $upstream_status $good_status {
    200 1;
    204 1;
}

match server_ok {
    require $good_status;
}
```

Figure 4.6: *match block*

Using **match** directive in the **health_check** directive:

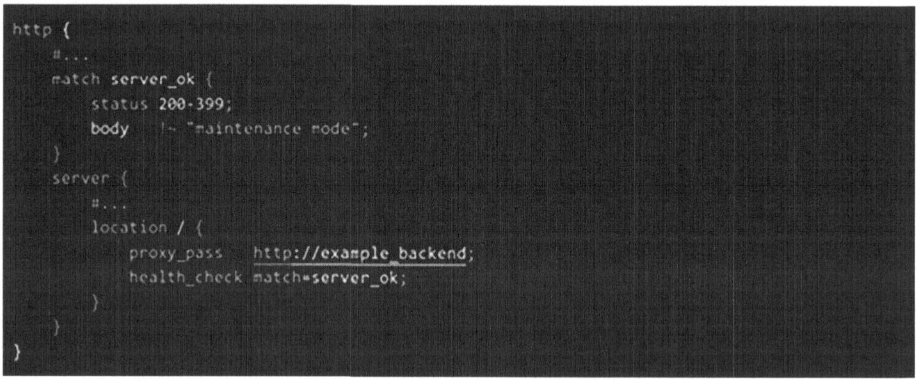

```
http {
    #...
    match server_ok {
        status 200-399;
        body   !~ "maintenance mode";
    }
    server {
        #...
        location / {
            proxy_pass   http://example_backend;
            health_check match=server_ok;
        }
    }
}
```

Figure 4.7: *health_check directive*

This code tells Nginx to send health check requests to this location, and the response is evaluated using the conditions defined in the **server_ok** match block in *Figure* 4.7.

```
match server_ok {
  require $good_status;
}
```

This is a smart match. It depends on the map block.

```
map $upstream_status $good_status {
  200 1;
  204 1;
}
```

If **`$upstream_status`** was **`200`** or **`204`** → **`$good_status`** is **`1`** → this match passes. If not, health check fails. This gives a flexible, indirect way to control what's considered "**`healthy`**."

Mandatory Health Checks

```
    server {
        #...
        location / {
            proxy_pass   http://example_backend;
            health_check mandatory persistent;
        }
    }
}
```

***Figure 4.8**: mandatory*

In a complex network infrastructure where the servers can be dynamically added or removed to scale up and scale down the network, it is always a best practice to mandate the health checks of the server before a server is marked live to accept client traffic. This can be done using the "**`mandatory persistent`**" parameter along with the **`health_check`** directive.

When the mandatory health check feature is combined with the "**`slow_start`**" directive, it gives a new server added to the upstream group more time to establish connections and "**`warm up`**" before being fully tasked with handling a complete share of the traffic. This gradual approach allows the server to progressively ramp up without immediately handling the full traffic load, ensuring a smoother transition and avoiding potential performance issues.

The "**`persistent`**" parameter for mandatory health checks ensures that the previous state of server is remembered when the Nginx Plus configuration is reloaded. This feature helps maintain continuity and stability in service, particularly during configuration changes or updates.

TCP Health Check

Transmission Control Protocol (TCP) connections can be used for streaming data, such as video or audio content. TCP ensures reliable and ordered delivery of data, which is essential for streaming applications where the order and integrity of the data are critical.

Just like the HTTP health check, TCP health check is also configured in the same way, except that it is defined inside the "**`stream`**" block instead of the "**`http`**" block.

Passive Health Checks

The Nginx configuration to configure passive health checks for the TCP requests are same as that of HTTP requests as previously explained.

For TCP requests, passive health also relies on the **actual client traffic** to determine the health of backend servers.

We define the **`max_fails`**, **`fail_timeout`**, and **`slow_start`** parameters in the upstream block server directive, along with the server name. The Nginx configuration example is as follows:

Nginx Configuration

```
stream {
    #set the upstream same way as the HTTP Health Check
    upstream stream_backend {
        server server1.example.com:12345 max_fails=2 fail_timeout=30s;
        server server2.example.com:12345 max_fails=2 fail_timeout=30s;
        server server3.example.com:12345 max_fails=2 fail_timeout=30s;
    }

    #server block
    server {
        listen      12345;
        proxy_pass stream_backend;
    }
}
```

***Figure 4.9**: TCP health check*

Active Health Checks

The configuration to configure active health checks for the TCP requests are same as that of HTTP requests.

Even for TCP requests, the active health check capability is only available in the commercial version of the Nginx, that is, Nginx Plus.

NGINX Plus sends a periodic TCP request to the servers in the upstream group to ensure it responds with an expected response code and content.

Nginx Configuration

- We define the health check using **`health_check`** directive in the location block which is enclosed in the stream block.

```
    #server block
    server {
        listen      12345;
        proxy_pass stream_backend;
        health_check;
    }
}
```

Figure 4.10: TCP health check

- We define a shared memory zone with the "**zone**" directive in the upstream block. In the following example, the zone is named "**stream_backend**".

  The zone is shared among all worker processes and stores the configuration of the upstream group. This enables the worker processes to use the same set of counters to keep track of responses from the servers in the group.

```
stream {
    #set the upstream same way as the HTTP Health Check
    upstream stream_backend {
        zone stream_backend 64k;
        server server1.example.com:12345 max_fails=2 fail_timeout=30s;
        server server2.example.com:12345 max_fails=2 fail_timeout=30s;
        server server3.example.com:12345 max_fails=2 fail_timeout=30s;
    }

    #server block
    server {
        listen     12345;
        proxy_pass stream_backend;
        health_check;
    }
}
```

Figure 4.11: stream_backend

- To reduce a timeout between two consecutive health checks, we can define the "**health_check_timeout**" directive. This directive overrides the **proxy_timeout** value for health checks.

proxy_timeout Versus health_check_timeout

proxy_timeout defines the maximum time the proxy will wait for a response from the upstream server when processing a client request. If the upstream does not respond within this period, the request fails, and an error is returned to the client.

health_check_timeout sets the maximum time to wait for a response to a health check request sent to an upstream server. If the upstream does not respond within this timeframe, the health check is considered a failure, which may eventually mark the server as unhealthy.

- **`health_check_timeout`**

Syntax	`health_check_timeout timeout;`
Default	health_check_timeout 5s;
Context	`stream, server`

***Table 4.3**: health_check_timeout*

```
    #server block
    server {
        listen      12345;
        proxy_pass stream_backend;
        health_check;
        health_check_timeout 3s;
    }
}
```

***Figure 4.12**: health_check_timeout*

Nginx Plus uses the port mentioned in the listen directive in the server block to send health check. To specify a particular port for health check request, we can specify using the port directive.

```
    #server block
    server {
        listen      12345;
        proxy_pass stream_backend;
        health_check port=12346;
        health_check_timeout 3s;
    }
}
```

***Figure 4.13**: port directive*

The other parameters to customize the health check requests are same as the HTTP request. The example of the configuration is given as follows:

```
    #server block
    server {
        listen      12345;
        proxy_pass stream_backend;
        health_check interval=10 passes=2 fails=3;
        health_check_timeout 3s;
    }
}
```

***Figure 4.14**: configuration*

Using `match` directive in the `health_check` directive

The **`match`** directive is used to define custom health checks just like for the HTTP requests. *However, the definition to configure match directive is different to that of* **`match`** *directive for* HTTP *requests.*

- **`match name`**

Syntax	`match name { ... }`
Default	–
Context	`stream`

Table 4.4: *match name*

The following parameters can be configured to set the **`match`** definition:

`send string`

Sends a string or a hexadecimal character ("**\x**" followed by two hex digits) to the server.

`expect string | ~ regex;`

A string or a regular expression that expected to match with the response from the server. The regular expression is specified with the preceding "**~***" modifier.

Note

- *Both send and expect parameters can contain hexadecimal literals with the prefix "**\x**" followed by two hex digits.*
- *If `expect` parameter is specified, the server is expected to unconditionally send data first.*
- *Not more than one send and one expect parameter can be specified at a time.*

Health check is passed if:

- *No send or expect parameters are specified, the ability to connect to the server is tested, that is, the TCP connection was successfully established.*
- *The string from the send parameter, if specified, was sent.*
- *The response obtained from the server matched the string or regular expression in the expect parameter, if specified.*
- *The time elapsed does not exceed the value specified in the `health_check_timeout` directive.*

Nginx Configuration

1. On the stream block, specify the **`match`** block with a custom name **`health_test`**.

```
stream {
    match health_test {

    }
}
```

Figure 4.15: *health_test*

2. Define send parameter. When the "**send**" parameter is specified, it is expected that the connection will be successfully established, and the specified string will be sent to the server.

```
match health_test {
    send "GET / HTTP/1.0\r\nHost: localhost\r\n\r\n";
}
```

Figure 4.16: *send*

3. Define **expect** parameter.

```
match health_test {
    expect ~* "200 OK";
}
```

Figure 4.17: *expect*

4. Putting **send** and **expect** parameters together.

```
stream {
    #...
    upstream stream_backend {
        zone stream_backend 64k;
        server server1.example.com:12345 max_fails=2 fail_timeout=30s;
        server server2.example.com:12345 max_fails=2 fail_timeout=30s;
        server server3.example.com:12345 max_fails=2 fail_timeout=30s;
    }

    match health_test {
        send      "GET / HTTP/1.0\r\nHost: localhost\r\n\r\n";
        expect ~* "200 OK";
    }
    server {
        listen       12345;
        health_check match=http;
        proxy_pass   stream_backend;
    }
}
```

Figure 4.18: *send and expect parameters*

UDP Health Check

Unlike TCP, UDP is connectionless. This means that it does not establish a persistent connection before sending data. Instead, it sends data packets, called datagrams, which contain information about the sender and receiver, as well as the transmitted data.

Similar to TCP health checks, UDP health checks are configured within the "**stream**" block using the **health_check**, **send**, and **expect** parameters.

Passive Health Checks

The Nginx configuration for passive health checks of TCP requests are same as that of HTTP requests, as explained previously.

For TCP requests, passive health checks relies on the **actual client traffic** to determine the health of backend servers.

Similar to the TCP upstream block definition, we define the **max_fails**, **fail_timeout**, and **slow_start** parameters along with the servers in the upstream block to enable the passive **health_check**. To configure the UDP datagram, we need to mention **udp** keyword in the listen directive line (as discussed in the last chapter).

The Nginx configuration example is as follows:

```
stream {
    # ...
    server {
        listen  127.0.0.1:8080 udp;
    }
}
```

```
upstream upd_upstream {
    server 192.168.136.130:53 max_fails=2 fail_timeout=60s;
    server 192.168.136.131:53 max_fails=2 fail_timeout=60s;
}
```

***Figure 4.19**: udp keyword*

Active Health Checks

The active health checks are defined in an exact way as we do for TCP health checks except for the keyword 'udp' in the listen directive. We define the health check in the server block using the **health_check** parameter. We define the send and expect parameters to further customize the health checks. All these are enclosed inside a stream block.

```
stream {
    #...
upstream upd_upstream {
    server 192.168.136.130:53 max_fails=2 fail_timeout=60s;
    server 192.168.136.131:53 max_fails=2 fail_timeout=60s;
}

match health_test {
   expect ~* "200 OK";
}

match health_test {
    send "GET / HTTP/1.0\r\nHost: localhost\r\n\r\n";
}
    server {
        listen 53 udp;
        health_check match=health_test;
        proxy_pass    upd_upstream;
    }
}
```

***Figure 4.20**: TCP health checks*

gRPC Health Check

As the name suggests, RPC stand for Remote Procedure Call and g stands for Google. gRPC was initially developed to serve as the communication protocol in their internal microservices architecture. gRPC is a modern, efficient, and highly scalable RPC framework that allows developers to build fast and reliable APIs with ease. Its support for streaming, interoperability, code generation makes it a popular choice for building microservices, cloud-native applications, and other distributed systems.

gRPC health checking protocol is supported by only Nginx Plus commercial version.

Defining upstream to handle gRPC request

1. The upstream group of servers to handle gRPC traffic is defined in the stream block, similar to TCP and UDP protocol.

```
stream {
    upstream grpc_backend {
        zone   grpc_backend 64k;
        server 10.0.0.1:50051;
        server 10.0.0.2:50051;
    }
}
```

Figure 4.21: *gRPC request*

2. Define the location block and send the request to the **grpc_backend** upstream group as follows:

```
location /grpc {
    grpc_pass grpc://grpc_backend;
}
```

Figure 4.22: *grpc_backend*

3. To define the health checks for gRPC request, we use the same **health_check** directive, except it is mandatory to specify **type=grpc** parameter in the **health_check** definition.

```
location /grpc {
    grpc_pass grpc://grpc_backend;
    health_check type=grpc;
}
```

Figure 4.23: *type=grpc*

4. We can specify the "**mandatory**" parameter to ensure that the health check is a must when any new server is onboarded before any request is sent to the upstream group of servers.

```
location /grpc {
    grpc_pass grpc://grpc_backend;
    health_check mandatory type=grpc;
}
```

Figure 4.24: *mandatory*

5. We can check for a specific status code using the **grpc_status** parameter.

```
location /grpc {
    grpc_pass grpc://grpc_backend;
    health_check mandatory type=grpc grpc_status=12;
}
```

Figure 4.25: *grpc_status*

Conclusion

Health checks in Nginx are critical for the continuous monitoring and maintenance of server health. By detecting and addressing issues promptly, these checks help ensure the uninterrupted availability and reliability of applications and services. With the ability to prevent traffic from being routed to unhealthy instances, Nginx improves fault tolerance and enhances overall system resilience.

Now that we know how to define health checks, we are good to go for a full-fledged Nginx configuration.

Example Configuration

Write an Nginx configuration to configure only active health check on the https://www.example.com/health on a group of upstream servers. The servers will be declared healthy only if a "`healthy`" response is sent by the servers. Additionally, the health checks should be done every 5 seconds.

Answer:

```
http {

match sever_ok {
    body ~ "healthy";
}

upstream example_backend{
    zone example_backend 64k;
    server example.server1.com:443 max_fails=0 slow_start=10s;
    server example.server2.com:443 max_fails=0 slow_start=10s;
}

server {
    listen 80;
    listen 443;
    server_name www.example.com
    #define ssl certs

    loaction / {
        proxy_pass https://example_backend;
        health_check matchh=server_ok uri=/healthy interval=5s fails=3 passes=2;
    }
}
}
```

Figure 4.26: *Output*

CHAPTER 5
Nginx Plus API

Introduction

Amidst the myriad of options available for a trusted webserver or a proxy server, Nginx stands out as the preferred solution. This is largely because of its dynamic management capabilities through the NGINX Plus API. While this functionality is exclusive only to the paid commercial edition, but the extended features it provides, such as real-time configuration changes, proactive monitoring, and seamless scalability, make Nginx Plus a worthwhile investment. This kind of flexibility is indispensable for modern, high-demand environments. The API enables automation of tasks such as configuring Nginx, monitoring its performance, and integrating it with other systems with a powerful interface. Through this interface, we can **perform** tasks including marking upstream servers up or down in a server group without hard-deploying configuration files, **auto scaling** the network by adding and removing servers, and **monitoring** server status, active connection, downtime, health check pass and fails.

Structure

In this chapter, the following topics will be covered:

- Sharing Data with Multiple Worker Processes
- Enabling the Nginx Plus API
- Accessing the API
- Setting Authentication on Nginx API
- Key Value Store in Nginx API
- Reading and Modifying Values in Nginx PLUS API with Precision

Before we understand how to enable Nginx Plus API, we should know the importance of sharing the state information across all worker process using shared zones.

Sharing Data with Multiple Worker Processes

In the first chapter, we learned that the worker process is single-threaded and is responsible for executing new connections and processing them. There is always only one master process and one or more worker processes. Each worker process keeps its own copy of the server group configuration and maintains its own set of information. The information includes:

- Current number of connections to each server in the upstream group.
- Number of failed attempts to pass a request to a server.
- Number of passes and failures in a health check
- Key-value store of the Nginx variables value and many more

Hence to dynamically modify the configuration, the information between the worker processes needs to be shared. To explain the same with an example, let us say:

- We have **`server1.example.com`** and **`server2.example.com`** in an upstream group.
- We have 4 worker processes: WP1, WP2, WP3, and WP4.
- We initiate a task of marking down **`server1.example.com`**.
- WP1 executes the task and marks down **`server1.example.com`**.
- Parallelly, while the system is also executing the client traffic, the information that WP1 has marked down server1.example.com and is no more available to execute requests should be shared with WP2, WP3, and WP4 to avoid failed requests.

This can be done by using the **`zone`** directive. When the zone directive is included in an upstream block, the state of the upstream group is kept in a memory area that is shared among all worker processes.

- **`zone`**

Syntax	`zone name [size];`
Default	–
Context	`upstream`
Example	`zone  testzone 64k;`

***Table 5.1**: zone*

Nginx configuration

```
upstream example_backend {
    server server1.example.com:443 max_fails=0 slow_start=60s;
    server server2.example.com:443 max_fails=0 slow_start=60s;
    zone testzone 64k;
}
```

***Figure 5.1**: zone*

In the preceding example, the testzone is the shared memory zone and size is 64k. It stores the run-time state of the upstream group **`example_backend`** that are shared between all the worker processes.

How zone sync helps the health checks?

When Nginx is configured, each worker process independently tracks the number of times it has failed to send a request to a server (as set by the `**max_fails**` parameter). In this setup, if the zone sync is unavailable , each incoming request is handled by only one worker process. When the chosen worker process fails to forward the request to a server, the other worker processes remain unaware of this failure.

This situation can lead to inconsistencies because while one worker process may mark a server as unavailable due to repeated failures, other worker processes may still attempt to send requests to the same server.

However, when using the `**zone**` directive, Nginx shares the state information across all worker processes, guaranteeing that if a server reaches the maximum number of failed attempts within the specified time, it is marked as unavailable for all worker processes simultaneously. This ensures more reliable handling of failed server connections across Nginx instances.

How zone sync helps the least connection load balancing?

Least Connections load-balancing method passes a request to the server that has least number of active connections.

If the configuration of the group is not shared, each worker process uses its own counter for the number of connections and might send a request to the same server that another worker process just sent a request to. Therefore, zone sync is very important for least connection load balancing algorithm to work.

Enabling the Nginx Plus API

Some important directives to enable Nginx Plus API are:

- **`api`**

Syntax	`api [write=on|off];`
Default	–
Context	`location`

Table 5.2: *api*

The **`api`** directive turns the Nginx Plus REST API on. We define it inside a location block.

The **`'write'`** parameter determines whether the API is read-only or read-write. By default, the API is read-only. Usually access to this location should be limited.

The current Nginx Plus API version is "9".

- **`limit_except`**

Syntax	`limit_except method ... { ... }`
Default	–
Context	`location`
Example	`limit_except GET {…}`

***Table 5.3**: limit_except*

This directive defines the allowed HTTP methods for the Nginx Plus API. The method parameter can be one of the following: **`GET`**, **`HEAD`**, **`POST`**, **`PUT`**, **`DELETE`**, **`MKCOL`**, **`COPY`**, **`MOVE`**, **`OPTIONS`**, **`PROPFIND`**, **`PROPPATCH`**, **`LOCK`**, **`UNLOCK`**, or **`PATCH`**.

Allowing the GET method implicitly allows the **`HEAD`** *method.*

- **`allow address`**

Syntax	`allow address | CIDR | unix: | all;`
Default	–
Context	`http, server, location, limit_except`
Example	`allow all;`

***Table 5.4**: allow address*

This directive allows access for the specified network or IP address. If the special value **`unix:`** is specified, it allows access for all UNIX-domain sockets.

- **`deny address`**

Syntax	`deny address | CIDR | unix: | all;`
Default	–
Context	`http, server, location, limit_except`
Example	`deny 10.12.13.14;`

***Table 5.5**: deny address*

This directive denies access for the specified network or IP address. If the special value **`unix:`** is specified, it denies access for all UNIX-domain sockets.

Sample Nginx Configuration putting the preceding directive together:

```
#Nginx Dashboard
server {
    listen 8080;
    access_log off;

    location = / {
        return 301 /dashboard.html;
    }
    location /api {
        client_max_body_size 20M;
        limit_except GET {
            auth_basic "USERNAME";
            auth_basic_user_file /etc/nginx/.httpasswd;
        }
        api write=on;
        allow 10.0.0.0/8;
    }
    location /dashboard.html {
        root /usr/share/nginx/html;
    }
}
```

Figure 5.2: *Sample Nginx Configuration*

In the preceding example,

1. We have defined the api location block on 8080 port. It is better to define location block for api on a separate, unique port.
2. **`access_log off;`** allows for the enabling or disabling of api access logs.
3. The following location block enables the Nginx Plus API using the /api, indicating the URI http://{IPAddress}:8080/api to be used to access the API.

```
Location /api {
        client_max_body_size 20M;
        limit_except GET {
            auth_basic "USERNAME";
            auth_basic_user_file /etc/nginx/.httpassword;
        }
        api write=on;
        allow 10.0.0.0/8;
    }
```

4. The **`limit_except`** GET excludes the GET method from the authentication defined inside the **`{}`**. This means to access **`POST/PATCH/DELETE`**, we would need a username and password. The username realm would be "**`USERNAME`**" and the password is encrypted in **`.httpassword`** file. The authentication is a Basic HTTP authentication.
5. **`api write=on`** allows the API to dynamically change the value.
6. Allow 10.0.0.0/8 allows the changes can be done only by localhost.
7. There is no **`server_name`** defined, hence you can access the API either from host machine or to reach the API remotely, you can access it using the box/ server name where Nginx Plus is installed. Example: http://{BOXNAME}:8080/ api/9/
8. The following location block enables the Nginx Plus dashboard (we will discuss more about it later):

```
        location = / {
        return 301 /dashboard.html;
    }
```

Accessing the API

The Nginx Plus API provide access to various aspects of the Nginx Plus server, including status information, configuration details, and monitoring metrics.

Here is an example of what you can add after the root URL **`http://{BOXNAME}:8080/ api/9/`** to fetch specific information.

- `` `/` ``: General API information.

  `http://{BOXNAME}:8080/api/9/`

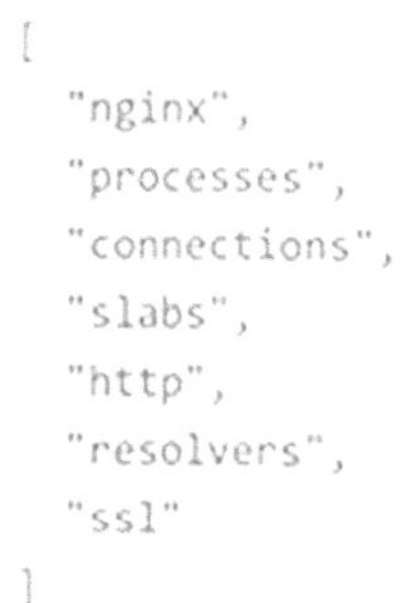

Figure 5.3*: General API information*

- `` `/nginx` ``: Information about the Nginx Plus server including version, buildpack, IP address of host machine, process id and others.

`http://{BOXNAME}:8080/api/9/nginx`


```json
{
  "version": "1.21.6",
  "build": "nginx-plus-r27",
  "address": "10.174.113.32",
  "generation": 19,
  "load_timestamp": "2024-01-10T05:55:57.884Z",
  "timestamp": "2024-03-28T10:57:49.175Z",
  "pid": 101974,
  "ppid": 2561
}
```


Figure 5.4: */nginx*

- `/processes`: Information about Nginx Plus processes.

  `http://{BOXNAME}:8080/api/9/processes`


```json
{
  "respawned": 0
}
```


Figure 5.5: */processes*

- `/connections`: Information about active, idle, dropped connections.

  `http://{BOXNAME}:8080/api/9/connections`


```json
{
  "accepted": 466091301,
  "dropped": 0,
  "active": 10,
  "idle": 1343
}
```


Figure 5.6: */connections*

- `/slabs/`: Information about memory slabs.

  `http://{BOXNAME}:8080/api/9/slabs`

```json
{
  "split": {
    "pages": {
      "used": 5,
      "free": 10
    },
    "slots": {
      "8": {↔},
      "16": {↔},
      "32": {↔},
      "64": {↔},
      "128": {↔},
      "256": {↔},
      "512": {↔},
      "1024": {↔},
      "2048": {↔}
    }
```

```json
{
  "ngx_zone_sync_shared": {
    "pages": {
      "used": 2,
      "free": 5
    },
    "slots": {
      "8": {
        "used": 0,
        "free": 0,
        "reqs": 0,
        "fails": 0
      },
      "16": {
        "used": 0,
        "free": 0,
        "reqs": 0,
        "fails": 0
      },
      "32": {
        "used": 1,
        "free": 126,
        "reqs": 1,
        "fails": 0
      },
      "64": {
        "used": 17,
        "free": 47,
        "reqs": 17,
        "fails": 0
      },
```


Figure 5.7: */slabs/*

- `/http/`: Statistics and information for all the HTTP requests

  `http://{BOXNAME}:8080/api/9/http`


```json
[
  "requests",
  "server_zones",
  "location_zones",
  "caches",
  "limit_conns",
  "limit_reqs",
  "keyvals",
  "upstreams"
]
```


Figure 5.8: */http/*

- **`/http/requests`** : Information about total HTTP requests.

  `http://{BOXNAME}:8080/api/9/requests`

```
{
  "total": 2862332484,
  "current": 10
}
```

Figure 5.9: */http/requests*

- **`/http/server_zones/`**: Information about HTTP server zones.

  `http://{BOXNAME}:8080/api/9/requests/server_zones`

```
▼ object {3}
    ▶ hg.nginx.org {7}
    ▶ lxr.nginx.org {6}
    ▶ trac.nginx.org {7}
```

Figure 5.10: */http/server_zones/*

- **`/http/location_zones/`**: Information about HTTP traffic for each location block.

  `http://{BOXNAME}:8080/api/9/requests/location_zones`

```
{
  "swagger": {
    "requests": 138,
    "responses": {
      "1xx": 0,
      "2xx": 133,
      "3xx": 5,
      "4xx": 0,
      "5xx": 0,
      "codes": {
        "200": 133,
        "304": 5
      },
      "total": 138
    },
    "discarded": 0,
    "received": 96497,
    "sent": 9548848
  },
  "api-calls": {
    "requests": 2063982,
    "responses": {
      "1xx": 0,
      "2xx": 1985855,
      "3xx": 0,
      "4xx": 78127,
      "5xx": 0,
      "codes": {
        "200": 1985855,
        "404": 78015,
        "405": 112
      },
      "total": 2063982
    },
    "discarded": 0,
    "received": 820744016,
    "sent": 2334836210
  }
}
```


Figure 5.11: */http/location_zones/*

- `/http/caches/`: Information about HTTP caches and its size, hit, miss, and other details.

  `http://{BOXNAME}:8080/api/9/caches`

```
{
  "http_cache": {
    "size": 67096576,
    "max_size": 67108864,
    "cold": false,
    "hit": {
      "responses": 1279905,
      "bytes": 159211508584
    },
    "stale": {
      "responses": 0,
      "bytes": 0
    },
    "updating": {
      "responses": 0,
      "bytes": 0
    },
    "revalidated": {
      "responses": 0,
      "bytes": 0
    },
    "miss": {
      "responses": 16180,
      "bytes": 2008544512,
      "responses_written": 16180,
      "bytes_written": 2008544512
    },
    "expired": {
      "responses": 1950,
      "bytes": 239985568,
      "responses_written": 1950,
      "bytes_written": 239985568
    },
    "bypass": {
      "responses": 0,
      "bytes": 0,
      "responses_written": 0,
      "bytes_written": 0
    }
  }
}
```


Figure 5.12: */http/caches/*

- `/http/limit_reqs/`: Information about HTTP request rate limited connections about the passed, failed, and delayed requests.

  `http://{BOXNAME}:8080/api/9/http/limit_reqs`

```
{
  "one": {
    "passed": 1300541,
    "delayed": 0,
    "rejected": 718,
    "delayed_dry_run": 0,
    "rejected_dry_run": 0
  },
  "ban": {
    "passed": 0,
    "delayed": 0,
    "rejected": 0,
    "delayed_dry_run": 0,
    "rejected_dry_run": 0
  }
}
```


Figure 5.13: */http/limit_reqs/*

- `/http/upstreams/`: Information about HTTP upstream servers and its details.

```
▼ object {4}
    ▶ demo-backend {4}
    ▶ trac-backend {4}
    ▶ hg-backend {4}
    ▶ lxr-backend {4}
```

Figure 5.14: */http/upstreams/*

You can further extract details of each upstream with the following URL.

/http/upstreams/demo-backend/servers/

- `/http/keyvals/`: Information about all Key-value pairs defined for HTTP requests.
- `/resolvers/`: Information about DNS resolvers.

```
▼ resolver-http {2}
    ▶ requests {3}
    ▶ responses {8}
▼ resolver-stream {2}
    ▶ requests {3}
    ▶ responses {8}
```

Figure 5.15: */resolvers/*

- `/ssl`: SSL/TLS related information.


```
{
  "handshakes": 463295560,
  "handshakes_failed": 19312,
  "session_reuses": 99786590
}
```


***Figure 5.16**: /ssl*

- `/workers/`: Information about number of Nginx worker processes, it's process id and real-time connections handled by each worker process.

```
▼ 0 {4}
      id  : 0
      pid : 460434
    ▶ connections {4}
    ▶ http {1}
▼ 1 {4}
      id  : 1
      pid : 460433
    ▶ connections {4}
    ▶ http {1}
```

***Figure 5.17**: /workers/*

Note: *All the above screenshots are taken from https://demo.nginx.com/. It is the demo Nginx Plus dashboard available publicly.*

Setting Authentication on Nginx API

The Nginx Plus API is a flexible yet very powerful tool to change the network settings or routing configurations with a simple **POST**, **PATCH**, or **DELETE**.

Hence, authentication of the API becomes paramount, as it provides **security** and **access control.** Well, you cannot risk to bring the whole website down due to a silly error right!

Authentication ensures that only authorized users or clients can access the API endpoints. It helps protect sensitive data and resources from unauthorized access, reducing the risk of data breaches or misuse, thereby making the API secure.

Authentication also allows you to enforce access control policies, such as restricting certain endpoints to specific user roles or groups. This helps ensure that users only have access to the resources they are authorized to use, thus limiting the access to the API.

How can we make the API secure?

We can do it by implementing basic authentication. Basic authentication is a simple method to provide a username and password when making a request to a server. It is commonly used in web-based applications and APIs as a means of verifying the identity of a user or client.

The client encodes the username and password using **Base64 encoding** and includes them in an "`Authorization`" header in the request. The header has the format: "`Authorization: Basic <credentials>`", where `<credentials>` is the Base64-encoded string of "`username:password`".

How to create the username and password?

1. Create a password file and username:

   Let us say the username is `user1`.

   Run the following `htpasswd` utility in the Linux terminal:

   ```
   sudo htpasswd -c /etc/nginx2/.htpasswd user1
   ```

   a. `-c` creates a new file

   b. The file pathname `/etc/nginx2/.htpasswd` is the first argument

   c. username `user1` is the second argument

   Press *Enter* and type the password for `user1` at the prompts.

2. You can also create multiple user-password pairs for role specific access. In that case, we can omit the `-c` flag in the command as `.htpasswd` file already exists.

   ```
   sudo htpasswd /etc/nginx2/.htpasswd user2
   ```

3. After these steps, confirm that the file contains paired usernames and hashed passwords using the `cat` command to view the file:

   ```
   $ cat /etc/nginx2/.htpasswd
   user1:$apr1$/woC1jnP$KAh0SsVn5qeSMjTtn0E9Q0
   user2:$apr1$QdR8fNLT$vbCEEzDj7LyqCMyNpSoBh/
   user3:$apr1$Mr5A0e.U$0j39Hp5FfxRkneklXaMrr/
   ```

How to include the Basic authentication in the API?

Let us go first through the directive needed to enable the authentication.

- **`auth_basic`**

Syntax	auth_basic string | off;
Default	auth_basic off;
Context	http, server, location, limit_except
Example	auth_basic "NGINX REST API";

***Table 5.6**: auth_basic*

This directive enables validation of username and password using the "**`HTTP Basic Authentication`**" protocol. This parameter sets the realm name that will be displayed in the authentication prompt. By default, it is disabled.

- **`auth_basic_user_file`**

Syntax	auth_basic_user_file file;
Default	–
Context	http, server, location, limit_except
Example	/etc/nginx2/.htpasswd

***Table 5.7**: auth_basic_user_file*

The file that stores the username and password in an encrypted format in a file, example **`/etc/nginx2/.htpasswd`** which we include using **`auth_basic_user_file`**.

```
http {
    server {
        listen 8080;
        access_log off;

        location = / {
            return 301 /dashboard.html;
        }
        location /api {
            limit_except GET {
            auth_basic "NGINX REST API";
            auth_basic_user_file /etc/nginx2/.httpasswd;
        }
            api write=on;
        }
        location /dashboard.html {
            root /usr/share/nginx/html;
        }
    }
}
```

***Figure 5.18**: Example Configuration*

Once the Nginx Plus API is enabled, the possibilities for dynamic configuration and automation expand dramatically. We can extend our Nginx configuration to support advanced setups such as enabling a key-value store that can be further integrated with Nginx maps. This integration allows us to modify values on the fly without having to deploy Nginx configurations and having to do Nginx reload and restart.

Imagine being able change the amount of traffic that should be allowed as per rate limiting policy on a fly that responds to changing traffic patterns on Nginx. Moreover, we can automate routine operations such as marking the upstream servers up or down, or updating configuration parameters through the API.

Let us explore these one by one.

Key Value Store in Nginx API

A **key-value store** is a simple database that stores data as a collection of key-value pairs. Each key is unique and is used to retrieve its associated value, much like looking up a word in a dictionary.

The key value store in Nginx allows us to maintain an in-memory mapping of keys to values that we can refer within our configuration using variables. This functionality is provided by the **ngx_http_keyval_module**. It enables us to define a key-value zone where dynamic data such as user sessions, customs flags, or configuration parameters can be stored and updated at runtime.

It is stored in shared memory zone (remember the concept of all worker processes being able to access it!). It can be enabled using directives such as **keyval_zone**, **keyval**, and **keyval_zone_variable**.

Let us first understand the directive definition.

- **keyval**

Syntax	keyval key $variable zone=name;
Default	–
Context	http

***Table 5.8**: keyval*

This directive is used to set key-value pairs in the specified shared memory zone defined by the keyword *zone*.

zone specifies the name of the shared memory zone.

key is a parameter that specifies the unique "**key**" of the key-value pair. It can also be a variable that already has a value assigned.

Example:

```
keyval $request_id $upstrean_name zone=myzone;
```

***Figure 5.19**: keyval*

In the preceding example, a key-value pair in the zone name '**myzone**' is set where each request id, that is, **$request_id** is the **key** and **$upstream_name** would be a dynamic value to be picked up from the key-value datastore in the shared memory zone, that is, myzone.

- **keyval_zone**

Syntax	keyval_zone zone=name:size [state=file] [timeout=time] [type=string|ip|prefix] [sync];
Default	–
Context	http

***Table 5.9**: keyval_zone*

This directive defines a shared memory zone where key-value pairs are stored. A unique name for the zone should be specified along with its size.

The optional state parameter specifies a file that keeps the current state of the key-value database in the JSON format and makes it persistent across nginx restarts. Changing the file content directly should be avoided. It can be done using Nginx Plus API.

Example:

```
keyval_zone zone=myzone:64k state=/etc/nginx/state_files/myzone.json;
```

***Figure 5.20**: keyval_zone*

In this example, myzone is the name of the shared memory zone, and 64k specifies the size of the shared memory zone.

Let us take an example to understand this better.

Imagine a scenario where we want to dynamically choose an upstream represented by a variable, that is, **$upstream_name** based on certain conditions, that is, **$request_id** for each incoming HTTP requests.

Setting a Variable: To establish a key-value pair, you must define the key. This key can be either a static name or string, a custom variable, or a pre-defined Nginx variable.

- Using a **pre-defined Nginx** variable, that is, **$request_id**

```
keyval $request_id $upstrean_name zone=myzone;
```

Figure 5.21: *$request_id*

- We can also use a **custom variable** as follows:

```
set $my_variable $request_uri;
```

Figure 5.22: *custom variable*

- We can use custom variables **`$my_variable`** as key in the keyval as:

```
keyval $my_variable $upstrean_name zone=myzone;
```

Figure 5.23: *$my_variable*

- It can also be a custom string value, as shown here:

```
keyval "blue" $upstream_name zone=myzone;
```

Figure 5.24: *custom string value*

This way, we can have multiple data in your key value store with different unique keys. The value will be corresponding to whatever matches the key.

Once we have defined the **`keyval`**, we need to define the **`keyval_zone`** which will be a shared memory zone that would be accessible to each Nginx worker process.

```
keyval_zone zone=myzone:64k state=/etc/nginx/state_files/myzone.json;
```

Figure 5.25: *keyval_zone*

Here, in the **`myzone`** memory zone, **`myzone.json`** file will be created that will store the key-value in **`json`** format, since we have defined the state file to be **`.json`** extension. You can also use a .txt format as per the requirement.

We personally use the **`.json`** format as it facilitates remote operations such as **`POST/PATCH/DELETE/GET`**.

The JSON file data could be represented as **`$request_id: $upstream_name`**

For example:

```
{
"myzone": {
    "1234": "blue",
    "4321": "green",
    "test": "brown"
  }
}
```

Figure 5.26: myzone

Employing these directives enables us to efficiently manage and manipulate data for various purposes, such as caching, routing, or applying access controls, enhancing the flexibility and functionality of our NGINX configuration.

Nginx Maps

Nginx maps allow developers to create key-value mappings within the Nginx configuration file. These mappings enable the transformation of input values (keys) into corresponding output values (values) based on predefined rules. With Nginx maps, developers can efficiently handle complex routing logic, manipulate request URIs, and customize server responses.

Maps are defined at the http `{}` block level and are used in the same way "`set`" directive for variables are used.

The only difference is that Nginx maps are only processed when referenced. If a request flow does not touch the section of a configuration where a map variable defined in the map is used, that map variable lookup will not be performed. As a result, Nginx maps add no overhead to requests until the variable is required. Therefore, maps are a great way to create low overhead variables.

Maps are defined using the **`map`** directive.

- **`map string`**

Syntax	`map string $variable { ... }`
Default	–
Context	`http`

Table 5.10: *map string*

Let us understand this better using a **conditional if example**.

Nginx If

In Nginx, the **`if`** derivative functions similarly to conditional statements in other coding languages, such as C, C++, Java, or Python.

Syntax	`if (condition) { ... }`
Default	–
Context	`server, location`

Table 5.11: *Nginx If*

Imagine a scenario, we want to conditionally respond with a **200** if the request method is **GET**, **405** if the request method is **POST**, and **305** if the request method is **PATCH**. Using **Nginx if,** our configuration would appear as follows:

```
if ($request_method = POST ) {
  return 405;
}
if ($request_method = GET ) {
  return 200;
}
if ($request_method = PATCH ) {
  return 305;
}
```

Figure 5.27: *Nginx if*

Well, there is no '**else**' in Nginx, hence use the cascaded **if**.

map Versus if

For the preceding **if** example, maps would render the same conditional logic but in a more comprehensive and simpler manner. To see how we can rewrite the same logic using maps, the preceding example can be rewritten as:

```
map $request_method $return_code {
  GET 200 ;
  POST 405;
  PATCH 305;
}
```

Figure 5.28: *map $return code*

This variable can be then referenced in location block as follows:

```
location / {
  return $return_code;
}
```

Figure 5.29: *$return code*

Some More Examples for Maps

Example 1: Conditional Routing

Suppose we want to route requests based on the request URI to different backend servers. We can use Nginx maps as:

```
http {
    map $uri $backend_server {
        /app1  backend1.example.com;
        /app2  backend2.example.com;
        default backend_default.example.com;
    }

    server {
        listen 80;

        location / {
            proxy_pass http://$backend_server;
        }
    }
}
```

Figure 5.30: *Conditional routing*

Example 2: URI Rewriting

Suppose we want to rewrite specific URIs to new paths and proxy the same to the backend. We can use Nginx maps along with the `rewrite` directive for URI rewriting as:

```
http {
    map $uri $new_uri {
        /old-path  /new-path;
        /old-page  /new-page;
        default    $uri;
    }

    server {
        listen 80;

        location / {
            rewrite ^ $new_uri permanent;
        }
    }
}
```

Figure 5.31: *URI Rewriting*

Example 3: Dynamic Content Generation

Suppose we want to add a response header for the request based on the client URL. We can define the map as follows and refer the variable in **`add_header`** directive:

```
http {
    map $uri $custom_header {
        /page1  "Custom Header Value for Page 1";
        /page2  "Custom Header Value for Page 2";
        default "Default Custom Header Value";
    }

    server {
        listen 80;

        location / {
            add_header X-Custom-Header $custom_header;
            ...
        }
    }
}
```

***Figure* 5.32**: *Dynamic Content Generation*

Example 4: Cascaded map

We can define map in such a way that one map will refer to second map for the further value.

```
# First map: Determine the device type from the User-Agent header
map $http_user_agent $device_type {
    default desktop;
    "~Mobile" mobile;
}

# Second map: Choose an upstream based on the device type from the first map
map $device_type $upstream_backend {
    desktop backend_desktop.example.com;
    mobile  backend_mobile.example.com;
}

server {
    listen 80;
    server_name example.com;

    location / {
        proxy_pass http://$upstream_backend;
    }
}
```

***Figure* 5.33**: *cascaded map*

Example 5: Integrating `map` and `key_val`

```
#key-val store that can be managed by API http://{Boxname}:8080/api/9/http/keyvals/device_type
{
    "Chrome":desktop,
    "Mobile":mobile,
    "ipad":Ipad
}

#Define key-val zone in Nginx
keyval_zone zone=device_type:64k state=/etc/nginx/state_files/device_type.json;
keyval $$http_user_agent $device_type zone=split;

# Choose an upstream based on the device type.
map $device_type $upstream_backend {
    desktop backend_desktop.example.com;
    mobile  backend_mobile.example.com;
}

server {
    listen 80;
    server_name example.com;

    location / {
        proxy_pass http://$upstream_backend;
    }
}
```

***Figure 5.34**: map and key_val*

These examples demonstrate how Nginx maps can be utilized for conditional routing, URI rewriting, and dynamic content generation within Nginx configurations.

Nginx if is Evil!

While the `if` directive in Nginx provides conditional logic for request processing, it comes with certain pitfalls and performance implications that can lead to unexpected behavior. Here is why the `if` directive is often considered "**evil**":

- **Increases Evaluation Time:** Nginx evaluates `if` conditions at runtime for each request, which can impact performance, especially in configurations with high traffic volume.
- **Configuration Complexity:** Overuse of `if` directives can lead to complex and difficult-to-maintain configurations. It can be challenging to understand the request flow if scattered through the configuration.
- **Blocking Behavior:** Certain `if` conditions can introduce blocking behavior, causing Nginx to process requests sequentially rather than concurrently. This can result in performance bottlenecks and decreased throughput.
- **Scope and Context:** `if` conditions in Nginx have limited scope and context to where it is defined. Whereas the maps are defined in http block and can be referred anywhere in the configuration whenever necessary.

Note: *Whenever possible, alternative directives such as* `try_files`, `rewrite`, *or* `map` *should be favored for implementing conditional logic to ensure optimal performance and maintainability of Nginx configurations.*

Now that we have learned how to implement keyval and keyval zone, let us now learn how to dynamically change values using Nginx API. We can use any API management tool such as Postman, SoapUI, or others available in the market.

Reading and Modifying Values in Nginx PLUS API with Precision

At its core, the Nginx API serves as a bridge between external systems and the Nginx server. Through the API, developers can query server status, retrieve configuration settings, and even modify server behavior in real time, all with a few simple HTTP requests.

Let us now embark on a hands-on journey to manipulate key-value stores, leveraging the API's capabilities to post, patch, and retrieve values dynamically.

Example Scenario: Let us consider a scenario where we manage a key-value DB with book names and its author. Each book name will be a unique identifier, and author would be the value mapped to each book. Our goal is to demonstrate how to post, patch, and retrieve authors for specific books using the Nginx Plus API.

Let us first define the keyval zone in the Nginx Configuration.

```
keyval_zone zone=keyvalDB:64k state=/etc/nginx/state_files/keyvalDB.json;
keyval $book_name $author zone=keyvalDB;
```

***Figure 5.35**: keyval zone*

Now we will try **`posting/patching`** and deleting a value in the **`keyvalDB`**.

Let us assume the **`keyvalDB.json`** has the following values:

```
{"Secret Seven": "Enid Blyton",
 "Pinocchio": "Carlo Collodi",
 "If Tomorrow Comes": "Sydney Sheldon"
}
```

***Figure 5.36**: keyvalDB.json values*

1. **Posting Values: Adding new value**

   To post a new value for a key in the key-value store, we craft an **`HTTP POST`** request with the key and its corresponding value as the payload and send the request to the API endpoint.

   ```
   HTTP REQUEST: http://{NGINXBOXNAME}:8080/api/5/http/keyvals/key-
   valDB
   PAYLOAD - {"Malory Towers":"Enid Blyon"}
   ```

Figure 5.37: Adding a new value

2. **Patching Values: Editing existing value**

   To update an existing value for a key in the key-value store, we craft an **`HTTP PATCH`** request with the key and its updated value as the payload and send the request to the API.

   ```
   HTTP REQUEST - http://{NGINXBOXNAME}:8080/api/5/http/keyvals/key-
   valDB
   PAYLOAD - {"Malory Towers":"Enid Blyton"}
   ```

Figure 5.38: Editing existing value

3. **Deleting Values: Removing a value**

   To delete the value associated with a specific key in the key-value store, we craft an HTTP "**`PATCH`**" request to the API with null as a value to delete the desired key value.

   ```
   HTTP REQUEST - http://{NGINXBOXNAME}:8080/api/5/http/keyvals/key-
   valDB
   PAYLOAD - {"Malory Towers":""}
   ```

Figure 5.39: *Removing a value*

Note: *With the delete request, it may delete the whole key value store. So, it is better to use the* **PATCH HTTP** *request with a null value.*

Conclusion

Through hands-on experiments and clear examples, we have learned how to work with key-value stores and maps using the NGINX Plus API. By mastering how to post, patch, and retrieve values dynamically, we can easily manage advanced server configurations. This makes us ready for our further chapters involving canary testing and rate limiting.

Chapter 6
Canary Testing with Nginx

Introduction

As design trends evolve and customer expectations continue to rise, the demand for new features in software is relentless. However, when managing a high-value website or software worth millions, simply rolling out a new feature without careful consideration can spell disaster. The risk of website or software downtime and potential loss of business looms large in such scenarios.

How do developers add new features while dealing with unexpected problems, especially when software is so complex, and time is limited?

This is where various testing methodologies and deployment strategies come into play, each designed to validate changes in such a way that there is almost no down time and bad customer experience. Among these methodologies, Canary testing, A/B testing, and Blue-Green testing stand out as effective approaches.

Canary testing, A/B testing, and Blue-Green may sound very similar but each serves a distinct purpose. Let us delve into the specifics of each methodology to understand their unique characteristics and applications.

Structure

In this chapter, the following topics will be covered:

- A/B Testing
- Blue Green Deployments
- Canary Testing
- Canary or Blue-Green or A/B Testing Using `split_client` Module
- Use Case to Implement `split_client` Module
- Using Nginx Plus API to Dynamically Switch Traffic Percentage for Canary

A/B Testing

In simple terms, A/B testing is a way to compare two versions of something to determine which performs better.

Imagine you have a website, and you are launching a new feature with a button. Version A is how the website looks now, and Version B is how it could look in the future with new button.

With A/B testing, you randomly send some users to A code and the other set of users to B code. After a while, you compare the two versions with parameters including scalability, usability, and performance metrics, and how those factors influence the website.

This helps the developers figure out if users like a new feature, such as a button. It is like giving people a test drive of cars before letting them decide which one to buy.

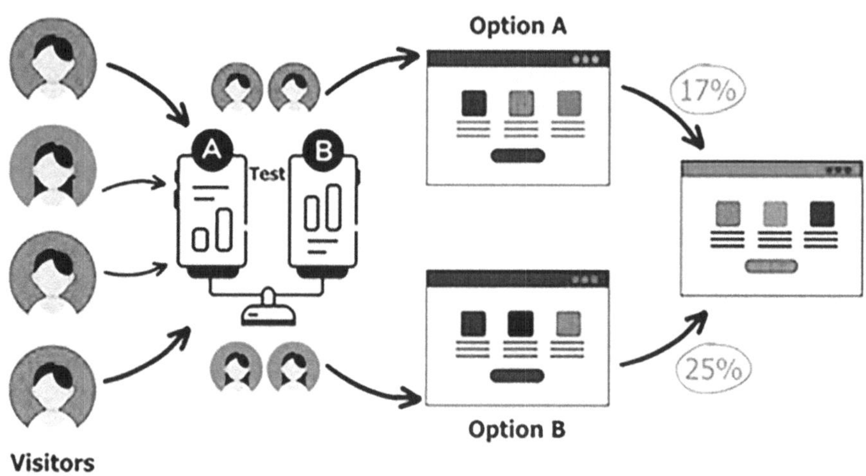

Figure 6.1: *A/B Testing*

Blue Green Deployments

Blue-green deployments are a strategy to minimize downtime and risk when rolling out new features or updates in production specially for a high serving client software or websites.

Imagine having two nearly identical production environments:

- **Blue Environment**: The current, stable version serving all user requests. Let us call the version of code as N.
- **Green Environment**: The new version, ready to receive traffic. Let us call the version of code as N1.

The developers continuously develop new code and deploy in the green environment where they perform "*down the layer testing*" - which means sending dummy traffic or test traffic to check the feature with depended applications in a production-like environment.

As a new release undergoes final testing in the green environment, once validated, a simple Nginx switch redirects incoming client traffic to the green environment, rendering the blue environment as idle. After final validations, if any issues arise, we can quickly revert back to the blue environment by simply switching the configuration back, ensuring that user experience remains uninterrupted.

In essence, blue-green deployments with Nginx allow for a smooth transition between application versions by maintaining two separate environments and dynamically controlling traffic routing, thereby ensuring **continuous availability** and **reducing deployment risks**.

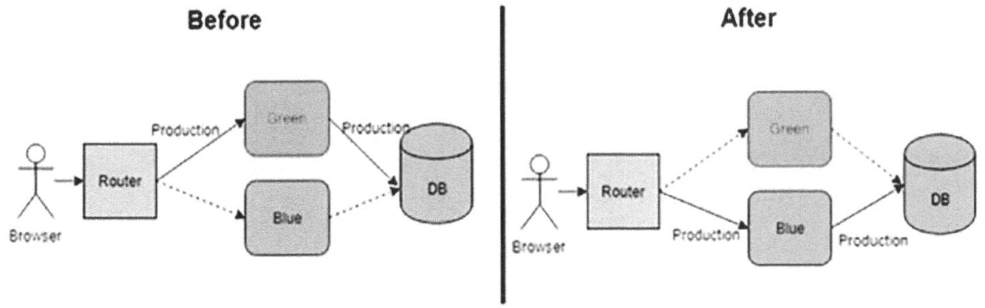

Figure 6.2: *Blue Green Deployments*

Canary Testing

"*Canary testing*" originates from coal mining, where the bird - canaries were used to detect toxic gases in the coal mines. Their distress or death signalled danger, prompting miners to evacuate.

Similarly in software development, it involves releasing updates or new features to a small group of *predefined* users, monitoring for issues or adverse effects. This method serves as an early warning system, allowing developers to detect problems before a wider rollout.

Formerly, after developers completed coding a feature, they conducted initial testing to catch general bugs. Subsequently, the feature underwent scrutiny in a testing environment with dedicated testers and dependent clients. Despite these efforts, variations of testing environment with production environments, such as operating systems bandwidth, or application setups leaked bugs in production.

Canary testing involves deploying a feature to a small subset of users, typically around 5%, who experience and assess the new features. By closely monitoring this user group, developers swiftly detect and resolve any bugs, minimizing the chances of encountering production issues later. This targeted approach lessens the number of users affected by bugs, thereby ensuring seamless releases and uninterrupted customer experience.

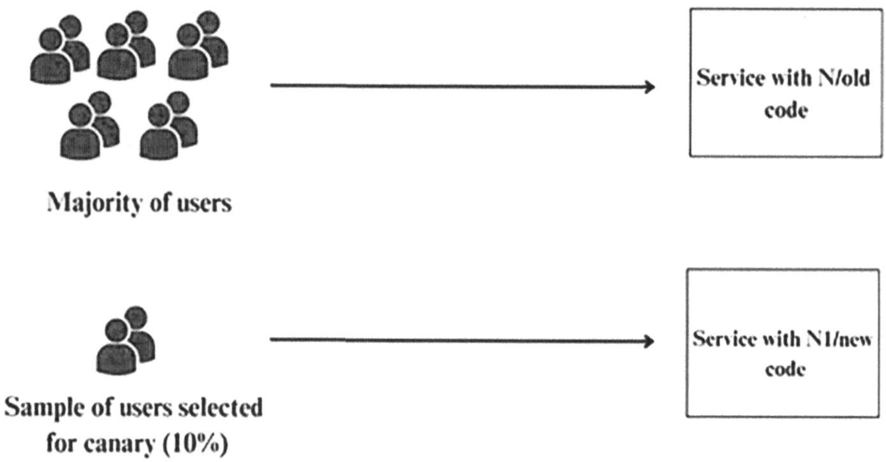

***Figure 6.3**: Canary Testing*

Canary or Blue-Green or A/B Testing Using `split_client` Module

When it comes to canary, blue-green, or A/B testing with Nginx, the **`split_client`** module is very a handy tool. The **`split_client`** module allows us to divide incoming traffic into different groups based on various criteria, such as IP address, request URL, **`request_id`**, timestamp, or HTTP headers. This can be useful for directing a portion of client traffic to an N1 version of the code while the rest of the traffic continues to route to the stable version.

Let us learn the syntax for the **`split_client`** module:

Syntax	`split_clients $variable $target {`
	`    percent_group1 value1;`
	`    percent_group2 value2;`
	`    ...`
	`}`

Default	–
Context	`http`

Example	`split_clients $request_id $target {`
	`    90% value1;`
	`    10% value2;`
	`}`

***Table 6.1**: split_client module*

- **`$variable`** is the key that will help to distinguish each request. Common variables include **`$remote_addr (client IP address)`**, **`$http_user_agent (User-Agent header)`**, **`$request_id`**, and so on.
- **`$target`** is the value that each request will be assigned according to the percentage defined in the **`split_client`**.
- **`percent_group1`** and **`percent_group2`** are the percentages of requests that should fall into each group. The sum of all percentages should be 100%.

The **`$target`** can be referred in the other parts of Nginx configuration, similar to the variables referred in maps and proxy directives. Example:

```
http {

  split_clients $request_id $target {
      90% value1;
      10% value2;
  }
  map $target $app_upstream {
    value1 app-blue;
    value2 app-green;
  }

  server {
    ..
    location / {
      proxy_pass https://$app_upstream;
    }
  }

}
```

***Figure 6.4**: split_client*

The **`split_clients`** module provides a flexible way to segment traffic and apply different behaviors based on certain criteria. It is commonly used for canary testing, A/B testing, blue-green deployments, and more. However, we should be cautious with its usage, especially in high-traffic scenarios, as it involves calculating hashes for each request, which can add overhead.

Use Case to Implement `split_client` Module

Scenario: We have just finished writing a new feature for our website **yourwebsite.com**. We want to roll the feature gradually to ensure it does not introduce any unexpected issues.

Let us assume:

- Blue is the current version or the N version of the code
- Green is the version with new feature or N1 version of the code

We will try to write the Nginx configuration to perform canary and release the new feature.

Note: *The* **`split_client`** *module is available only on Nginx Plus or commercial Nginx version.*

Step 1. Create a file named **`split.config`** and add the following configuration:

```
#Create a split_client zone where each request with a unique request_id will be assigned either Blue or Green upstream
    split_clients $request_id $app_upstream {
        95%   Blue-app;
        5%   Green-app;
    }

#upstream Blue-app and upstream Green-app defined.
    upstream Blue-app {
        server 10.0.0.1;
    }

    upstream Green-app {
        server 10.0.0.2;
    }

    server {
        listen 80;
        server_name yourwebsite.com;

        location / {
            proxy_connect_timeout 75s;
            proxy_send_timeout 120s;
            proxy_read_timeout 120s;
            send_timeout 120s;
            proxy_set_header Connection "";
            proxy_set_header HOST $host;
            proxy_set_header X-Forwarded-For $proxy_add_x_forwarded_for;
            add_header X-Upstream $proxy_host always;
# Here in the proxy pass we used the $app_upstream defined in the split client.
            proxy_pass http://$app_upstream;
        }
    }
```

Figure 6.5: *split.config*

Step 2. Include **split.conf** file in the **nginx.config** using **include** directive:

```
user  user;
worker_processes  auto;

error_log  /var/log/nginx/error.log;
pid        /var/run/nginx.pid;

# worker_rlimit_nofile in most cases should be set to 2 *
worker_connections
worker_rlimit_nofile 16192;
events {
    worker_connections  8096;
}

http {
    include /etc/nginx/mime.types;
    default_type  application/octet-stream;

    log_format  main    '$remote_addr - $remote_user [$time_
local] "$request" '
                         'connection:$connection '
                         'connection_requests:$connection_
requests '
                         'pid:$pid '
                         'url=$request_uri '
                        'status="$status" $body_bytes_sent
"$http_referer" '
                        'protocol=$scheme '
                        'useragent="$http_user_agent"
hostheader="$http_host" '
                        'virtualserver=$host '
                        'method=$request_method '
                        'request_length=$request_length '
                        'rt="$request_time" uct="$upstream_
connect_time" uht="$upstream_header_time" urt="$upstream_
response_time" '
                        'xff="$http_x_forwarded_for" '
                        'gzip_ratio="$gzip_ratio" '
                        'X_Upstream="$proxy_host" ';

    access_log  /var/log/nginx/access.log  main;

    sendfile        on;
    #tcp_nopush     on;
    keepalive_timeout  100s;
    gzip  on;
```

```
    gzip_proxied any;
    gzip_types text/plain text/css text/xml text/javascript
application/x-javascript application/xml application/json
application/javascript;
    gzip_disable "msie6";
    resolver 10.8.8.8 10.7.7.7;
    proxy_http_version 1.1;
    proxy_set_header Connection "";
    proxy_connect_timeout 75s;
    proxy_read_timeout 100s;
    variables_hash_max_size 2048;
    variables_hash_bucket_size 128;
    map_hash_max_size 128;
    map_hash_bucket_size 128;

    client_body_buffer_size 16k;
    client_header_buffer_size 1k;
    client_max_body_size 0;
    large_client_header_buffers 16 32k;

    proxy_buffer_size 128k;
    proxy_buffers 4 256k;
    proxy_busy_buffers_size 256k;

    server_tokens off;

    # To avoid any unintended file usage, including each file
rather than a regex to include all.
    #include /etc/nginx/conf.d/environment-file/*.conf;

    # Include the split.conf file
    include /etc/nginx/conf.d/split.conf;

}
```

How does Nginx route requests with `split_client` module?

1. **Client Identification:** When a request arrives at Nginx, the **`split_clients`** module identifies the client based on the specified variable; here **`$request_id`**.
2. **Hash Calculation**: After identifying the client, the **`split_clients`** module calculates a hash based on the value of the specified variable. This hash function ensures that clients are evenly distributed among the defined groups; here blue-app or green-app.
3. **Group Assignment:** Once the hash is calculated, Nginx uses the result to determine which group the client belongs to. The **`split_clients`** directive defines the groups based on their corresponding percentages.

4. **Routing:** After assigning the client to a group, Nginx can use conditionals or variables to route the request accordingly to either the Blue-app or the Green-app.
5. **Request Processing**: Finally, Nginx processes the request based on the routing decision and serves the appropriate response to the client.

Using Nginx Plus API to Dynamically Switch Traffic Percentage for Canary

Using the NGINX Plus API, we can dynamically adjust traffic splitting between different versions of our application, facilitating controlled rollouts and monitoring. Here is a basic overview of how we can leverage the Nginx API to gradually route the traffic from blue to green.

Scenario: You have just finished writing a new feature for our website. We want to roll switch the client to the green route with new feature gradually. We will first divert 25% of the client to green. After some time, we will divert 50% and 75%. At the end, we will finally switch the entire traffic, that is, 100% to green.

Let us assume:

- Blue is the current version or the N version of the code
- Green is the version with new feature or N1 version of the code

We will try to write the Nginx configuration to perform percentage wise throttle and release the new feature.

Create a file **`split.config`** and add the following configuration.

Step 1. Since we want to remotely switch the traffic, we will enable the Nginx Plus API as follows:

```
##Create a keyval zone that will help to change the canary
percentage using nginx plus api
keyval_zone zone=split:64k state=/etc/nginx/state_files/split.
json;
keyval $server_name $split_level zone=split;

map $split_level $app_upstream {

##For blue-green
    blue0_green100 $split_blue0_green100;
    blue25_green75 $split_blue25_green75;
    blue50_green50 $split_blue50_green50;
    blue75_green25 $split_blue75_green25;
```

```
    blue100_green0 $split_blue100_green0;
}

#Create a split_client zone where each request with a unique
request_id will be assigned either Blue or Green upstream
split_clients $request_id $split_blue0_green100 {
    100% green;
    * blue;
}

split_clients $request_id $split_blue75_green25 {
    75% blue;
    25% green;
}

split_clients $request_id $split_blue50_green50 {
    50% blue;
    50% green;
}

split_clients $request_id $split_blue25_green75 {
    25% blue;
    75% green;
}

split_clients $request_id $split_blue100_green0 {
    100% blue;
    * green;
}

#upstream Blue-app and uptstream Green-app defined.
    upstream Blue-app {
        server 10.0.0.1;
    }

    upstream Green-app {
        server 10.0.0.2;
    }

    server {
        listen 80;
        server_name yourwebsite.com;

        location / {
            proxy_connect_timeout 75s;
            proxy_send_timeout 120s;
            proxy_read_timeout 120s;
```

```
            send_timeout 120s;
            proxy_set_header Connection "";
            proxy_set_header HOST $host;
            proxy_set_header X-Forwarded-For $proxy_add_x_
forwarded_for;
            add_header X-Upstream $proxy_host always;
# Here in the proxy_pass we used the $app_upstream defined in the
split_client.
            proxy_pass http://$app_upstream;
        }
    }
```

Step 2. Include **split.conf** file in the **nginx.config** using include directive.

```
user  user;
worker_processes  auto;

error_log  /var/log/nginx/error.log;
pid        /var/run/nginx.pid;

# worker_rlimit_nofile in most cases should be set to 2 *
worker_connections
worker_rlimit_nofile 16192;
events {
    worker_connections  8096;
}

http {
    include /etc/nginx/mime.types;
    default_type  application/octet-stream;

    log_format  main    '$remote_addr - $remote_user [$time_
local] "$request" '
                         'connection:$connection '
                         'connection_requests:$connection_
requests '
                         'pid:$pid '
                         'url=$request_uri '
                        cstatus="$status" $body_bytes_sent
"$http_referer" '
                        'protocol=$scheme '
                        'useragent="$http_user_agent"
hostheader="$http_host" '
                        'virtualserver=$host '
                        'method=$request_method '
                        'request_length=$request_length '
                        'rt="$request_time" uct="$upstream_
```

```
connect_time" uht="$upstream_header_time" urt="$upstream_
response_time" '
                        'xff="$http_x_forwarded_for" '
                        'gzip_ratio="$gzip_ratio" '
                        'X_Upstream="$proxy_host" ';

    access_log  /var/log/nginx/access.log  main;

    sendfile        on;
    #tcp_nopush     on;
    keepalive_timeout  100s;
    gzip  on;
    gzip_proxied any;
    gzip_types text/plain text/css text/xml text/javascript
application/x-javascript application/xml application/json
application/javascript;
    gzip_disable "msie6";
    resolver 10.8.8.8 10.7.7.7;
    proxy_http_version 1.1;
    proxy_set_header Connection "";
    proxy_connect_timeout 75s;
    proxy_read_timeout 100s;
    variables_hash_max_size 2048;
    variables_hash_bucket_size 128;
    map_hash_max_size 128;
    map_hash_bucket_size 128;

    client_body_buffer_size 16k;
    client_header_buffer_size 1k;
    client_max_body_size 0;
    large_client_header_buffers 16 32k;

    proxy_buffer_size 128k;
    proxy_buffers 4 256k;
    proxy_busy_buffers_size 256k;

    server_tokens off;

    #Enable Nginx Dashboard and enable write on for the api to
allow changes
    server {
        listen 8080;
        access_log off;

        location = / {
            return 301 /dashboard.html;
        }
```

```
            location /api {
                api write=on;
            }
            location /dashboard.html {
                root /usr/share/nginx/html;
            }
        }

        # To avoid any unintended file usage, including each file
    rather than a regex to include all.
        #include /etc/nginx/conf.d/environment-file/*.conf;

        # Include the split.conf file
        include /etc/nginx/conf.d/split.conf;
    }
```

Step 3. We will post values using Nginx Plus API for the first time. In the **keyval**, we defined **$server_name $split_level** (*Figure* 6.6). The value of **$split_level** is defined in the map (*Figure* 6.7) as follows:

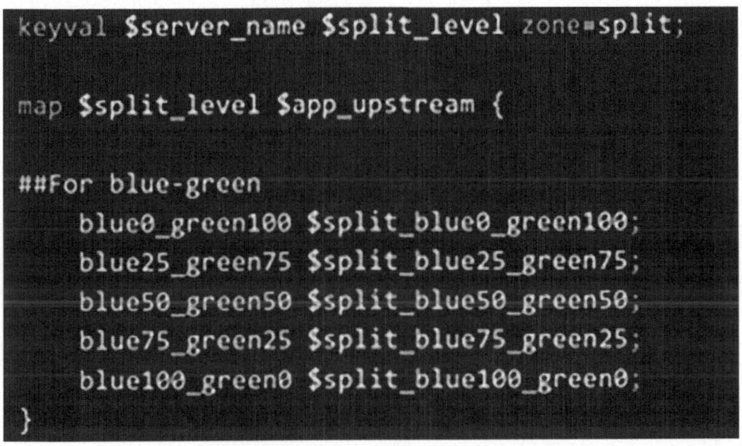

Figure 6.6: *$server_name $split_level*

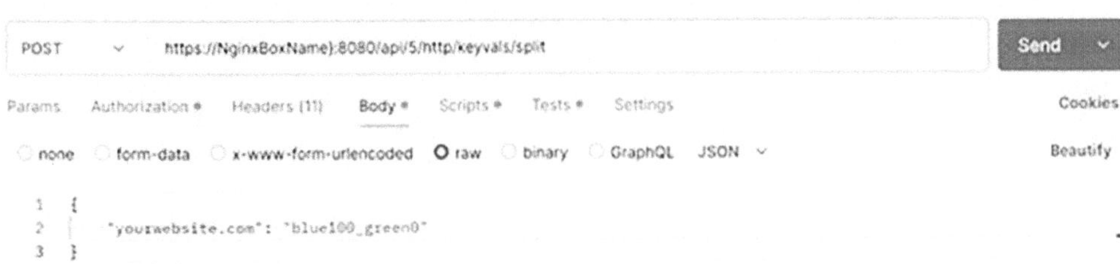

Figure 6.7: *$split_level*

Step 4. Routing 25% of the traffic from Blue to Green:

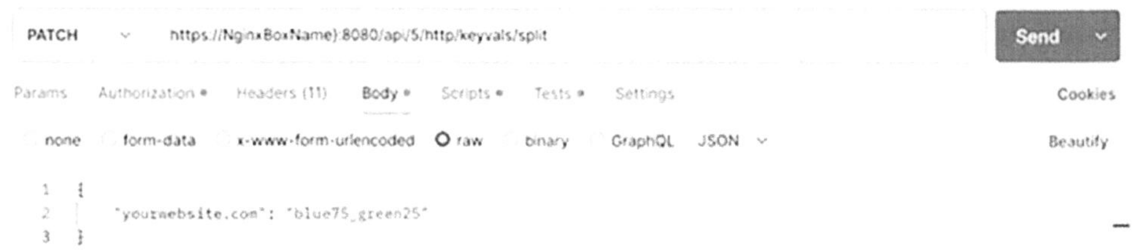

Figure 6.8: *Routing 25%*

Step 5. Routing 50% of the traffic from Blue to Green:

Figure 6.9: *Routing 50%*

Step 6. Routing 75% of the traffic from Blue to Green:

Figure 6.10: *Routing 75%*

Step 7. Routing 100% traffic from Blue to Green:

***Figure 6.11**: Routing 100%*

Conclusion

In this chapter, we delved into the essential aspects of canary testing using Nginx, a powerful tool for managing and distributing web traffic. By mastering canary testing with Nginx, we can achieve greater reliability and stability in our deployment processes. This approach not only safeguards user experience but also empowers development teams to innovate and deploy new features with confidence. As we continue to refine our deployment strategies, the principles and techniques covered in this chapter will serve as a foundation for maintaining high availability and performance in your web applications. In the next chapter, we will explore how Nginx stands as a robust and versatile web server.

CHAPTER 7
Nginx as a Web Server

Introduction

As discussed previously, Nginx's event-driven and asynchronous architecture allows Nginx to manage thousands of connections with a small and predictable amount of memory, significantly reducing the overhead and improving scalability. Indeed, the adoption of Nginx has surged across various industries, driven by its impressive capabilities as both a web server and a reverse proxy.

In the realm of web servers, the most critical functions include efficiently serving static and dynamic content, implementing caching strategies, and applying compression techniques. Nginx excels in all these areas, making it a powerful tool for modern web infrastructure.

In this chapter, we will explore how Nginx handles these essential tasks.

Structure

In this chapter, the following topics will be covered:

- Serving Static Content
- Compression Decompression

Serving Static Content

Static content consists of files that do not change frequently, such as HTML, CSS, JavaScript, and images. It refers to any web content that can be delivered to an end user exactly as stored, without any need for generation, modification, or processing by the server. This type of content is the same for every user, making it one of the simplest and most efficient forms of content to transmit over the Internet.

Although static content is less interactive than dynamic content, its simplicity often translates to faster load times and reduced server load.

Nginx is exceptionally well-suited for serving static files because of its high-performance, event-driven architecture, which allows it to handle numerous concurrent connections efficiently.

How Static Content Works

Fetching a static content from a web server is one of the fundamental functions of the web. For instance, when a user types a URL such as http://www.example.com/index.html into a web browser, the browser fetches the index.html file from the web server hosting example.com.

Here are the steps involved in requesting static content from a server:

Step1. Client Request:

When we type a URL such as http://example.com/index.html into our browser, the browser sends an **`HTTP GET`** request to the Nginx server.

Step 2. Request Handling:

Nginx receives the request and checks its configuration. Within the configuration, the location block that handles the requested URI (in this case, `/index.html` or simply / if index.html is the default file) is selected.

Step 3. File System Lookup:

Nginx uses the root or alias directive specified in the configuration to determine the file's location on disk. For instance, if the configuration includes:

```
location / {
    root /var/www/html;
    index index.html;
}
```

***Figure 7.1**: file system lookup*

Nginx will look for the file at **`/var/www/html/index.html`**.

Step 4. Serving the File:

Once the file is found, Nginx reads the contents of **`index.html`** from the disk and sends it back to the client as the HTTP response. This process is optimized for static content, meaning it can quickly serve files without additional processing or interfacing with application servers.

Step 5. Response to the Client:

The client's browser receives the response, interprets the HTML content, and renders the page. Since the content is static and stored on the server, this process is usually very fast and efficient.

To summarize, Nginx serves static content such as index.html by directly retrieving the file from a specified directory on the disk and sending it over the network to the client.

How Nginx Serves Static Content

Let us start by understanding some Nginx directives, which we will later see in the Nginx configuration for handling static files.

- **`root`**

Syntax	`root path;`
Default	`root html;`
Context	`http, server, location, if in location`
Example	`root index.html`

***Table* 7.1:** *root*

The **`root`** directive in Nginx specifies the directory from which the server should serve static files. It defines the base directory on the filesystem where the requested file is located.

Example:

For the following configuration,

```
location /img/ {
    root /files/images;
}
```

***Figure* 7.2:** *root*

For the request, **`/img/pic.png`**, Nginx looks for the file at **`/files/images/`** and respond with **`/img/files/images/pic.png`** to the client.

A path to the file is constructed by merely adding a URI to the value of the root directive. If a URI has to be modified, the alias directive should be used.

- **`alias`**

Syntax	`alias path;`
Default	–
Context	`location`

***Table* 7.2:** *alias*

The alias directive in Nginx is used to map a specific URI to a ***different*** directory on the filesystem.

When a request matches a location block with an alias directive, Nginx replaces the matched portion of the URI with the specified path by the alias directive. This allows Nginx to serve content from a directory that does not directly correspond to the request URI structure.

root Versus alias

Let us understand this with an example:

If we use the **root** directive, the location's prefix is appended to the root directory. For example,

```
location /images/ {
    root /var/www/html;
}
```

***Figure 7.3**: root example*

A request for **/images/picture.jpg** is mapped to **/var/www/html/images/picture.jpg**.

With **alias**, the matched part of the URL is replaced by the alias value. For example,

```
location /images/ {
    alias /data/pictures/;
}
```

***Figure 7.4**: alias example*

A request for **/images/picture.jpg** is mapped directly to **/data/pictures/picture.jpg**, ignoring the **/images/ portion** from the filesystem path.

Note: *When the location matches the last part of the directive's value, it is often better to use the root directive instead of alias. Example scenario:*

```
location /images/ {
    alias /data/w3/images/;
}
```

***Figure 7.5**: images*

Using `alias` with Regular Expressions

If the **`alias`** directive is used inside a location block defined with a regular expression, the regular expression should contain captures, and the alias should refer to these captures. This approach allows Nginx to correctly map the requested URI to the filesystem path.

Example: The location block uses a regular expression to match URLs that point to image files within the **`/users/ directory`**. The **`alias`** directive maps the captured part of the URI (**`$1`**) to the **`/data/w3/images/ directory`**.

```
location ~ ^/users/(?:gif|jpe?g|png)$ {
    alias /data/w3/images/$1;
}
```

Figure 7.6: *regular expressions capturing*

- **`index`**

Syntax	`index file ...;`
Default	`index index.html;`
Context	`http, server, location`
Example	`index index.html;`

Table 7.3: *index*

The index directive in Nginx specifies the default file to serve when a client requests a directory rather than a specific file. This directive is commonly used to define the main entry points for directories, such as **`index.html`** for HTML-based websites, or **`index.php`** for PHP-based applications.

How the index Directive Works: When a client requests a URL that corresponds to a directory, Nginx uses the index directive to determine which file within that directory to serve. If the specified index file exists, Nginx serves it. If it does not exist, Nginx will follow other configured rules or return an error, depending on the configuration.

Example,

```
index index.html index.htm;
```

`Index.html`, **`index.htm`** are the filenames that Nginx will look for in the specified order when a directory is requested.

Note:

Order of Files: *The order in which files are listed in the index directive is important. Nginx will serve the first file it finds.*

Performance: *If a directory contains a large number of files, specifying multiple index files may have a slight performance impact due to the additional file existence checks.*

- **`try_files`**

Syntax	`try_files file ... uri;` `try_files file ... =code;`
Default	–
Context	`server, location`
Example	`try_files $uri $uri/ /index.php;`

Table 7.4: *try_files*

When a request comes in, **`try_files`** evaluates a list of file paths in order. It uses the first file that exists on the disk and serves it to the client. If none of the files exist, it can either return a specified error code or pass the request to an internal location.

In the preceding example,

1. For **`$uri`** parameter, Nginx first checks if the requested URI corresponds to an existing file.
2. For **`$uri/`** parameter, Nginx checks if a directory with that name exists if the file in **`$uri`** is not found.
3. For **`index.php`** parameter, if neither the file nor the directory exists, the request is passed to **`/index.php`**.

The **`try_files`** directive is a powerful tool in Nginx configuration, allowing for flexible file handling, fallbacks, and integration with dynamic content. It enhances the ability to serve static content efficiently while providing mechanisms to handle various edge cases gracefully.

We can use **`try_files`** in the following scenario in different ways:

- Simple Static File Handling
- Fallback to Index File
- Fallback to Another Location
- Custom Error Page

Simple Static File Handling

```
server {
    listen 80;
    server_name www.example.com;

    root /var/www/example;

    location / {
        try_files $uri $uri/ =404;
    }
}
```

***Figure 7.7**: Static File Handling*

In this scenario, Nginx will try to serve the requested file directly. If the file does not exist, it will return a **`404`** error.

a. The file will be searched in the location **`/var/www/example`**, as defined in root directive.

b. **`$uri`** represents the requested file, **`$uri/`** checks if a directory exists, and **`=404`** returns a **`404`** error if neither exists.

Fallback to Index File

```
server {
    listen 80;
    server_name www.example.com;

    root /var/www/example;

    location / {
        try_files $uri $uri/ /index.html;
    }
}
```

***Figure 7.8**: Index File*

In the preceding example, **`/index.html`** is the fallback file served if the requested file or directory does not exist.

Fallback to Another Location

```
server {
    listen 80;
    server_name www.example.com;

    root /var/www/example;

    location / {
        try_files $uri $uri/ /index.php?$query_string;
    }

    location ~ \.php$ {
        include snippets/fastcgi-php.conf;
        fastcgi_pass unix:/var/run/php/php7.4-fpm.sock;
    }
}
```

Figure 7.9: *fallback*

Nginx will try to serve the requested file. If the file does not exist, it will pass the request to another location block, such as a PHP script for dynamic processing.

In the preceding example, **`index.php?$query_string`** passes the request to **`index.php`** along with the query string if the file or directory does not exist.

Custom Error Page

Nginx will try to serve the requested file and a directory index file. If neither exists, it will serve a custom error page.

```
server {
    listen 80;
    server_name www.example.com;

    root /var/www/example;

    location / {
        try_files $uri $uri/ /custom_404.html;
    }

    error_page 404 /custom_404.html;

    location = /custom_404.html {
        internal;
    }
}
```

Figure 7.10: *error page*

In the preceding example, **/custom_404.html** is the custom 404 error page. The **error_page** directive sets the custom error page for 404 status code. The internal directive inside the location block ensures that **custom_404.html** page is not directly accessible by clients.

Compression Decompression

One of the pivotal roles in achieving the lightning-fast load for a website is played by compression and decompression of files. At its core, compressing files before transmission and efficiently decompressing them upon arrival, we streamline the data exchange process between servers and clients. This process is crucial for improving load times, reducing bandwidth consumption, and ultimately providing a better user experience.

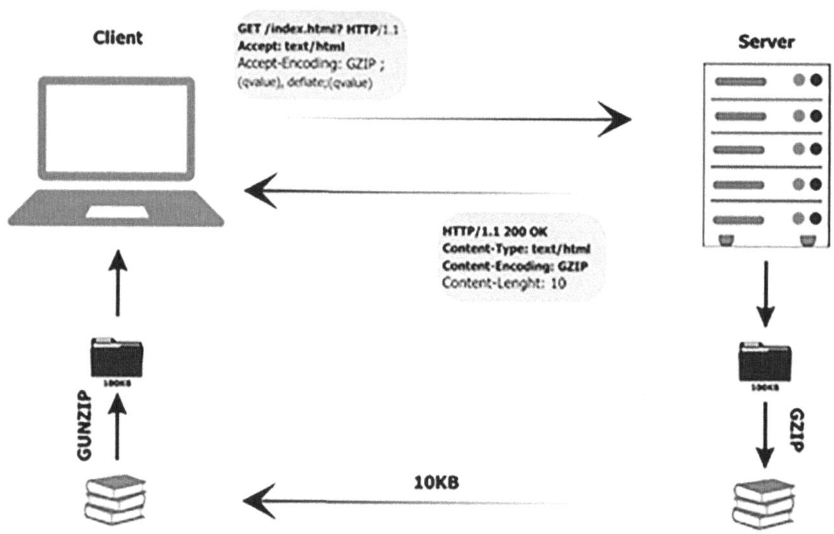

Figure 7.11: *Compression Decompression*

The necessity of file compression for websites contributes to several critical factors:

- **Improved Load Times:** Compressed files are smaller in size, which means they can be downloaded faster. This reduction in load time is particularly beneficial for users with slower internet connections or those accessing websites from mobile devices.
- **Reduced Bandwidth Usage:** Smaller file sizes mean less data is transmitted between the server and the client. This reduction in data transfer not only speeds up communication but also reduces the bandwidth usage, which can result in cost savings, especially for websites with high traffic volumes.
- **Enhanced User Experience:** Faster load times lead to a smoother and more responsive browsing experience. Users are more likely to stay on a website

that loads quickly, reducing bounce rates and increasing engagement and conversions.

- **SEO Benefits:** Search engines such as Google take page load speed into account when ranking websites. Faster websites tend to rank higher in search results, making file compression an essential part of SEO strategies.
- **Lower Server Load:** Efficient file compression reduces the load on the web server by minimizing the amount of data it needs to handle. This efficiency can lead to better server performance and the ability to serve more concurrent users.

Types of Compression

There are two main types of compression used in web development:

- **Lossless Compression:** This type of compression reduces file size without losing any data. When decompressed, the file is restored to its original state. Common formats include GZIP and Brotli.
- **Lossy Compression:** This method reduces file size by permanently eliminating some data, especially redundant or less important information. This type is commonly used for images, videos, and audio files. Formats such as JPEG and MP3 are examples of lossy compression.

Compression Algorithm

The two prominent compression algorithms that are widely used are **Gzip** and **Brotli**, each offering distinct advantages in the world of web optimization.

Gzip

Gzip identifies repetitive patterns within the data stream and replaces them with shorter representations, effectively compressing the file without compromising its integrity. Gzip is widely adopted compression algorithm.

Enabling Gzip in Nginx: To enable Gzip compression in Nginx, the **`gzip`**, **`ngx_http_gzip_module`**, is installed by default during Nginx installation. Here are some important directives to implement the **`gzip`** compression in Nginx:

- **`gzip`**

Syntax	`gzip on | off;`
Default	`gzip off;`
Context	`http, server, location, if in location`
Example	`gzip on;`

Table 7.5: *Gzip*

The **gzip** directive enables or disables Gzip compression of the client responses. By default, **gzip** is disabled.

- **gzip_buffers**

Syntax	gzip_buffers number size;
Default	gzip_buffers 32 4k (for 32-bit systems) gzip_buffers 16 8k (for 64-bit systems)
Context	http, server, location
Example	gzip_buffers 32 4k;

Table 7.6: *gzip_buffers*

This directive sets the number and size of buffers used to hold compressed data when **gzip** compression is enabled.

gzip_buffers 32 4k instructs Nginx to allocate 32 buffers, each of 4 kilobytes, for the compressed data.

- **gzip_comp_level**

Syntax	gzip_comp_level level;
Default	gzip_comp_level 1;
Context	http, server, location
Example	gzip_comp_level 5;

Table 7.7: *gzip_comp_level*

This directive sets the Gzip compression level. Acceptable values range from 1 (fastest, least compression) to 9 (slowest, most compression).

- **gzip_disable**

Syntax	gzip_disable regex ...;
Default	–
Context	http, server, location

Table 7.8: *gzip_disable*

This directive disables gzipping of responses for specific "**User-Agent**" header fields matching any of the specified regular expressions.

Example: Disabling Gzip for Internet Explorer 6

Internet Explorer 6 (IE6) is known to have issues with Gzip compression. Therefore, to disable Gzip for IE6, we can use the following configuration:

```
http {
    gzip on;
    gzip_disable "msie6";

    server {
        listen 80;
        server_name www.example.com;

        location / {
            root /var/www/html;
            index index.html;
        }
    }
}
```

***Figure 7.12**: Disabling Gzip for Internet Explorer*

`gzip_disable "msie6"` disables gzip compression when the User-Agent header matches the pattern "**`msie6`**", which is typically present in Internet Explorer 6 requests. The special mask "**`msie6`**" corresponds to the regular expression "**`MSIE [4-6]\.`**", but works faster.

- **`gzip_http_version`**

Syntax	`gzip_http_version 1.0 | 1.1;`
Default	`gzip_http_version 1.1;`
Context	`http, server, location`
Example	`gzip_http_version 1.1;`

***Table 7.9**: gzip_http_version*

This directive sets the minimum HTTP version of a request to be compressed.

- **`gzip_proxied`**

Syntax	`gzip_proxied off | expired | no-cache | no-store | private | no_last_modified | no_etag | auth | any ...;`
Default	`gzip_proxied off;`
Context	`http, server, location`
Example	`gzip_proxied any;`

***Table 7.10**: gzip_proxied*

This directive enables or disables compression for proxied requests based on the following conditions:

- **off**: Disables Gzip compression for all proxied requests.
- **expired**: Compresses responses even if they have an expired header.
- **no-cache**: Compresses responses with a "**Cache-Control: no-cache**" header.
- **no-store**: Compresses responses with a "**Cache-Control: no-store**" header.
- **private**: Compresses responses with a "**Cache-Control: private**" header.
- **no_last_modified**: Compresses responses without a "**Last-Modified**" header.
- **no_etag**: Compresses responses without an "**ETag**" header.
- **auth**: Compresses responses to requests that require HTTP authentication.
- **any**: Compresses all responses to proxied requests.

Syntax	gzip_types mime-type ...;
Default	gzip_types text/html;
Context	http, server, location
Example	gzip_types image/png;

Table 7.11: *gzip_types*

This directive specifies the MIME types of responses that should be compressed.

gzip_types image/png directs Nginx to compress all **png** format images only.

What are MIME types?

MIME types define the nature and format of a file by associating file extensions with a specific content type. In the context of Nginx, MIME types are used to inform browsers and clients about the kind of content being served, ensuring that files are rendered or handled appropriately. For example, when a browser receives a file with the MIME type **text/html**, it understands that the file should be displayed as an HTML document.

In Nginx, MIME types are typically configured in a file such as **mime.types**, which is then included in **nginx.conf**. This file maps common file extensions to their respective MIME types. For example:

```
types {
    text/html                    html htm shtml;
    text/css                     css;
    text/javascript              js;
    image/jpeg                   jpeg jpg;
    image/png                    png;
    application/json             json;
    application/javascript       js;
    ##Additional mappings...
}
```

***Figure 7.13**: mime.types*

- **`gzip_vary`**

Syntax	`gzip_vary on	off;`
Default	`gzip_vary off;`
Context	`http, server, location`

***Table 7.12**: gzip_vary*

This directive adds or removes the "**`Vary: Accept-Encoding`**" header to the response when Gzip compression is used.

This header is important for caching proxies and CDNs because it signals that the response varies based on the client's "**`Accept-Encoding`**" request header. When enabled, caches will store both compressed and uncompressed versions of a resource, ensuring to serve the correct version (compressed or uncompressed) to different clients.

- **`gzip_min_length`**

Syntax	`gzip_min_length length;`
Default	`gzip_min_length 20;` (20 is bytes here)
Context	`http, server, location`

***Table 7.13**: gzip_min_length*

This directive sets the minimum length in bytes of a response that will be compressed before it is considered for gzip compression. This setting helps avoid the overhead of compressing very small responses, which may not yield significant savings in size,

Putting all the compression directives together, following is the sample Nginx example configuration:

```
http {
    # Enable gzip compression
    gzip on;
```

```
    # Set the minimum length of a response that will be
compressed
    gzip_min_length 256;

    # Allocate 16 buffers of 8 KB each for compression
    gzip_buffers 16 8k;

    # Set the gzip compression level (1 = fastest, 9 = best
compression)
    gzip_comp_level 5;

    # Compress the following MIME types
    gzip_types text/plain text/css application/json application/
javascript text/xml application/xml application/xml+rss text/
javascript;

    # Disable gzip for certain user agents, here IE
    gzip_disable "MSIE [1-6]\.";

    # Set the HTTP version for compressed responses
    gzip_http_version 1.1;

    # Add the «Vary: Accept-Encoding» header
    gzip_vary on;

    # Enable gzip compression for proxied requests with specific
conditions
    gzip_proxied expired no-cache no-store private auth;

    # Default server configuration
    server {
        listen 80;
        server_name www.example.com;

        # Location for serving static files
        location / {
            root /var/www/html;
            index index.html;
        }

        # Location for handling API requests
        location /api {
            proxy_pass http://backend_server;
            proxy_set_header Host $host;
            proxy_set_header X-Real-IP $remote_addr;
            proxy_set_header X-Forwarded-For $proxy_add_x_
forwarded_for;
```

```
                proxy_set_header X-Forwarded-Proto $scheme;
            }
        }
    }
```

Brotli

Brotli compression is a modern algorithm that compresses web content even more efficiently than gzip. This can lead to faster page loads and lower bandwidth usage. Nginx can leverage Brotli through modules such as **ngx_brotli** (open-source) or via built-in support in NGINX Plus. This makes it an essential tool for improving web performance.

The **ngx_brotli** module enables Brotli compression in Nginx Plus and consists of the following two modules:

```
#for compressing responses on-the-fly
load_module modules/ngx_http_brotli_filter_module.so;
# for serving pre-compressed files
load_module modules/ngx_http_brotli_static_module.so;
```

***Figure 7.14**: ngx_brotli*

We define these two **brotli** modules in **nginx.conf** "**main**" context, using the **load_module** directives specified in the top-level (" **main**") context.

The following list explains Nginx Brotli directive along with an example for each:

Syntax	`brotli_static on|off|always`
Default	`brotli_static off;`
Context	`http, server, location`
Example	`brotli_static on;`

***Table 7.14**: brotli_static*

This directive enables serving pre-compressed **.br** files if they exist, bypassing on-the-fly compression.

Syntax	`brotli on|off`
Default	`brotli off;`
Context	`http, server, location`
Example	`brotli on;`

***Table 7.15**: brotli*

This directive activates Brotli compression for HTTP responses.

Syntax	brotli_types <mime_type> [..]
Default	brotli_types text/html;
Context	http, server, location
Example	brotli_types images/png;

Table 7.16: *brotli_types*

This directive specifies the MIME types that should be compressed using Brotli.

Syntax	brotli_buffers <number> <size>
Default	brotli_buffers 32 4k|16 8k;
Context	http, server, location
Example	brotli_buffers 64 4k;

Table 7.17: *brotli_buffers*

This directive sets the number and size of buffers used to store Brotli-compressed data before sending it to the client.

Syntax	brotli_comp_level <level>
Default	brotli_comp_level 6;
Context	http, server, location
Example	brotli_comp_level 2;

Table 7.18: *brotli_comp_level*

This directive determines the compression level (typically between 1 and 11), where 1 is the least amount of compression and 11 is the maximum amount of compression.

Syntax	rotli_min_length <length>
Default	rotli_min_length 20;
Context	http, server, location
Example	rotli_min_length 10;

Table 7.19: *brotli_min_length*

This directive sets the minimum length of a response that will be compressed. The length is determined only from the Content-Length response header field.

Putting all the **`brotli`** directives together, the sample Nginx configuration example is given as follows:

```
http {
    brotli on;
    brotli_comp_level 6;
    brotli_types text/html text/css application/javascript application/json;

    server {
        listen 80;
        server_name example.com;

        location / {
            root /var/www/html;
            index index.html;
        }
    }
}
```

Figure 7.15: *brotli*

Conclusion

While Nginx can serve static files on its own, it often acts as a reverse proxy for dynamic content. We have seen in this chapter how it stands as a robust and versatile web server, capable of efficiently delivering both static files and dynamic content. Whether serving simple HTML pages or acting as a reverse proxy that intelligently routes and balances traffic across backend servers, Nginx delivers exceptional performance, security, and scalability. Its flexible architecture empowers administrators to fine-tune every aspect of content delivery, making it an indispensable tool in modern web infrastructure. In the next chapter, we will examine how to further enhance the performance of Nginx by caching most accessed content.

CHAPTER 8
Caching in Nginx

Introduction

Let us go back to the pizza shop analogy from *Chapter 1, Introduction to Nginx.*

Imagine you own a pizza shop that gets hundreds of orders every day. Each time an order comes in, you make the pizza from scratch. That would take time and delay the customer when you have a very busy day with hundreds of orders lined up. Instead, you can decide to prepare a batch of popular pizzas in advance and keep them warm in an oven. When an order arrives, you pull out one of the ready-made pizzas, rather than starting the dough, sauce, and toppings all over again. This is essentially what caching does. It keeps frequently requested data "*ready to serve*" so that it can be delivered quickly without having to fetch all data from the application servers each time.

One of the key factors contributing to faster website performance is caching. Caching ensures that content is always readily available, reducing load times and providing a seamless user experience.

In this chapter, we will dive deeper into what types of content can be cached and how to enable caching effectively in Nginx. By the end, you will have a solid understanding of how caching plays a vital role in optimizing website speed and retaining audience in our websites.

Structure

In this chapter, the following topics will be covered:

- Understanding Caching
- Benefits of Caching
- Different Types of Cache
- Understanding CDN
- DNS Cache Server
- Caching with Nginx
- Nginx Processes Involved in Caching

- Configuring Caching in Nginx
- Purging Content from The Cache

Understanding Caching

Caching is the process of storing copies of frequently accessed data or files in a temporary storage location known as cache. By caching data, software applications, servers, and web browsers can store essential information, reducing the need for users to download or reprocess it every time they access a website or application. This significantly improves loading times and enhances the overall user experience.

A typical example of caching can be seen in web browsers, which store page content locally on a user's device for a set time period.

When a user first visits a website, the browser downloads the static content (that do not change frequently) from the web server and saves it to a local directory. On subsequent visits, instead of fetching the content from the server again, the browser retrieves it from the local cache. This dramatically speeds up page load times, saving the user valuable time, reducing network traffic, and lightening the load on the web server.

Benefits of Caching

Caching offers numerous benefits across various layers of technology, significantly enhancing performance, efficiency, and user experience. Here are the key benefits of caching:

- **Faster Load Times:** Caching allows frequently requested content to be stored in a cache, enabling quicker access and reducing the time it takes to load a website or application. This provides users with a smoother experience, particularly on content-heavy sites.
- **Reduced Server Load:** By serving cached data instead of regenerating the content for every request, caching reduces the strain on application servers. This frees up resources, allowing servers to handle other traffic and requests, thus improving scalability.
- **Bandwidth Savings:** Cached content minimizes the amount of data transferred between the server and client. This reduces bandwidth usage and saves costs, particularly for high-traffic websites.
- **Improved User Experience:** Faster response times translate to a more seamless and enjoyable user experience. Websites that load quickly tend to retain users longer, reduce bounce rates, and have higher engagement levels.
- **Increased Scalability:** Caching makes websites and applications more scalable

by alleviating pressure on back-end infrastructure. During periods of high traffic, caches help to maintain performance and prevent the system from being overwhelmed.

- **Lower Latency:** Caching data at points closer to the user, such as using Content Delivery Networks (CDNs), reduces latency. Users receive data from a geographically closer cache rather than from the origin server, which leads to faster load times, especially for global audiences.
- **Optimized Database Performance:** Caching frequently requested database queries reduces the number of times the database has to process the same request. This improves database efficiency and lowers the risk of performance bottlenecks, especially in read-heavy applications.
- **Cost Efficiency:** By reducing server load, bandwidth usage, and the need for repeated computations, caching helps save on infrastructure and operational costs. This is especially beneficial for businesses with large-scale applications that serve millions of requests.
- **Enhanced Application Performance:** Compute-intensive applications, such as those running recommendation engines or performing real-time analytics, benefit from caching as it speeds up data access. By leveraging in-memory caching, these applications can operate more efficiently without relying on slower disk-based storage.
- **Improved Availability:** In cases where the origin server is down or experiencing issues, cached content can still be served, maintaining the availability of the site or application to some extent. This adds a layer of resilience to the system.

Different Types of Cache

Caching can be applied across various layers of technology, including operating systems, networking layers such as Content Delivery Networks (CDN) and DNS, web applications, and databases. It plays a critical role in reducing latency and improving I/O Operations Per Second (IOPS) for many read-heavy workloads, such as Q&A platforms, gaming, media sharing, and social networks. Cached data can encompass database query results, computationally intensive calculations, API responses, and web assets including HTML, JavaScript, and image files.

The following image illustrates a complete website architecture, showcasing how caching can be applied at each layer between the:

- web browser,
- application server including the browser's own cache,
- intermediary caches,

- content delivery networks (CDNs),
- load balancer or reverse proxy, and

Caching at any of these levels, especially at the reverse proxy or load balancer, can significantly boost performance.

Layer	Client-Side	DNS	Web	App	Database
Use Case	Accelerate retrieval of web content from websites (browser or device)	Domain to IP Resolution	Accelerate retrieval of web content from web/app servers. Manage Web Sessions (server side)	Accelerate application performance and data access	Reduce latency associated with database query requests
Technologies	HTTP Cache Headers, Browsers	DNS Servers	HTTP Cache Headers, CDNs, Reverse Proxies, Web Accelerators, Key/Value Stores	Key/Value data stores, Local caches	Database buffers, Key/Value data stores
Solutions	Browser Specific	Amazon Route 53	Amazon CloudFront, ElastiCache for Redis, ElastiCache for Memcached, Partner Solutions	Application Frameworks, ElastiCache for Redis, ElastiCache for Memcached, Partner Solutions	ElastiCache for Redis, ElastiCache for Memcached

Figure 8.1: *Different Level of Caching in Network Architecture*

Understanding CDN

A Content Delivery Network (CDN) is a distributed network of servers strategically located across various geographic locations to deliver web content, such as images, videos, stylesheets, JavaScript files, and other resources. The primary goal of a CDN is to reduce latency and improve the response times by serving content from a server that is geographically closer to the user. This way the data reduces the distance that it needs to travel, minimizes the load on the origin server, and provides a better overall experience for end-users. For example, if you are sitting in India, the data center in Mumbai will be closer than the one in Texas.

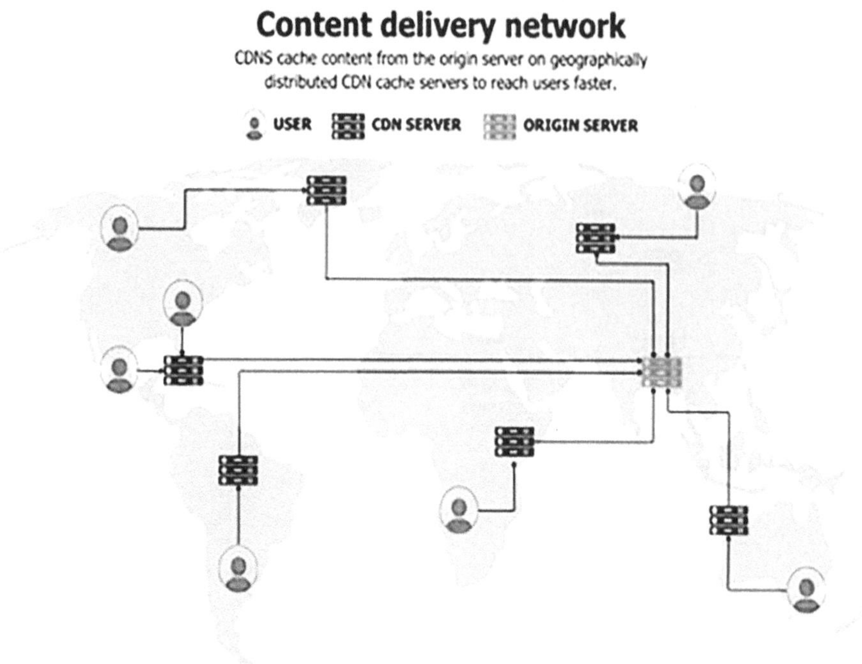

***Figure 8.2**: Content Delivery Network*

Akamai is one of the world's leading CDN providers, offering a comprehensive suite of content delivery and cloud services. Founded in 1998, Akamai has grown to manage a vast, globally distributed network of servers, making it one of the largest and most robust CDN platforms.

Netflix, a leading streaming platform, utilizes Akamai's CDN services to deliver its vast library of movies and TV shows to millions of users worldwide. By caching its content close to users and optimizing network paths, Akamai significantly reduces latency and enhances the user experience for Netflix viewers.

DNS Cache Server

A DNS cache server is a type of DNS server that temporarily stores (caches) the DNS query results for a domain name to improve the efficiency and speed of future DNS queries. When a DNS server resolves a domain name (for example, example.com) to an IP address (for example, 192.0.2.1), it caches this information so that if another query for the same domain is made, it can respond more quickly without needing to resolve the domain name again from the scratch.

Unbound is a popular open-source DNS cache server and recursive resolver that provides a fast and secure way to resolve DNS queries and cache results. It is widely used by ISPs, enterprises, and individuals to speed up DNS resolution and improve privacy.

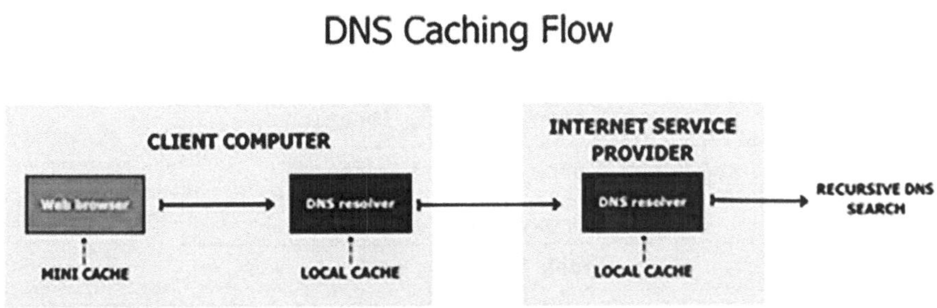

Figure 8.3: *DNS Cache Server*

Caching with Nginx

Nginx offers a comprehensive set of caching features.

A cache server sits between the client and the origin server. The origin server is the application servers. The cache server stores the copies of content it encounters. When client requests content already saved in the cache, the cache serves it directly, bypassing the origin server. This boosts performance, as the cache is closer to the client, and reduces the load on application servers by eliminating the need to regenerate pages for every request.

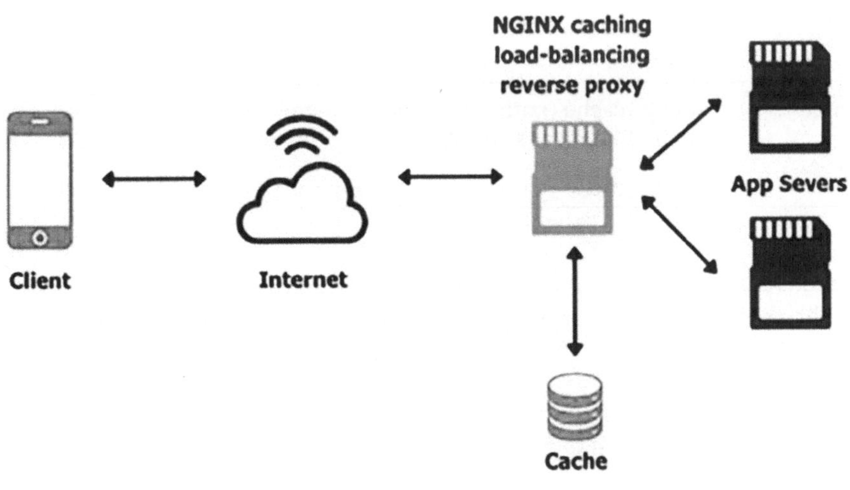

Figure 8.4: *Cache Server*

To enable caching in Nginx, let us first dive into few important Nginx directives:

- **`proxy_cache`**

<table>
<tr><td>Syntax</td><td>proxy_cache zone | off;</td></tr>
<tr><td>Default</td><td>proxy_cache off;</td></tr>
<tr><td>Context</td><td>http, server, location</td></tr>
<tr><td>Example</td><td>proxy_cache mycache;
proxy_cache off;</td></tr>
</table>

***Table 8.1**: proxy_cache*

This directive is used to enable or disable caching of responses from the proxied server. The zone parameter is used to specify the shared memory zone where the cached data is stored, so all worker processes can access it.

In the preceding example, **`proxy_cache mycache; 'mycache'`** is the shared memory zone where the cached data is stored.

- **`proxy_cache_path`**

<table>
<tr><td>Syntax</td><td>proxy_cache_path <path> [parameters];
where parameters can be [levels=levels] [use_temp_path=on|off] keys_zone=name:size [inactive=time] [max_size=size] [min_free=size] [manager_files=number] [manager_sleep=time] [manager_threshold=time] [loader_files=number] [loader_sleep=time] [loader_threshold=time] [purger=on|off] [purger_files=number] [purger_sleep=time] [purger_threshold=time];</td></tr>
<tr><td>Default</td><td>–</td></tr>
<tr><td>Context</td><td>http</td></tr>
<tr><td>Example</td><td>proxy_cache_path /data/nginx/cache levels=1:2 keys_zone=my_cache:10m max_size=10g inactive=60m use_temp_path=off;
proxy_cache_path /var/cache/nginx keys_zone=my_cache:10m;</td></tr>
</table>

***Table 8.2**: proxy_cache_path*

This directive defines the path on the file system where cached data will be stored along with cache settings, such as size, inactive time, and cache zone. Let us understand the different **`proxy_cache_path`** parameters that can be set.

- **`<path>`**

  Description: Specifies the file system directory where the cache will be stored in Nginx.

  Example: `proxy_cache_path /data/nginx/cache;`

This means the cached files will be stored in the **`/data/nginx/cache`** directory on the server.

- **`levels=<levels>`**

  Description: Defines how many subdirectory levels will be created in the cache directory. Nginx stores cached files using a hash, and the '**`levels`**' parameter breaks the hash into directories to avoid having too many files in a single directory which could slow down performance.

  Example: `levels=1:2;`

  This creates one directory from the first character of the hash and two subdirectories from the next two characters. For instance, if the hash is **`a1b2c3`**, the cached file could be stored in **`/a/1b/2c3`**.

- **`keys_zone=<name>:<size>`**

  Description: Defines the shared memory zone where cache keys are stored. The **`<name>`** identifies the cache zone, and **`<size>`** sets the memory allocated for storing cache metadata.

  Example: `keys_zone=my_cache:10m;`

  This creates a cache zone called **`my_cache`** with 10 MB of memory. The memory holds metadata about cached items, such as keys and their expiration times, but not the cached content itself.

- **`max_size=<size>`**

  Description: Specifies the maximum size of the cache. When the cache exceeds this size, Nginx will remove the least recently used (LRU) items to free up space.

  Example: `max_size=10g;`

  This sets a limit of 10 GB for the cache. When this size is reached, older cached content will be purged automatically.

- **`inactive=<time>`**

  Description: Defines the duration that if cached data is stored and not accessed, it will be removed from the cache.

  Example: **`inactive=60m;`**

  This means cached content that hasn't been accessed in 60 minutes will be removed. It helps prevent the cache from storing stale data that is no longer needed.

- **`use_temp_path=on|off`**

  Description: Controls whether Nginx uses a temporary path when writing files to the cache. By default, cached files are first written to a temporary directory and then moved to the cache directory. This parameter allows to bypass writing to temporary directory to reduce disk I/O.

  Example: `use_temp_path=off;`

  When off, cached files are written directly to the cache directory without using a temporary location. This is often more efficient for systems with high disk I/O requirements.

- **`loader_threshold=<time>`**

  Description: Defines the percentage of the cache loader process that is allowed to run at a time. It controls how many items are loaded from disk into the cache index at server startup.

  Example: `loader_threshold=300ms;`

  This means the cache loader will be allowed to run for a maximum of 300 milliseconds before pausing and allowing other processes to run.

- **`loader_files=<number>`**

  Description: Specifies the number of files that Nginx will process (load from disk) during each run of the cache loader. This is used to limit the impact of cache loading on server startup.

  Example: `loader_files=200;`

  This tells Nginx to load 200 cache files during each cycle of the cache loader process.

- **`loader_sleep=<time>`**

  Description: Defines the amount of time Nginx waits between cache loading cycles. It is useful for systems that need to manage cache loading without overwhelming server resources.

  Example: `loader_sleep=50ms;`

  Nginx will pause for 50 milliseconds between loading cycles.

- **`purger=<boolean>`**

  Description: Enables or disables automatic purging of expired cache files. When set to on, Nginx will automatically remove expired files without manual intervention.

  Example: `purger=on;`

This ensures that Nginx automatically purges old cached files as they expire.

- **proxy_cache_key**

Syntax	`proxy_cache_key string;`
Default	`proxy_cache_key $scheme$proxy_host$request_uri;`
Context	`http, server, location`
Example	`proxy_cache_key "$host$request_uri$cookie_user";`

Table 8.3: *proxy_cache_key*

This directive defines the key used to identify a cached response. The key can include variables such as the request URI, headers, or cookies.

- **proxy_cache_valid**

Syntax	`proxy_cache_valid [statuscode] time;`
Default	–
Context	`http, server, location`

Example	`proxy_cache_valid 200 302 10m;`
	`proxy_cache_valid 404 1m;`
	`proxy_cache_valid 5m;`
	`proxy_cache_valid any 1m;`

Table 8.4: *proxy_cache_valid*

It sets the duration for which responses with specific HTTP status codes are considered valid in the cache.

In the preceding example, **proxy_cache_valid 200 302 10m;** responses with status code 200 and 302 are cached for 10 minutes.

In the preceding example, **proxy_cache_valid 5m;** where only caching time is specified without any status code then by default 200, 301, and 302 responses with status code are cached.

In the preceding example, **proxy_cache_valid any 1m;** any parameter specifies all the status response codes will be cached.

- **proxy_cache_use_stale**

Syntax	`proxy_cache_use_stale error | timeout | invalid_header | updating | http_500 | http_502 | http_503 | http_504 | http_403 | http_404 | http_429 | off ...;`
Default	`proxy_cache_use_stale off;`

Context	`http, server, location`
Example	`proxy_cache_use_stale error timeout updating http_500 http_502 http_503 http_504;`

***Table 8.5:** proxy_cache_use_stale*

This directive specifies conditions under which Nginx should serve stale cached content, such as when the backend server is unavailable or slow. The parameters match the parameters of the **proxy_next_upstream** directive.

The `**error**` parameter allows the use of a stale cached response if the proxied server cannot be selected to process the request.

The `**updating**` parameter enables the use of a stale cached response while it is being refreshed. This helps reduce the number of requests made to proxied servers during the cache update process.

- **proxy_cache_bypass**

Syntax	`proxy_cache_bypass string ...;`
Default	–
Context	`http, server, location`
Example	`proxy_cache_bypass $http_cookie    $http_authorization;`

***Table 8.6:** proxy_cache_bypass*

This directive determines conditions under which Nginx will bypass the cache and send the request to the origin server. For example, we can bypass the cache for requests with **$http_cookie**.

This directive can be used with **proxy_no_cache**.

Syntax	`proxy_no_cache string ...;`
Default	–
Context	`http, server, location`
Example	`proxy_no_cache $http_pragma  $http_authorization;`

***Table 8.7:** proxy_no_cache*

This directive specifies the conditions when responses should not be cached, based on conditions such as specific headers or cookies. For example, requests will be checked for **$http_pragma** and will not be cached.

- **`proxy_cache_lock`**

Syntax	`proxy_cache_lock on | off;`
Default	`proxy_cache_lock off;`
Context	`http, server, location`
Example	`proxy_cache_lock on;`

Table 8.8: *proxy_cache_lock*

This directive in Nginx prevents a "**`thundering herd`**" problem when multiple requests for the same uncached resource hit your server simultaneously. With this directive enabled, if one request triggers a cache fill, other concurrent requests for the same resource wait until the cache is populated instead of all being sent to the backend. This helps reduce unnecessary load on the upstream server and improves overall performance.

- **`proxy_cache_lock_timeout`**

Syntax	`proxy_cache_lock_timeout time;`
Default	`proxy_cache_lock_timeout 5s;`
Context	`http, server, location`
Example	`proxy_cache_lock_timeout 5s;`

Table 8.9: *proxy_cache_lock_timeout*

This directive sets a timeout for **`proxy_cache_lock`**. When the time expires, the request will be passed to the proxied server.

`proxy_cache_lock_timeout 5s;` sets the maximum time that requests will wait for the cache to be filled before proceeding.

- **`proxy_cache_min_uses`**

Syntax	`proxy_cache_min_uses number;`
Default	`proxy_cache_min_uses 1;`
Context	`http, server, location`
Example	`proxy_cache_min_uses 100;`

Table 8.10: *proxy_cache_min_uses*

This directive sets the minimum number of times a request must be made before it is cached, which helps prevent caching rarely accessed content.

`proxy_cache_min_uses 100;` indicated the cached content should be at least hit 100 times before selecting it for caching.

- **`proxy_cache_revalidate`**

Syntax	`proxy_cache_revalidate on | off;`
Default	`proxy_cache_revalidate off;`
Context	`http, server, location`

Table 8.11: *proxy_cache_revalidate*

This directive forces Nginx to revalidate cached content with the origin server before serving it to ensure freshness.

- **`proxy_cache_methods`**

Syntax	`proxy_cache_methods GET | HEAD | POST ...;`
Default	`proxy_cache_methods GET HEAD;`
Context	`http, server, location`

Table 8.12: *proxy_cache_methods*

This directive specifies which requests with HTTP methods (for example, **`GET`**, **`POST`**) are eligible for caching when using the **`proxy_cache`** directive.

Note: *By default, NGINX only caches responses for GET and HEAD requests because these methods are generally safe and idempotent, meaning they do not alter the state of the server. However, there may be cases where we want to cache responses for other methods, such as POST. In that case, we will have to specify those with **`proxy_cache_methods`** directives.*

Nginx Processes Involved in Caching

Nginx's caching process involves two additional critical processes:

- cache manager
- cache loader

These processes help manage the cache effectively without overloading the system or exceeding resource limits.

- **Cache Manager:** The cache manager process runs periodically and ensures that the cache does not exceed the size limit set by the `**max_size**` parameter in the `**proxy_cache_path**` directive. If the cache grows beyond this limit, the cache manager deletes the least recently accessed data to free up space. However, the cache size can temporarily exceed the limit between cache manager activations, so this process ensures that the system eventually adheres to the specified size.

- **Cache Loader**: The cache loader process is responsible for loading metadata about cached content into the shared memory zone when Nginx starts or reloads. However, loading the entire cache at once can consume too many resources, slowing down Nginx performance in the initial minutes after startup. To prevent this, Nginx allows for iterative cache loading, using the **`loader_threshold`**, **`loader_files`**, and **`loader_sleeps`** parameters explained in the `**proxy_cache_path**` directive above.

  In the following example, each iteration lasts 300 milliseconds or loads up to 200 items, whichever occurs first. This ensures that cached data is gradually reloaded, avoiding any performance bottleneck.

  ```
  proxy_cache_path /data/nginx/cache keys_zone=mycache:10m load-
  er_threshold=300 loader_files=200 loader_sleeps=50?
  ```

Configuring Caching in Nginx

Let us begin with Nginx server setup to proxy all incoming requests directly to the backend server with no caching involved. The basic Nginx configuration would be as follows:

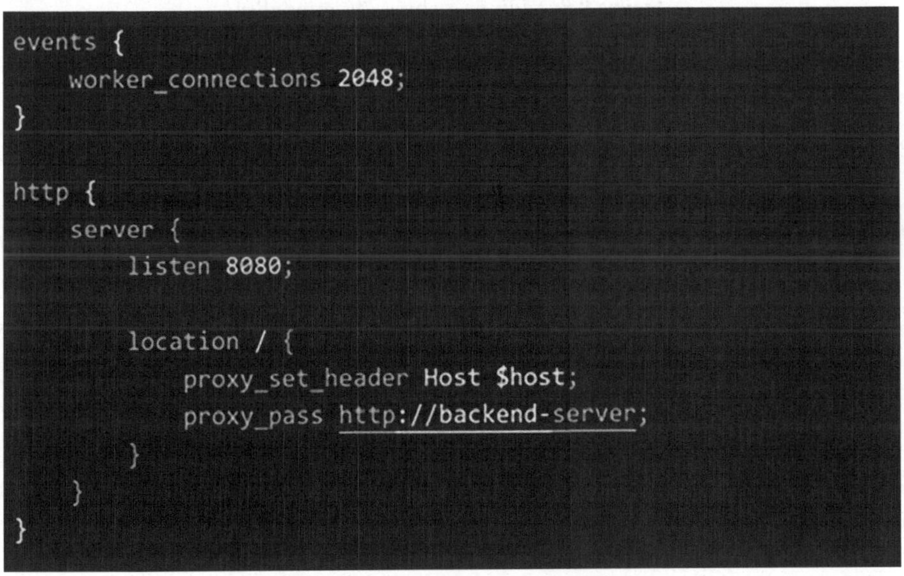

Figure 8.5: *Caching configuration*

Now, let us enhance the previous configuration by **adding caching functionality**. This will allow Nginx to store responses from the backend service, reducing the load on the server and improving response times for repeated requests.

```
events {
    worker_connections 2048;
}

http {
    proxy_cache_path /var/cache/nginx keys_zone=my_cachezone:10m;

    server {
        listen 8080;
        proxy_cache my_cachezone;

        location / {
            proxy_set_header Host $host;
            proxy_pass http://backend-server;
            proxy_cache_key $scheme://$host$uri$is_args$args;
            proxy_cache_valid 200 10m;
        }
    }
}
```

***Figure 8.6**: Adding Caching Functionality*

1. The `**proxy_cache_path**` directive specifies the directory **/var/cache/nginx** where cached responses will be stored.
2. The `**proxy_cache**` directive defines the shared memory zone '**my_cachezone**' used to store cache keys and related metadata.
3. The `**proxy_cache_key**` **$scheme://$hosturiis_args$args;** sets the key used to identify cached content.
4. The `**proxy_cache_valid**` **200 10m;** controls the cache expiration time. Once the cache expires, responses are considered "**stale**" and are no longer treated as fresh content.

In some cases, we might need to **temporarily bypass the cache** for a particular nature of request and directly hit the backend servers. We can use the **proxy_cache_bypass**, as shown in the following example.

```
http {
    proxy_cache_path /var/cache/nginx keys_zone=my_cachezone:10m;

    server {
        listen 8080;
        proxy_cache my_cachezone;

        location / {
            proxy_set_header Host $host;
            proxy_pass http://backend-server;
            proxy_cache_key $scheme://$host$uri$is_args$args;
            proxy_cache_valid 200 10m;
            proxy_cache_bypass $cookie_bypasscache;
        }
    }
}
```

Figure 8.7: *proxy_cache_bypass*

In this example, we introduced the **proxy_cache_bypass** directive, using the **$cookie_bypasscache** cookie variable. If a request includes the cookie '**bypasscache**', the cache read will be bypassed, forcing Nginx to fetch fresh data from the backend.

Let us now learn how we can **serve cached data when the backend is down or responding slowly.**

Nginx provides mechanisms to deliver stale content. This can be achieved using the **proxy_cache_use_stale** directive, which allows Nginx to serve cached (stale) data under certain conditions, such as when the backend is down or timing out.

```
events {
    worker_connections 2048;
}

http {
    proxy_cache_path /var/cache/nginx keys_zone=my_cachezone:10m;
    proxy_cache_path /var/cache/nginx keys_zone=my_cachezone:10m inactive=1w;

    server {
        listen 8080;
        proxy_cache my_cachezone;

        location / {
            proxy_set_header Host $host;
            proxy_pass http://backend-server;
            proxy_cache_key $scheme://$host$uri$is_args$args;
            proxy_cache_valid 200 10m;
            proxy_cache_bypass $cookie_bypasscache;
            proxy_cache_use_stale error timeout http_500 http_502 http_503 http_504 http_429;
        }
    }
}
```

Figure 8.8: *proxy_cache_use_stale*

In the preceding example, we added the `**proxy_cache_path**` directive to include the `**inactive**` parameter and configured the `**proxy_cache_use_stale**` directive with the following parameters:

1. '**error**' which will serve stale content when the backend server is unreachable.
2. '**timeout**' which will serve stale content if the backend server takes too long to respond.
3. '**http_5xx and http_429**' which will serve stale content when the backend returns specific HTTP status codes.

This is how we can setup caching in Nginx and take advantage of its benefits to improve the performance and reliability of our web applications. Let us move to the next section to learn about removing expired, outdated, or unwanted cache data.

Purging Content from The Cache

While managing a web server with Nginx and caching enabled, purging content from the cache becomes an essential task. This process allows us to remove outdated, unwanted, or sensitive content that may have been stored in the cache.

Why Purge the Cache?

Purging the cache is necessary when:

- **Content Updates**: New content or updates need to be reflected immediately on the website.
- **Data Sensitivity:** Sensitive or personal information may have been cached unintentionally.
- **Troubleshooting**: Solving issues related to outdated content being served.

Enabling Purging of Cache in Nginx

To enable purging in Nginx, **proxy_cache_purge** directive is used.

- **proxy_cache_purge**

Syntax	proxy_cache_purge string ...;
Default	–
Context	http, server, location

Table 8.13: *proxy_cache_purge*

This directive defines conditions under which the request will be considered a cache purge request. The result of successful operation is indicated by returning the 204 (No Content) response.

Sample Nginx Configuration

```
proxy_cache_path /data/nginx/cache keys_zone=cache_zone:10m;

map $request_method $purge_method {
    PURGE   1;
    default 0;
}

server {
    ...
    location / {
        proxy_pass http://backend_server;
        proxy_cache cache_zone;
        proxy_cache_key $uri;
        proxy_cache_purge $purge_method;
    }
}
```

***Figure 8.9**: Nginx Configuration*

In the preceding example, we have enabled the purging of cache with **proxy_cache_purge $puirge_method**. We can now send a '**PURGE**' request to remove specific content from the cache. Following is a sample curl command that sends a PURGE request to Nginx. If the URL matches cached content, it will be removed.

```
curl -X PURGE http://yourdomain.com/purge/some/path/to/content
```

Restricting Access to the Purge Command

Purging content from the Nginx cache is a critical task for web administrators and developers. It is recommended that we limit the number of IP addresses that are allowed to send a cache-purge request.

```
proxy_cache_path /data/nginx/cache keys_zone=cache_zone:10m;
```

```
server {
    ...
    location / {
        proxy_pass http://backend_server;
        proxy_cache cache_zone;
        proxy_cache_key $uri;
        proxy_cache_purge $purge_method;
    }
}

geo $purge_allowed {
   default          0;  # deny from other
   10.0.0.1         1;  # allow from 10.0.0.1 address
   192.168.0.0/24   1;  # allow from 192.168.0.0/24
}

map $request_method $purge_method {
   PURGE    $purge_allowed;
   default 0;
}
```

***Figure 8.10**: Purge Command*

In the preceding example, Nginx first checks if the request is a **PURGE**. If yes, it jumps to the geo directive, which checks the client IP address from where the **PURGE** request was initiated. If the IP address is whitelisted, the **$purge_allowed** is set to value 1. This value is further mapped to **$purge_method**, permitting purging. If the value evaluated to 0, purging is denied.

Conclusion

Nginx caching is a must-have tool for any web server setup looking to balance performance and resource usage. When implemented correctly, it results in faster content delivery, reduced bandwidth usage, and a more responsive user experience—all key factors for the success of modern web applications.

In the next chapter, we will learn how to setup advanced Nginx monitoring for Nginx servers and how to understand and analyze the server errors and performance.

Chapter 9
Advanced Activity Monitoring

Introduction

One of the key differences between the open-source Nginx and the commercial Nginx Plus is the Activity Monitoring Dashboard capability. While open-source Nginx requires external tools and plugins for detailed monitoring, Nginx Plus offers built-in, interactive, and real-time dashboard that provides powerful insights into system performance and application traffic which is the '*Nginx Plus dashboard*'.

This dashboard is designed to give administrators a comprehensive view of critical metrics, such as active connections, requests per second, bandwidth usage, and server health. With NGINX Plus, the monitoring is not just limited to the basic data; it also includes advanced metrics on upstream servers, SSL/TLS status, session persistence, caching efficiency, and security details, all in a single interface.

This real-time visibility into traffic, load balancing, and system health enables proactive issue detection, security monitoring, and capacity planning, making NGINX Plus an essential choice for enterprises that require comprehensive operational insights to maintain application performance and availability. The Activity Monitoring Dashboard is a key differentiator that enhances NGINX Plus's value for production environments, making it more robust than the open-source version.

Structure

In this chapter, the following topics will be covered:

- Nginx Plus Demo Dashboard
- Enable Nginx Dashboard
- Limit Access to Nginx Plus Dashboard
- Defining `status_zone` in Nginx Plus
- `status_zone` versus zone

Nginx Plus Demo Dashboard

To get a live preview of the Nginx Plus Dashboard, you can visit the official **Nginx Plus Demo** page at https://demo.nginx.com/.

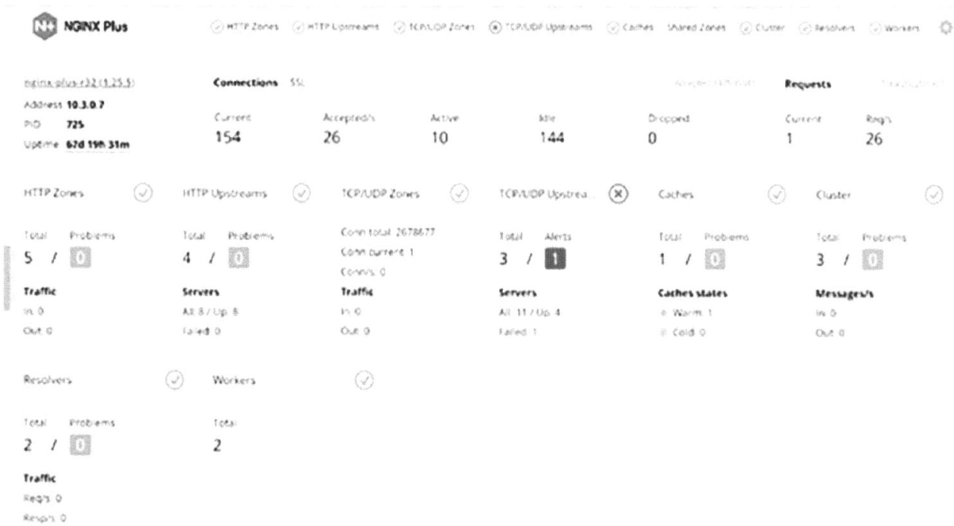

***Figure 9.1**: Nginx Plus Demo Dashboard*

This demo provides a real-time visualization of Nginx Plus's advanced monitoring features, illustrating how it tracks vital performance metrics for managing application traffic. When we visit the demo dashboard, we will encounter an interactive display of metrics that reflect the full range of Nginx Plus's capabilities, including:

- **Active Connections**: A live view of the number of client connections currently handled by the server.
- **Requests per Second (RPS)**: Real-time data on the number of HTTP requests processed, helping to visualize traffic trends.
- **Upstream Server Health**: A detailed breakdown of how Nginx Plus is distributing traffic across backend servers, along with health check indicators for each backend server.
- **SSL/TLS Handshakes and Certificates**: Insights into secure traffic, showing how SSL connections are being managed, including details about certificate status.
- **TCP/UDP Zones**: Visualizes metrics for TCP/UDP traffic handling, showcasing Nginx Plus's ability to load balance not just HTTP but also non-HTTP protocols for real-time applications and databases.
- **Cluster**: Metrics showing how NGINX Plus is operating in a **clustered**

environment, with load balancing and synchronization across multiple nodes to ensure high availability and fault tolerance.

Let us learn about how we can enable the dashboard for your Nginx.

Enabling Nginx Dashboard

To enable the NGINX Plus Dashboard, perform the following steps to configure it on your NGINX Plus server.

Prerequisites: Ensure Nginx plus is installed.

Step 1. Enable the Nginx Plus API

The Nginx Plus Dashboard relies on the Nginx Plus API to fetch real-time data. We need to enable the API in our Nginx configuration file, as learned in *Chapter* 5, *Setup Nginx* API.

Step 2. Open the NGINX Configuration File (**`nginx.conf`**) located at:`**/etc/nginx/nginx.conf**`

```
sudo vim /etc/nginx/nginx.conf
```

Step 3. Configure the API and Dashboard

In **`nginx.conf`** file, add a `**server**` block in the `**http**` context that defines the API and dashboard location with a unique port, for example, **`8080`**.

```
http {
  server {
    listen 8080;
     # API location block will be defined here
  }
}
```

Figure 9.2: *Configure API and Dashboard*

Step 4. Add the API location block

The **`/api`** exposes the Nginx Plus API, which provides the data for the dashboard.

```
http {
    # ...
    server {
        listen 8080;
        # ...
        location /api {
            api;
            # ...
        }
    }
}
```

Figure 9.3: *API Location Block*

Step 5. Add the dashboard location block (`/dashboard.html`)

This serves the actual HTML page for the dashboard from the default NGINX HTML directory which comes by default with the Nginx Plus package. The dashboard html file is located in the root directory (for example, **`/usr/share/nginx/html`**) specified by the root directive.

```
http {
    # ...
    server {
        listen 8080;
        # ...
        location /api {
            api;
            # ...
        }

        location = /dashboard.html {
            root   /usr/share/nginx/html;
        }
    }
}
```

Figure 9.4: *Dashboard Location Block*

Step 6. Save and Close the Configuration File and reload Nginx configuration using **`nginx -s reload`** command

You can now access your dashboard in your browser with http://[NginxBoxName]:8080/dashboard.html URL.

Limit Access to Nginx Plus Dashboard

To make the dashboard more secure, we can enable read-write mode for the NGINX Plus API and ensure secure access following these detailed steps.

Step 1. Enable Read-Write Mode for the API

The default NGINX Plus API operates in read-only mode. To enable modifications such as resetting statistics or managing upstream servers, you need to enable write access. Add the **`write=on`** along with **`api`** directive to enable the changes on Nginx Plus Dashboard.

```
http {
    server {
        listen 8080;

        # API with write access enabled
        location /api {
            api write=on;  # Enable read-write mode for the API

            # Restrict access to specific IP addresses
            allow 127.0.0.1;  # Example: allow local access only
            deny all;
        }
    }
}
```

Figure 9.5: *Enable Read-Write Mode*

Step 2. Restrict Access to the API

For security reasons, limit access to the API location to only trusted networks. This can be done using `**allow**` and `**deny**` directives inside the **`/api`** location block, as shown in the following figure, allowing only specific IP ranges.

```
http {
    server {
        listen 8080;

        # API with write access enabled
        location /api {
            api write=on;  # Enable read-write mode for the API

            # Restrict access to specific IP addresses
            allow 192.168.1.0/24;  # Example: allow local access only
            deny all;
        }
    }
}
```

Figure 9.6: *Restrict access to API*

Step 3. Secure API Methods with Basic Authentication

It is recommended to protect sensitive HTTP methods, such as **PATCH**, **POST**, and **DELETE** by requiring authentication. We can set up HTTP Basic Authentication as follows:

[We have learned this in detail in the section 'Setting Authentication on Nginx API']

a. Create a Password File

Use **htpasswd** command to create a password file:

```
sudo htpasswd -c /etc/nginx/.htpasswd admin
```

b. Configure Authentication in NGINX

Add authentication to the API location in the configuration inside the **/api** location block with username and password using **auth_basic** and **auth_basic_user_file** directives:

- **auth_basic**

Syntax	`auth_basic string | off;`
Default	`auth_basic off;`
Context	`http, server, location, limit_except`

***Table 9.1**: auth_basic*

The **auth_basic** directive in Nginx is used to enable **HTTP Basic Authentication** which is a simple authentication method that requires users to enter a username and password to access a specific resource or location on a web server.

- **auth_basic_user_file**

Syntax	`auth_basic_user_file file;`
Default	–
Context	`http, server, location, limit_except`

***Table 9.2**: auth_basic_user_file*

This directive specifies a file that keeps usernames and passwords, in the following format:

```
# comment
name1:password1
name2:password2:comment
name3:password3
```

Example Nginx Configuration with authentication enabled in location block.

```
location /api {
    api write=on;
    auth_basic "Nginx Plus API";
    auth_basic_user_file /etc/nginx/.htpasswd;
}
```

Figure 9.7: *Nginx Configuration with Authentication*

Now you are set to enable Nginx Plus Dashboard. For advanced monitoring of upstreams, health checks and server zones, we need to enable **`status_zone`** in Nginx. Let us learn why and how in the next section.

Defining `status_zone` in Nginx Plus

The "**`status_zone`**" directive creates a shared memory zone for collecting and aggregating status or performance data from different worker processes. This shared memory zone allows various parts of Nginx to store and retrieve metrics in real time, which is essential for monitoring and load balancing.

To enable NGINX Plus dashboard, the **`status_zone`** directive is needed.

Key Functions of `status_zone` in NGINX Plus are:

Step 1. Tracking Metrics

The **`status_zone`** directive collects detailed statistics about traffic and performance for a specific server group or upstream group, including:

- Active and idle connections
- Requests per second
- Traffic (sent and received bytes)
- Response statuses (e.g., 2xx, 3xx, 4xx, and 5xx response codes)

These metrics are aggregated and displayed on the Nginx Plus dashboard and are available via the Nginx Plus API for further analysis or integration with monitoring tools.

Nginx Configuration Example to enable `status_zone`

To enable the collection of statistics using **`status_zone`**, we can define it in the server or upstream block as follows:

```
server {
    listen 80;
    server_name example.com;

    # Define a status zone to collect metrics for this server
    status_zone my_server_zone;

    location / {
        proxy_pass http://backend;
    }
}
```

Figure 9.8: *status_zone*

In this preceding example,

- **`status_zone my_server_zone;`** creates a **shared memory zone** called **`my_server_zone`** where the statistics for the server are stored and the Nginx Plus API collects the information from here.

Step 2. Real-Time Monitoring on the Nginx Plus Dashboard

The Nginx Plus dashboard provides a graphical interface that visualizes the data collected via **`status_zone`**. It displays live metrics such as:

- **Server load**: Active and idle connections
- **Throughput**: Traffic sent and received
- **Response statistics**: Breakdown of response statuses (e.g., 200, 404, and more)
- **Requests per second**: Rate of incoming requests
- **Health checks** of each upstream server
- **Bytes** sent and received.

This allows administrators to monitor the health and performance of their Nginx servers in real time, helping identify performance bottlenecks or troubleshooting issues quickly.

For example, if one of the upstream health checks starts failing, it will turn the upstream in the dashboard as red colour to signal the server as unhealthy and alert the admins to mark it down.

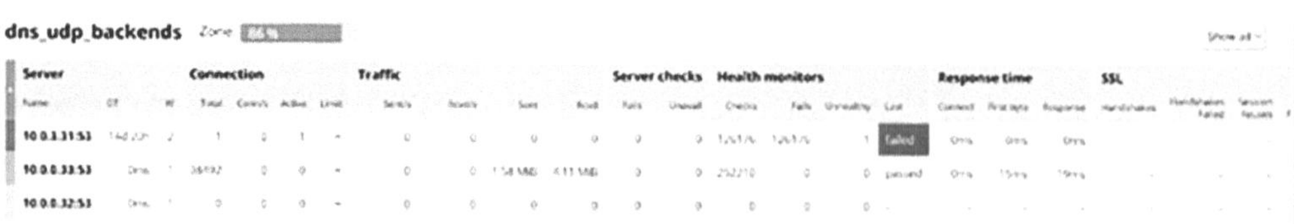

Figure 9.9: *Unhealthy Nginx Upstream*

Step 3. Integration with the Nginx Plus API

The **status_zone** metrics are also available via the Nginx Plus REST API, allowing us to integrate them with external monitoring systems such as Prometheus, Grafana, or other custom dashboards. This API provides JSON-formatted data, which can be queried programmatically for automation or detailed analysis.

status_zone Versus zone

In Nginx, both **status_zone** and **zone** are configuration directives used to define shared memory regions, but they serve different purposes and are used in distinct contexts. Here is a breakdown of their key differences:

Step 1. zone Directive

The zone directive is used to define a shared memory region where various states or data (such as, session persistence or cache metadata) are stored. This allows Nginx worker processes to share and synchronize information efficiently. It is commonly used in upstream configurations, caching, rate limiting, and load balancing scenarios.

Example of zone in an upstream block:

```
upstream backend {
    zone backend_zone 64k;
    server backend1.example.com;
    server backend2.example.com;
}
```

***Figure 9.10:** zone in an Upstream Block*

Key uses of zone:

- **Load balancing**: Stores load-balancing states for upstream servers, enabling features such as session persistence and consistent hashing.
- **Rate limiting**: Tracks client request data across worker processes to enforce consistent rate limiting.
- **Caching**: Stores cache keys and metadata, allowing multiple workers to share cached content.

Step 2. status_zone Directive

The **status_zone** directive is specific to **Nginx Plus** and is used to gather and report status metrics about a particular context. It defines a zone to store statistics that can be accessed via the Nginx Plus API or displayed in the Nginx Plus dashboard.

Example of `status_zone` in a server block:

```
server {
    listen 80;
    server_name example.com;
    status_zone my_server_status;

    location / {
        proxy_pass http://backend;
    }
}
```

***Figure 9.11**: status_zone in a Server Block*

Key uses of `status_zone`:

- **Monitoring and Metrics**: Tracks and reports server-level metrics, such as requests, connections, and traffic.
- **API Integration**: Makes this data available via the **Nginx Plus API** for real-time monitoring or external tools.
- **Dashboard Integration**: The **`status_zone`** data is visualized in the **Nginx Plus dashboard**, allowing users to see live stats about their Nginx server performance.

Conclusion

The dashboard is particularly useful for tracking performance trends, identifying bottlenecks, and ensuring the reliability of applications in real time. Its ability to integrate with external tools, such as Prometheus further enhances its utility, making it a must-have for anyone managing complex web environments with NGINX Plus. This visibility helps administrators proactively manage traffic, optimize performance, and troubleshoot issues more efficiently. In the next chapter, we will explore how to diagnose common Nginx issues through its extensive logging capabilities.

CHAPTER 10
Debugging and Troubleshooting Nginx

Introduction

Logs are an excellent way to track what's happening in your applications. They don't just help us understand normal activity–they are also extremely useful when we need to troubleshoot problems. Like any other application, Nginx keeps a record of important events, such as site visitors, client transaction, and any issues encountered on the website or Nginx servers which it writes in details to log files. By reviewing these logs, we can spot unusual patterns early and take proactive action before they turn into bigger problems.

Modern web applications demand reliability, performance, and clear visibility into their operational state. When things go wrong–be it a sudden spike in response time, intermittent 5xx errors, or unexpected user behavior–it is critical to understand what is happening inside the server. This is where logging, as well as a well-structured approach to debugging and troubleshooting becomes indispensable.

In this chapter, we will explore how to diagnose common Nginx issues through its extensive logging capabilities. We will begin with the fundamentals of logging–what it is, why it matters, and what makes logs so critical for troubleshooting. We will then delve into the specifics of Nginx's two primary log types: **Access Logs** and **Error Logs**. Finally, we will discuss strategies for correlating these logs to gain deeper insights into complex issues that might not be evident from examining a single log source in isolation.

Structure

In this chapter, we will cover the following topics:

- Nginx Logs
    - Access Logs
    - Error Logs
- Correlating Error and Access Logs

Nginx Logs

By default, NGINX records its activity in two main log files: **`error.log`** and the **`access.log`**. We can find these logs in **`/var/log/nginx`**, as long as they have been enabled in the main Nginx configuration file. In the following sections, we will take a closer look at both the access and error logs and show you how to enable them if you have not done so already.

Access Logs

Access logs track every request that Nginx processes. Each log entry generally includes the client's IP address, the requested URL, the HTTP method used, the response status code, the size of the response, and various timing and header details. Access logs form the baseline data set that answers questions like: Who is visiting my site? Which resources are most requested? How often do 4xx or 5xx errors occur?

Configuring Access Logs

Key directives to define logging for an application are:

- **`log_format`**

Syntax	`log_format name [escape=default|json|none] string ...;`
Default	`log_format combined "...";`
Context	`http`

Example	`log_format compression '$remote_addr - $remote_user [$time_local] '`
	`'"$request" $status $bytes_sent '`
	`'"$http_referer" "$http_user_agent" "$gzip_ratio"';`

Table 10.1: *log_format*

This directive defines the structure of the log entries for access.log file. We can create one or more named log formats and then refer them in **access_log** directives. By customizing the format, we decide which data points are included in each log entry and how they are arranged.

Why Customize log_format?

- **Flexibility:** If you need additional data such as request processing time, HTTP headers, or a custom variables and data, you can add corresponding variables in the log format.
- **Integration with Monitoring Tools:** Custom formats make it easier to parse logs with external tools or log management systems such as Splunk and Prometheus.
- **Focus on Relevant Data:** You can strip out unneeded details to keep logs simpler and more storage-friendly.

Syntax	`access_log path [format [buffer=size] [gzip[=level]] [flush=time] [if=condition]];` `access_log off;`
Default	`access_log logs/access.log combined;`
Context	`http, server, location, if in location, limit_except`

Table 10.2: *access_log*

The **access_log** directive tells Nginx which file to write its access logs and which predefined format of **log_format** it should use. Access logs record details about every request processed by the server, such as the client's IP address, the requested URL, response status codes, and user agent information. These details helps us understand who is accessing our application, what resources they are requesting, and how our server is responding.

By default, Nginx will append new entries to this file for each request it serves.

- The first argument '**path**' is mandatory.
- The second argument **format**, **buffer**, **gzip**, **flush**, and **if** is optional.

If we don't specify any format then logs will be written in default combined format.

In general, the **access_log** directive can be placed in the http block, server block, or even in location blocks within your Nginx configuration file. Placing it in http applies it globally, while configuring it in server or location allows for more targeted logging.

Note: *It is always better to segregate the access logs of all the virtual hosts by recording them in a separate file. To do that, we need to override the* ***access_log*** *directive that is defined in the http section with another* ***access_log*** *directive in the server context.*

Optional access log parameters

When configuring the **`access_log`** directive in NGINX, you have a few optional parameters that can adjust how logs are written. Among these are **`[gzip[=level]]`**, **`[flush=time]`**, and **`[if=condition]`**. They serve the following purposes:

- **`gzip[=level]`:** This option compresses the access logs using gzip, helping reduce disk space usage.
    - **Syntax: `gzip`** or **`gzip=level`** where level is a number from 1 (fastest, least compression) to 9 (slowest, most compression). If we just write gzip without a level, it defaults to a compression level of 1.
    - **Example:** `access_log /var/log/nginx/access.log main gzip=5;`

  Here, logs are compressed at a medium compression level of 5.

- **`flush=time`:** This setting controls how frequently buffered log data is written (flushed) to the disk. Without this directive, logs may be flushed at default intervals or when the buffer is full. Setting a flush interval ensures logs are written out regularly, even if the buffer is not filled yet.
    - **Syntax: `flush=time`** where time can be specified in units such as s (seconds), m (minutes), and so on.
    - **Example:** `access_log /var/log/nginx/access.log main flush=5m;`

  This instructs Nginx to flush the compressed log buffer every 5 minutes.

- **`if=condition`:** The **`if`** parameter lets us conditionally log requests based on a boolean-style check of a variable or expression. If the condition evaluates to a non-empty string that is not "**`0`**", the request is logged; otherwise, it is skipped.
    - **Syntax: `if=condition`** where condition can be any variable or expression supported by Nginx that evaluates to a truth or false value.
    - **Example:** You only want to log requests for Nginx API for any status code except 2xx and 3xx.

```
#Nginx Dashboard
server {
    listen 8080;
    access_log off;

    location = / {
        return 301 /dashboard.html;
    }
    location /api {
        access_log /var/log/nginx/apiaccess.log  api if=$loggable;
        client_max_body_size 20M;
        limit_except GET {
            auth_basic "NGINX Plus API";
            auth_basic_user_file /etc/nginx/.httpasswd;
        }
        api write=on;
        allow 10.0.0.0/8;
    }
    location /dashboard.html {
        root /usr/share/nginx/html;
    }
}

map $status:$request_method $loggable {
    ~^[23]:GET  0;
    default 1;
}
```

Figure 10.1: *if=condition example*

```
access_log /var/log/nginx/apiaccess.log api if=$loggable;
```

Here, the request is logged only if **`$loggable`** is 1 (that is, if the status code is 5xx or 4xx). Otherwise, Nginx skips logging that request.

Common Log Variables

The following table explains the variable included in the log format string. These variables capture details about the client, request, response, upstream timings, and security information.

	Variable	Description
1	`$remote_addr`	The client's IP address that made the request.
2	`$remote_user`	The username provided by HTTP Basic Authentication, if any.
3	`$time_local`	The local time and date on the server when the log entry was made.
4	`$request`	The full HTTP request line (e.g., GET /index.html HTTP/1.1).
5	`$connection`	A unique connection number assigned by Nginx, incremented for each new TCP connection.
6	`$connection_requests`	The number of requests made over this particular connection so far.
7	`$pid`	The process ID of the Nginx worker process that handled the request.
8	`$request_uri`	The requested URI (path and query string, if any) without the host name.
9	`$status`	The HTTP status code returned to the client (e.g., 200, 404, 500).
10	`$body_bytes_sent`	The number of bytes sent to the client (excluding the response headers).
11	`$http_referer`	The "Referer" header from the client's request, indicating the page that linked to this resource.
12	`$scheme`	The request scheme (http or https).
13	`$http_user_agent`	The user agent string sent by the client's browser or tool.
14	`$http_host`	The Host header from the client's request, indicating which domain was requested.
15	`$host`	The host name of the server handling the request. If not specified by the client, it uses the server's name.
16	`$request_method`	The HTTP method used in the request (e.g., GET, POST, PUT).
17	`$request_length`	The length of the request (including request line, headers, and body) in bytes.
18	`$request_time`	The total time taken to process the request, in seconds, from reading the first byte of the request to sending the last byte of the response.
19	`$upstream_connect_time`	The time it took Nginx to establish a connection to an upstream server.

20	`$upstream_header_time`	The time between establishing an upstream connection and receiving the first byte of the response header from the upstream server.
21	`$upstream_response_time`	The time taken to receive the full upstream response (header and body) after the connection was established.
22	`$http_x_forwarded_for`	The "X-Forwarded-For" header, showing the originating IP of the client if the request passed through proxies or load balancers.
23	`$gzip_ratio`	The compression ratio achieved if the response was compressed by Nginx.
24	`$ssl_protocol`	The SSL/TLS protocol used (e.g., TLSv1.2, TLSv1.3) for encrypted connections.
25	`$ssl_cipher`	The cipher suite used in the SSL/TLS connection.

***Table 10.3**: log variables*

All these variables are most logged variables and that give a comprehensive view of each request's details, performance, and security context.

Let us do an example analysis of a **`access.log`** entry.

Suppose you see these entries in **`access.log`**:

```
203.0.113.10 - - [10/Dec/2024:14:35:10 +0000] "GET /login HTTP/1.1" 200 612 "-" "Mozilla/5.0"
203.0.113.10 - - [10/Dec/2024:14:35:11 +0000] "POST /login HTTP/1.1" 401 30 "https://example.com/login" "Mozilla/5.0"
```

***Figure 10.2**: access log entry*

From these two lines, we learn that:

- The client at 203.0.113.10 accessed the /login page successfully (200 OK). And the type of request made by the client was GET from 5.0 version of Mozilla browser.

  The subsequent POST to /login returned a 401 Unauthorized error. If users are complaining about not being able to log in, this clue suggests authentication failure for the client. By correlating times and client addresses, we can further investigate whether this is a user problem, a configuration issue, or something else.

Putting It All Together

Step 1. Define a format

```
log_format custom '$remote_addr "$request" $status $request_
time';
```

Step 2. Use it in **`access_log`** directive

```
access_log /var/log/nginx/access.log custom;
```

Sample Nginx Configuration

```
http {
    log_format  main  '$remote_addr - $remote_user [$time_local] '
                      '"$request" $status $body_bytes_sent '
                      '"$http_referer" "$http_user_agent"';

   log_format custom '$remote_addr - $remote_user [$time_local] '
                 'connection:$connection '
                 'connection_requests:$connection_requests '
                 'pid:$pid '
                 'remote_port:$remote_port '
                 'host=$http_host '
                 'virtualserver=$host '
                 'url=$request_uri '
                 'method=$request_method '
                 'args:$args '
                 'request_length=$request_length '
                 'status="$status" bytes_sent=$bytes_sent '
                 '$body_bytes_sent '
                 '$http_referer '
                 'useragent="$http_user_agent" '
                 'ua="$upstream_addr" '
                 'us="$upstream_status" '
                 'rt="$request_time" '
                 'urt="$upstream_response_time" '
                 'uct="$upstream_connect_time" '
                 'uht="$upstream_header_time" '
                 'xff="$http_x_forwarded_for" '
                 'pipe:$pipe ';

    # default Nginx access log with main log_format
    access_log  /var/log/nginx/access.log  main;

    server {
        listen 80;
        server_name example.com;
   # custom Nginx access log with custom log_format
        access_log  /var/log/nginx/example.log  custom;
        # Additional server directives
    }
}
```

Figure 10.3: *Sample Nginx Configuration*

Error Logs

If Nginx encounters issues such as configuration errors, it writes them to the error.

log. For example, if Nginx fails to start or suddenly stops working, checking the error.log should be our first step.

Sometimes we may see warnings **[warn]** recorded in error.log file. While a warning does not necessarily mean there is an immediate problem, it could signal a potential issue that might become serious later.

Configuring Error Logs

By default, Nginx has an **error_log** directive that sets the path and level of detail (log level) for error messages.

The directive description for **error_log** is:

Syntax	`error_log file [level];`
Default	`error_log logs/error.log error;`
Context	`main, http, mail, stream, server, location`
Example	`error_log  /var/log/nginx/error_log  crit;`

***Table 10.4**: error_log directive*

The '**file**' argument defines the path of the log file.

The '**level**' argument defines the severity level of the log event to be recorded. By default, only log events with a severity level of ***error*** are recorded.

For example, `error_log  /var/log/nginx/error_log  crit;` sets the severity level of error messages to be logged to crit.

Further, the **error_log** if defined in the http context implies that the error log for all the virtual host will be available in a single file.

Note: *It is also possible to record error logs for all the* **server_block** *(virtual host) separately by overriding the* **error_log** *directive in the server context.*

In some situation, you might want to disable the error log. To do that, set the log file name to **/dev/null**.

```
error_log /dev/null;
```

Nginx Error Log Severity Levels

Error logs can be categorized with different log levels representing different priorities and severity. Here is the list of all the available levels:

- **debug:** Highly verbose, includes detailed internal processing.
- **info:** General informational messages, not used frequently.

- **notice**: Normal but significant events.
- **warn**: Potential issues that are not necessarily errors but should be heeded.
- **error**: An error that prevented a request from completing successfully.
- **crit**: Critical issues that often require immediate attention.
- **alert**: Very severe problems that need urgent fixing.
- **emerg**: The server is essentially unusable or in a catastrophic state.

In this hierarchy, debug is considered the highest priority, which means if we set debug as the chosen level, Nginx will also capture logs from every other level. For instance, if we set the log level to error, it will also include events labeled as crit, alert, and **emerg** (emergency).

Using Error Logs for Troubleshooting

When faced with server-side errors such as 502 Bad Gateway errors, checking the **error.log** often gives immediate clues. For instance, we might see:

```
2024/12/10 14:35:20 [error] 1234#0: *10 upstream timed out (110: Connection timed out) while connecting to upstream,
client: 203.0.113.10, server: example.com, request: "GET /api/v1/data HTTP/1.1", upstream: "http://127.0.0.1:8080/data",
host: "example.com"
```

Figure 10.4: *error.log clues*

From this message, we learn:

- The upstream server with **IP 127.0.0.1:8080** took too long to respond.
- A request to **/api/v1/data** triggered the timeout.
- The client **203.0.113.10** experienced this issue at a specific time.
- The DNS name is **example.com**

This information allows us to investigate the upstream application, network conditions, or Nginx server resource constraints causing delays.

Correlating Error and Access Logs

A failed request in the access log with **status=500** indicates a problem but does not explain why it failed. The error log may contain a corresponding entry that reveals the root cause which could be a timed-out upstream server, a missing file, or a permission error. By reviewing logs in tandem, we can link symptoms in access logs with causes in error logs.

Strategies for Correlation

In many logging scenarios, it can be challenging to connect information from access logs and error logs to form a full picture of what happened during a particular request. We may ideally try to trace back with time stamp and unique log information but that may not always be correct.

However, Nginx offers a unique and powerful way to correlate these logs. The Nginx variable that enables this is the **`$connection`** variable.

The **`$connection`** variable represents a unique number assigned to each TCP connection Nginx handles. As a request comes in, Nginx logs this $connection number in both the access and error logs. This creates a direct link between both the logs that would otherwise be difficult to associate especially if multiple requests and errors occur simultaneously.

Because **`$connection`** remains constant for the entire lifecycle of a connection, it provides a reliable "**`thread`**" that we can follow. If we see an error logged with connection:12345 in the error log, you can look up **`connection:12345`** in the access log to find the corresponding request details.

Figure 10.5: *Error.log and access.log*

This capability is learned solely from personal experience and extensive hands-on troubleshooting. It is a feature we might not find explained in the internet or other Nginx books.

Conclusion

Nginx logging is a vital component of managing and optimizing our web server. Its flexible logging system–comprising access logs, error logs, and customizable formats–empowers us to monitor traffic, diagnose issues, and enhance performance through detailed insights. By effectively leveraging these logging capabilities, we can quickly pinpoint bottlenecks, detect anomalies, and fine-tune our configurations to meet evolving demands. As we continue to refine our Nginx setup, we must remember that a robust logging strategy is not just about recording data; it is a proactive tool for ensuring reliability, security, and an exceptional user experience.

CHAPTER 11
Performance Enhancements

Introduction

Modern web infrastructures demand servers that can handle enormous workloads with minimal latency. The COVID-19 pandemic accelerated the shift to online services, transforming the way companies, educational institutions, and consumers operate. In just a few short months, the world embraced a digital-first approach–driven by the rise of remote work, the explosive growth of e-commerce and contactless services, increased media consumption, and the rapid adoption of telemedicine. This transformation underscores the critical importance of performance enhancements in NGINX to meet today's high-demand, high-availability requirements.

Structure

In this chapter, we will dive into various strategies and configurations to boost Nginx's performance, covering:

- Speed Matters More Than Ever
- The Role of Nginx in the New Normal
- Configuring Worker Processes and Worker Connections
- Keepalive Connections
- Nginx Buffers
- OS Tuning (CPU Cores, Hard, and Soft Limits)

Speed Matters More Than Ever

With everyone relying heavily on web-based services, **site performance** has become business-critical. Slow-loading pages or unresponsive services are not just inconvenient–they can result in lost revenue, poor user experiences, and damage to brand reputation. Several factors highlight why speed has become a top priority:

- **User Expectations:** The bar has been raised for digital experiences. Users now demand near-instant page loads, seamless video streaming, and quick response times.
- **Competition and Choice:** With more services going online, consumers have abundant alternatives. A slow website can push users directly to a competitor's faster site.
- **Search Engine Rankings:** Major search engines such as Google factor page speed and user experience into their ranking algorithms. Faster websites tend to rank higher and attract more organic traffic.
- **Global User Base:** As businesses expand to serve customers in multiple regions, latency and network inefficiencies become more pronounced. This can further slowdown response times for users far from a hosting location.

The Role of Nginx in the New Normal

Nginx stands out as a leading solution for delivering the **scalability and speed** required in this hyper-connected post-COVID era. Nginx excels at this challenge due to its event-driven, asynchronous architecture.

- **High Concurrency Model:** Its asynchronous, event-driven architecture allows Nginx to handle massive spikes in traffic with minimal slowdown.
- **Flexible Reverse Proxy Capabilities:** Nginx's built-in load balancing and caching features ensure that busy sites can distribute traffic efficiently and reduce latency, maintaining strong performance even under heavy loads.
- **Easy Integration with Modern Stack:** Whether you are running microservices, containers, or cloud-based platforms, Nginx is highly adaptable and integrates well with a variety of modern technologies.
- **Security and Reliability:** As more business moves online, so do security threats. Nginx offers features such as SSL termination, rate limiting, and integration with Web Application Firewalls (WAFs) to help protect high-traffic websites.

However, simply installing Nginx and letting it run with default settings often leaves optimization opportunities unexplored.

Configuring Worker Connections

As discussed in the first chapter, Nginx is built on an event-driven, non-blocking model. Typically, it spawns a single master process and multiple worker processes. The master process reads the configuration file, manages worker processes, and handles signals (for example, to reload the config or shut down). Worker processes do the "**real work**" of handling client requests.

- **Master Process**: Maintains global settings, monitors worker processes, and handles system signals.
- **Worker Processes**: Handle network connections asynchronously, allowing each worker to manage thousands of concurrent requests.

Best Practices

- **Match or Slightly Exceed CPU Cores:** A common rule of thumb is to align worker processes with the number of CPU cores. Some workloads benefit from having as many workers as cores; others might benefit from additional workers if hyperthreading is effective in your environment.
- **Load Testing:** Benchmark different worker counts to see which configuration yields the best throughput. More workers are not always better; too many can cause overhead from context switching. (Context switching in an operating system involves saving the context or state of a running process so that it can be restored later, and then loading the context or state of another process and run it).

Configuring Worker Connections

Each worker process can handle a specific number of simultaneous connections, defined by the **worker_connections** directive. Example:

```
worker_connections 1024;
```

Because each client typically consumes one connection (not accounting for keepalive or multiplexing scenarios), this number effectively caps the maximum concurrency per worker. To serve a large number of concurrent users:

1. **Increase worker_connections:** For example, **worker_connections 8192** (1024 × 8, where 8 is the number of CPU Core, discussed in *Chapter 1, Introduction to Nginx*); if you handle thousands of clients simultaneously.

2. **Check OS Limits:** Ensure your operating system allows enough open files (detailed discussion on OS Tuning). If the OS limits are lower, setting **worker_connections** higher won't help and you may need to increase the OS hard and sift limits.

Keepalive Connections

Nginx keepalive directive allow multiple HTTP requests to be sent over a single TCP connection, reducing the overhead of establishing a new connection for each request. One crucial optimization that often goes overlooked is the **HTTP Keepalive** feature (also known as persistent connections). Let us first begin with understanding how HTTP requests work.

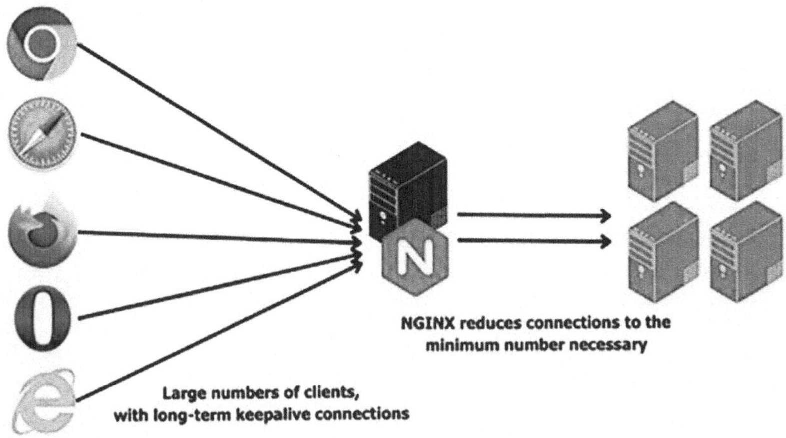

Figure 11.1: *NGINX Acting as an HTTP Proxy and Streamlining Client Requests*

Traditional HTTP Connection Model (Non-Persistent)

By default, older HTTP/1.0 behavior would open a separate TCP connection for every individual request and response. This meant if a web page referenced 50 images, the browser had to initiate 50 separate connection handshakes–leading to a slow user experience, especially on high-latency networks.

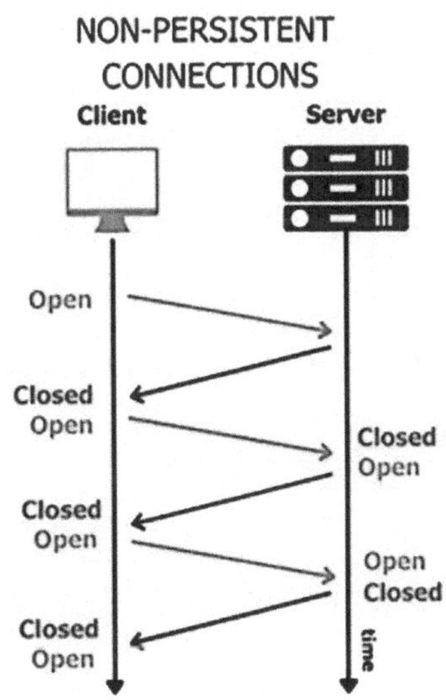

Figure 11.2: *Non-Persistent HTTP Connection*

Persistent Connections (Keepalives)

With HTTP/1.1, the specification introduced **persistent connections**, commonly known as "**`Keepalives`**." The idea is simple: after fulfilling a request, the server keeps the TCP connection open for a certain amount of time, allowing the client to send subsequent requests without the overhead of creating a new connection.

- **Reduction in Latency:** Reusing the same TCP connection avoids repeated round-trip times for connection setup and tear-down.
- **Resource Efficiency:** Because fewer total TCP connections are created, servers and networks handle less overhead in terms of CPU, memory, and networking resources.

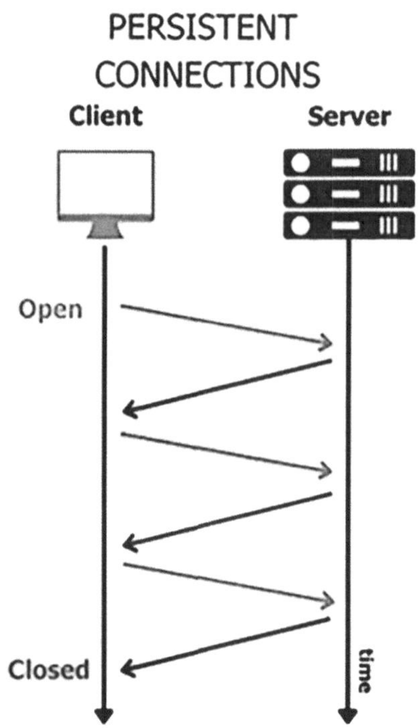

Figure 11.3: *Persistent HTTP Connection*

Why Keepalives Matter

In an age where every millisecond can impact user satisfaction, keepalives are a low-effort, high-impact performance improvement. They are especially beneficial for sites with multiple assets (CSS, JavaScript, images) that must be fetched in quick succession. By reducing the network chatter involved in establishing new connections, overall load time drops, and the browsing experience feels smoother.

Configuring Keepalive in Nginx

Let us first understand the important keepalive directives.

- **`keepalive`**

Syntax	`keepalive connections;`
Default	–
Context	`upstream`
Example	`Keepalive 15;`

***Table 10.1**: keepalive directive*

Keepalive directive defines the maximum number of connections to upstream servers.

The **`keepalive 15;`** line means that Nginx will keep maximum number 15 idle open to the backend server for reuse. This helps to improve performance by avoiding the overhead of repeatedly establishing new connections for subsequent requests.

If there are more connections than this number, Nginx may close some of the idle connections to maintain the specified limit.

- **`keepalive_requests`**

Syntax	`keepalive_requests number;`
Default	`keepalive_requests 1000;`
Context	`upstream`
Example	`keepalive_requests 500;`

***Table 10.2**: keepalive_requests*

- **`keepalive_requests`** directive defines how many requests can be served on a particular connection before it is closed.
- **`keepalive_requests 500;`** means that Nginx will serve 500 requests over a connection.

Note: *When using load balancing methods other than the default round-robin method, it is necessary to activate them before the keepalive directive.*

- **`keepalive_ timeout`**

Syntax	`keepalive_timeout timeout;`
Default	`keepalive_timeout 60s;`
Context	`upstream`
Example	`keepalive_timeout 90s;`

***Table 10.3**: keepalive_ timeout*

This directive will define the time till when the server will keep an idle connection open.

- **`keepalive_timeout 90s;`** defines the server will keep the idle connection to upstream server alive for 90 seconds before closing it.

Example Configuration:

```
http {
    .
    .
    .
    keepalive_timeout 65;
    keepalive_requests 100;

upstream backend {
    server backend1.example.com;
    server backend2.example.com;
    keepalive 32;
}

server {
    listen 80;
    server_name example.com;

    location / {
        proxy_pass http://backend;
        proxy_http_version 1.1;
        proxy_set_header Connection "";
    }
}
}
```

Figure 11.4: *keepalive_timeout*

In the preceding example, 32 keepalive connections to will be kept open per worker to each backend **`backend1.example.com`** and **`backend2.example.com`**.

- The server will wait 65 seconds of inactivity before closing the connection.
- The maximum 100 requests will be allowed per keepalive connection.

Choosing Appropriate Values

- **Time versus Resource Usage:** A longer `keepalive_timeout` can improve user experience for clients that frequently make multiple requests. However, if too many connections remain idle, memory and socket resources can be tied up unnecessarily.

  Best Practice: Set the `keepalive_timeout` to a moderate value. A very high timeout might keep connections open longer than necessary, consuming resources, while a very low timeout reduces the benefit of reuse.

- **Security Considerations:** In some environments, extremely long-lived connections can raise security or compliance questions, especially if an idle user session remains open. Balance performance gains with security policies.

Performance Benefits and Metrics

- **Reduced Latency and Faster Page Loads**

  Because each connection can handle multiple resource requests, end users benefit from fewer connection negotiations. The savings are particularly noticeable when:

  - Users connect from high-latency networks.
  - Sites with many static assets (images, CSS, JS).
  - Repeated AJAX calls or REST API requests in Single-Page Applications (SPAs).

- **Lower CPU and Memory Load**

  Every TCP handshake requires CPU cycles. By keeping connections open longer, you reduce the handshake frequency. This optimization can be especially beneficial under heavy loads or high concurrency situations.

Monitoring Key Metrics

- **Connection Reuse Rate:** How many requests per connection on average? A higher number means more benefit from keepalives.
- **Idle Connection Count:** Ensure Nginx and the OS are configured to handle a spike in idle connections if keepalive timeouts are relatively long.
- **Response Time and Throughput**: Tools such as JMeter or other load-testing suites can help measure real-world performance improvements.

Nginx Buffers

Nginx allocates buffers for incoming requests (client body buffers) and outgoing responses (proxy buffers). Proper buffer tuning can drastically affect memory usage, response times, and how much data spills to temporary files on disk.

Common Buffer Directives *(explained in detail in Chapter 2, Get Started with Nginx Configurations)*

- **`client_body_buffer_size`**: Sets the size of the buffer for reading client request bodies (e.g., form submissions).
- **`proxy_buffer_size /proxy_buffers/proxy_busy_buffers_size`**: Control how data from upstream servers is buffered in memory before being sent to clients.

  Note: *While larger buffers can reduce disk writes, they also consume more* RAM. *If you handle thousands of concurrent connections, each requiring large buffers, you might risk exceeding the available memory. So, you need to tune these parameters iteratively and observe system metrics* (CPU, *memory,* I/O) *while running multiple load tests to find the right balance.*

OS Tuning

File Descriptor Limits (Hard and Soft): When Nginx handles incoming connections, each open connection (socket) uses a file descriptor. By default, many Linux distributions cap file descriptors at 1024 per process, which becomes a bottleneck once traffic grows beyond a few hundred or thousand simultaneous connections. These limits are restricted using the following parameters:

Hard versus Soft Limits

- **Soft Limit:** The immediate, enforced limit on open files for a **`user/process`**.
- **Hard Limit:** The upper boundary to which you can raise the soft limit. (This setting can be typically changed only by the root user or via system configurations)

If your soft limit remains 1024 and you try to set **`worker_connections 16384`** in **`nginx.conf`**, the system cannot open more than 1024 sockets–leading to the most common seen error on very large traffic websites - "**`too many open files`**" errors.

How to Raise Limits

- **Edit `/etc/security/limits.conf`**

  ```
  (nginxuser) soft nofile 65536
  (nginxuser) hard nofile 65536
  ```

  Replace **`nginxuser`** with the user running Nginx (for example, **`richa_garg`** or **`serviceaccount`** running the nginx process), ensuring both soft and hard limits are set to a higher value, such as **`65536`**.

- **Configure `/etc/sysctl.conf`**

  ```
  fs.file-max = 2097152
  ```

  This increases the system-wide maximum of open files to 2,097,152. Apply it via **`sudo sysctl -p`**.

- **Verify**

  ```
  ulimit -n
  ```

  Make sure it matches or exceeds your desired **`worker_connections`**.

Note: *While raising file descriptors is vital for handling large numbers of simultaneous connections, each connection still uses memory and CPU resources. Always test carefully (e.g., with load-testing tools) to confirm your hardware can handle the new limits.*

Hence by aligning your file descriptor configuration with Nginx's **`worker_connections`** setting, you ensure the server can efficiently manage high-traffic loads without running into connection or resource errors.

Bringing It All Together

Step-by-Step Optimization Workflow

1. **Assess Baseline Performance:** After the initial Nginx configuration is set up, run a baseline test using any performance measurement tool, such as Jmeter. Measure the current throughput, latency, and resource usage with default Nginx settings.
2. **Tune Worker Processes and Connections:** Once we have the **`baselinem`**, we can align the number of workers with CPU cores, and raise **`worker_connections`** to handle expected concurrency.
3. **Enable Keepalives**: Enable keepalives to reduce the overhead of repeated TCP/SSL handshakes for both client and upstream connections.
4. **Optimize Buffers**: Increase or tweak buffers to reduce disk writes, while watching overall memory consumption.
5. **OS-Level Adjustments:** Raise file descriptor limits, consider CPU affinity, and tune network parameters.
6. **Use JMeter for Validation:** For each preceding step, we need to continuously measure the impact of each change by running standardized performance tests. We can compare metrics such as average response time, throughput, and errors to confirm real improvement.
7. **Iterate and Document:** Keep a record of the changes you make and the resulting performance. This practice ensures reproducibility and helps you roll back if a tweak negatively impacts other parts of the system.

Conclusion

HTTP Keepalives are a simple yet highly effective way to improve web performance. By letting clients and servers reuse TCP connections for multiple requests, you can reduce latency, lower CPU overhead, and enhance the user experience—especially for websites loaded with numerous assets.

As with all optimizations, the key is balance: excessive idle connections can strain system resources, but carefully tuned keepalives often yield substantial gains. By understanding how persistent connections work, configuring them properly in Nginx, and verifying the impact through load tests, you can ensure your site consistently delivers fast and efficient service to its users. In the next chapter, we will learn several ways Nginx can help protect your site and keep it running smoothly.

CHAPTER 12
Security with Nginx

Introduction

Imagine a malicious attacker is trying to break into your website with thousands of automated requests–perhaps through an AI-bot generating countless username-password permutations. What happens next? Very quickly, your server becomes overwhelmed, your network bandwidth clogs, and precious CPU and memory are squandered on illegitimate traffic. Real users who try to access your site start experiencing slow load times or error messages. Essentially, your site's performance suffers–and so does your reputation. How do you mitigate such threats? The answer is security. This chapter will show you several ways Nginx can help protect your site and keep it running smoothly.

Structure

In this chapter, the following topics will be covered:

- Rate Limiting
- Nginx Rate Limiting Algorithm
- Nginx Rate Limit Directives
- Understand Bursts and Nodelay
- Two Stage Rate limiting
- Restricting Access by Geographical Location
- Securing HTTP Traffic to Upstream Servers
- Securing TCP Traffic to Upstream Servers

Rate Limiting

One powerful yet frequently misunderstood feature of Nginx is **rate limiting**. In simple words, ratc limiting sets a cap on how many HTTP requests a single user can make over a certain span of time–whether it is a quick **GET** for your homepage or a **POST** on a login form.

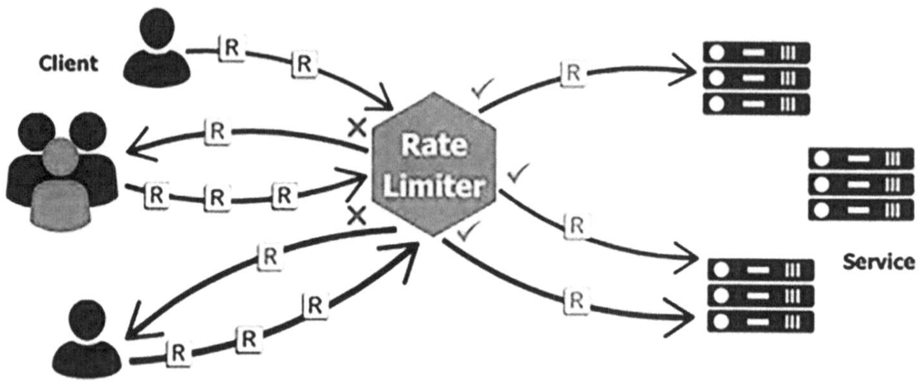

***Figure 12.1**: Rate Limiting*

Rate limiting has several important uses, including:

- **Security:** It slows down brute-force password-guessing attempts by limiting how quickly attackers can make guesses.
- **DDoS Protection:** By capping the rate of incoming requests at typical user levels, you can block suspiciously high traffic and log the URLs under attack.
- **Preventing Overload:** It helps ensure your backend services are not buried under too many simultaneous requests.
- **Restricting IPs:** Allow or block specific IP addresses to prevent suspicious hosts from connecting.

In this upcoming section, we will explore the basics of NGINX rate limiting and look at some advanced setups. **The concepts and configurations work the same way in Nginx and Nginx Plus.**

Nginx Rate Limiting Algorithm

Nginx rate limiting is based on the leaky bucket algorithm, a concept commonly used in telecommunications to manage bursts of traffic under limited bandwidth. Imagine a bucket with water poured in at different rates while water steadily leaks out from the bottom. If water flows in faster than it drains, the bucket eventually overflows.

Translating this to request processing:

- Incoming Requests are like water poured into the bucket.
- The Bucket itself is a queue where requests wait, managed in first-in, first-out (FIFO) order.
- Leaking water represents the steady rate at which requests leave the queue and are processed by the server.

- Overflowing is what happens when too many requests arrive too quickly, causing extra requests to be discarded (never reaching the server).

By controlling the rate at which requests "**leak**" from the bucket, NGINX keeps your server from getting overwhelmed by sudden surges in traffic.

Nginx Rate Limit Directives

The **limit_req_zone** sets up a shared memory zone, essentially a small in-memory "**bucket**" where Nginx tracks request rates per key (often the client's IP).

- **limit_req_zone**

Syntax	limit_req_zone key zone=name:size rate=rate [sync];
Default	-
Context	http
Example	limit_req_zone $binary_remote_addr zone=mylimit:10m rate=10r/s;

***Table 12.1**: limit_req_zone*

In the preceding example, **$binary_remote_addr** is the key that uniquely identifies the client IP for each request. The **zone=mylimit:10m** names the shared memory zone **mylimit** and allocates 10 MB of shared memory for tracking client states. The **rate=10r/s** indicates a maximum of 10 requests per second will be accepted for this zone.

- **limit_req**

Syntax	limit_req zone=name [burst=number] [nodelay | delay=number];
Default	–
Context	http, server, location
Example	limit_req zone=mylimit burst=20 nodelay;

***Table 12.2**: limit_req*

The **limit_req** directive applies the rate limit to a specific server or location block setting the shared memory zone and the maximum burst size of requests. If the rate of incoming requests exceeds the rate configured for a zone, their processing is delayed. Excessive requests are delayed until their number exceeds the maximum burst size in which case the request is terminated with an **error 503 status code** (https://nginx.org/en/docs/http/ngx_http_limit_req_module.html#limit_req_status). By default, the maximum burst size is equal to zero.

```
http {
    limit_req_zone $binary_remote_addr zone=mylimit:10m rate=10r/s;

    server {
    listen 80;
    server_name www.example.com;

    location /api/ {
        limit_req zone=mylimit burst=20 nodelay;
        proxy_pass http://backend_server;
    }
}

}
```

***Figure 12.2:** Example Configuration*

In the preceding configuration, a shared memory zone named **`mylimit`** is defined reserving 10 MB for tracking request rates.

`$binary_remote_addr` is a key used here for rate limiting to identify a unique client. **`Rate=10r/s`** specifies that 10 request per second will be accepted in this zone.

Please pay extra attention to the next section

How is the request distributed over a span of 1 second?

Nginx tracks requests at millisecond granularity, so this limit, that is, 10 r/s corresponds to 1 request every 100 milliseconds (ms). How 100 ms?

We know, 1 second = 1000 millisecond. So these 10 request is distributed over a span of 1000 milliseconds. 1 request will be executed in 1000/10 millisecond, that is, 100 milliseconds. **This means that a request is rejected if it arrives less than 100ms after the previous permitted one.**

Understanding Bursts and Nodelay

This section explains Bursts and Nodelay parameters.

Burst

In the preceding section, we learned that Nginx tracks requests in milliseconds. If the rate is 10 r/s, this indicates that the 1 request every 100 ms will be permitted. What if the requests arrive too quickly? Let us say, Nginx receives request at the rate of 20 r/s, that is, 2 request within 100 ms of each other? For the second request, Nginx will return status code 503 to the client. This will lead to too many 503 errors, as requests to an application is very unpredictable. Instead, we can buffer any excess requests and service them in a timely manner. This is where the burst parameter in **limit_req** helps.

For example, if 21 requests hit the server simultaneously, Nginx immediately processes the first request and queues the remaining 20. It then sends one request from that queue to the upstream server every 100ms. If a 22nd request shows up while the queue is still full (holding 20 requests), Nginx returns a 503 (Service Unavailable) because there is no room left in the queue.

```
+------------------------------+
| New Request Arrives          |
+--------------+---------------+
               |
               v
 Is Queue Slot Available?
   (burst limit not exceeded)
               |
  +------------+-------------+
  |                          |
  v                          v
Forward Request          Return 503 (Queue Full)
Mark Slot as "Taken"
(slot frees after 100ms)
```

Figure 12.3: *Understanding Bursts*

In the preceding example configuration, we defined **burst=20** in the **limit_req** defined in the location **/api/** block. This means, any request that arrives sooner than 100ms after the previous one is put in a queue, and here we are setting the queue size to **20**.

```
+----------+          Request #1 -> [Immediate to Upstream]
| Incoming |          Requests #2-21 -> [Queued in Burst (slots 1..20)]
| Requests | --->   Request #22 -> [Rejected with 503 if queue is full]
+----------+
```

Figure 12.4: *When burst is 20*

Nodelay

Using burst on its own helps control traffic smoothly, but it can make the site slow. In the example, if there are 20 requests in the queue, and 1 request is served every 100 seconds, and 10 request in 1 second, the 20th request in the burst queue will not be served until 2 seconds. Practically this is not possible and healthy for any website.

To fix this, we can add the **`nodelay`** parameter alongside burst, which lets Nginx forward requests right away as long as there is room in the queue, instead of spacing them out over time.

When we add nodelay parameter, Nginx still keeps track of extra requests in a queue (based on burst setting) and respects the same rate limit, but it does not slow each request down on purpose. Instead, if a request shows up sooner than the rate limit allows, Nginx immediately sends it on if there is a free slot in the queue. That slot remains taken for 100ms (if your rate is 10r/s), and then it becomes available again.

If 21 requests arrive at the same time and your burst queue is 20, Nginx sends all 21 right away. It marks **`20 "slots"`** in the queue as occupied, then frees them one by one every 100ms. If 4 more requests arrived instantly, it would allow 0 of them and return 503 for all 4, because the queue is still full.

After 101ms, only 1 queue slot has been freed, so if another 20 requests arrive at that moment, Nginx can only send 1 and rejects the remaining 19. If instead 501ms had passed—freeing 5 slots—then 5 of those new requests get forwarded immediately while the rest get 503.

Two-Stage Rate Limiting

Starting with **Nginx 1.15.7**, we can use a **two-stage rate limit** to give browsers a bit more flexibility when loading multiple resources at once, but still throttle excessive traffic. You enable two-stage rate limiting with the **`delay`** parameter in the **`limit_req`** directive.

Here is a simple example where we set a rate limit of **5 requests per second**. A typical page on this site loads **4–6 resources**, with a maximum of 12. Our configuration allows a burst of up to **12 requests**, but handles them in two stages:

1. **The first 8 extra requests** (set by **`delay=8`**) go through immediately, with no delay.
2. **The next 4 extra requests** (up to the total burst of **`12`**) are held back so we don't exceed 5 requests per second.
3. **Any requests beyond 12** are rejected.

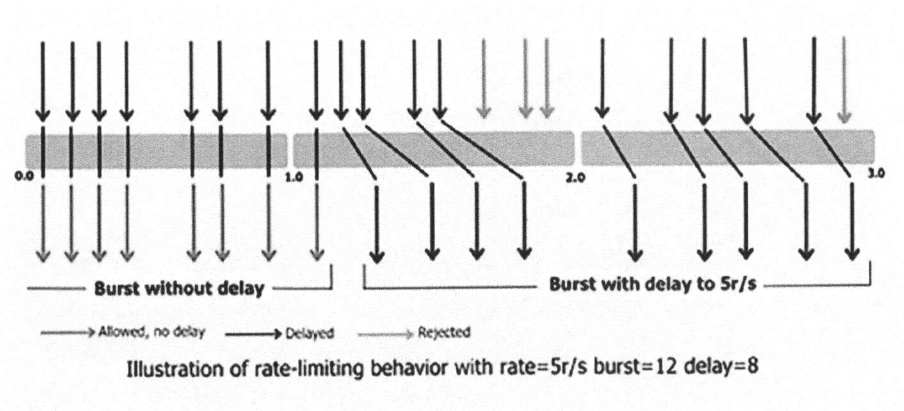

***Figure 12.5**: Illustration of Rate-Limiting Behavior with rate=5r/s, burst=12, and delay=8*

Can we define multiple `limit_req` and `limit_req_zone`?

Yes, we can have multiple **`limit_req`** and **`limit_req_zone`**. Let us understand how it is done with the following example.

Let us say you only want to rate-limit traffic from IP addresses **not** on an "**`allowlist`**."
Imagine you have two sets of users:

- **`Allowlisted IPs`:** These are trusted ranges that you want to allow more requests from (for example, internal corporate networks).
- **Everyone Else:** This might be the public whose request rates you want to cap more strictly.

```
geo $limit {
    default 1;          # By default, apply the rate limit
    10.0.0.0/8 0;       # These IP ranges are allowlisted
    192.168.0.0/24 0;
}

map $limit $limit_key {
    0 "";
    1 $binary_remote_addr;
}

http {
    # Create one zone for the public (5 requests/s)
    limit_req_zone $limit_key zone=req_zone:10m rate=5r/s;

    # Create another zone for allowlisted IPs (15 requests/s)
    limit_req_zone $binary_remote_addr zone=req_zone_wl:10m rate=15r/s;

    server {
        listen 80;
        server_name example.com;

        location / {
            # 1) Rate limit for everyone else
            limit_req zone=req_zone burst=10 nodelay;

            # 2) Rate limit for allowlisted IPs
            limit_req zone=req_zone_wl burst=20 nodelay;

            proxy_pass http://backend;
        }
    }
}
```

Figure 12.6: *Example Configuration*

How It Works

1. **Allowlisted IPs** do not match the first zone (**`req_zone`**) because **`$limit_key`** is an empty string for them (as per the **`geo/map config`**). They **do** match the second zone (**`req_zone_wl`**), so they get up to **15 requests per second** (with a burst of 20).
2. **Non-Allowlisted IPs** match **both** zones. Why?
   a. They match **`req_zone`** because **`$limit_key`** is set to their IP.
   b. They also match **`req_zone_wl`** because it uses **`$binary_remote_addr`** (the client's IP).

Note: *When a request matches two rate limits, Nginx uses the stricter one. Here, 5 requests per second is stricter than 15, so those IPs are effectively capped at 5 requests per second.*

Restricting Access by Geographical Location

This directive allows Nginx to assign values to a variable based on the client's IP address. This is most used to identify the geographical location of a request, but you can also tailor it for custom IP classification–such as **allowlists**, **denylists**, or specific network ranges.

- **geo**

Syntax	`geo [$address] $variable { ... }`
Default	–
Context	`http`

Table 12.3: *geo*

```
http {
    geo $country {
        default                "OTHER";             # Default for all unlisted IPs

        192.168.0.0/24         "LOCAL";            # Example subnet
        203.0.113.0/24         "CORP";             # Another subnet
        198.51.100.0/24        "PARTNER";          # A partner network
    }

    server {
        listen 80;
        server_name example.com;

        location / {
            # Possibly use $country in a condition
            if ($country = "CORP") {
                # Special handling for corporate traffic
            }

            proxy_pass http://backend;
        }
    }
}
```

Figure 12.7: *Example Configuration*

Use Cases

- **Geo-Blocking or Geo-Redirects:** If you integrate with a GeoIP database, you can block requests from certain countries or redirect users to region-specific content.
- **`Allowlisting and Denylisting`:** Restrict sensitive endpoints (e.g., admin panels) to traffic coming from a safe subnet.
- **Rate Limiting by Region:** Combine geo and **`limit_req`** to apply more aggressive or lenient rate limits based on the source IP's geographical designation.
- **Traffic Routing:** If you operate multiple datacenters, you can direct traffic from specific regions to the nearest server block for better performance.

Zone Sharing During Rate Limiting

In **NGINX Plus**, **`zone_sync_server`** and **`zone_sync`** are directives used to **synchronize shared memory zones across a cluster of NGINX Plus servers**.

This ensures **all nodes have the same view** of things like rate-limiting counters or sticky session data which is super useful in a **load-balanced environment**.

This is especially helpful when you have **multiple NGINX Plus instances (servers)** and want to **synchronize in-memory states** including:

- Rate limiting zones (**`limit_req_zone`**)
- Key-value zones (**`keyval`**)
- Sticky sessions
- Custom shared zones

Let's walk through **each directive**, explain what it does, and provide helpful context with examples.

- **`zone_sync`**

Syntax	`zone_sync`
Default	–
Context	`server`

Table 12.4: *zone_sync*

This **enables zone synchronization** on the instance.

It tells NGINX that it should synchronize zone data (such as rate limits, sticky session info, keyval data, and more) with one or more sync servers.

Think of this as a **global switch** – you must turn it on before configuring more details.

- **`zone_sync_server`**

Syntax	`zone_sync_server address [resolve];`
Default	–
Context	`server`

Table 12.5: *zone_sync_server*

Defines the **address and port** of the **remote server** to sync zones with.

- The address can be a domain or IP.
- The resolve flag tells NGINX to **dynamically resolve DNS** so it can respond to changes (like load balancer updates or DNS failover).
- **Example**: `zone_sync_server example-g2-nginx.com:9000 resolve;`

Syntax	`zone_sync_buffers number size;`
Default	`zone_sync_buffers 8 4k|8k;`
Context	`server, stream`

Table 12.6: *zone_sync_server*

Sets the **number** and **size** of buffers used to process zone sync data.

- **Example**: `zone_sync_buffers 512 4k;`
  where, 512: number of buffers and 4k: size of each buffer.
- Bigger values = more memory = better performance with high-frequency updates or many zones.

This is like tuning how much NGINX can "*hold in memory*" when reading sync updates before applying them.

- **`zone_sync_connect_retry_interval`**

Syntax	`zone_sync_connect_retry_interval time;`
Default	`zone_sync_connect_retry_interval 1s;`
Context	`server, stream`

Table 12.7: *zone_sync_connect_retry_interval*

Defines how long NGINX waits before retrying a failed connection attempt to the sync server.

- **Useful in unstable networks**: Set low for fast recovery, high to reduce CPU usage.

- If a sync server goes down, this controls how fast NGINX tries to reconnect.
- **Example**: `zone_sync_connect_retry_interval 100ms;`

Syntax	`zone_sync_connect_timeout time;`
Default	`zone_sync_connect_timeout 5s;`
Context	`server, stream`

***Table 12.8**: zone_sync_connect_retry_interval*

Sets the connection timeout for sync connections – how long NGINX waits for a response when trying to establish a connection to the sync server.

- **Example**: `zone_sync_connect_timeout 100ms;`

Syntax	`zone_sync_interval time;`
Default	`zone_sync_interval 1s;`
Context	`server, stream`

***Table 12.9**: zone_sync_connect_retry_interval*

This controls how often **changes** to zone data are **sent** to other nodes.

- Lower = more frequent syncing (more consistent, higher CPU/network)

  Higher = less frequent (less load, possibly stale state for a bit)
- **Example**: `zone_sync_interval 100ms;` NGINX will check for and send delta updates every 100ms.

Syntax	`zone_sync_timeout timeout;`
Default	`zone_sync_timeout 5s;`
Context	`server, stream`

***Table 12.10**: zone_sync_connect_retry_interval*

This defines the **maximum time** NGINX waits for a response to a zone sync update before considering the operation failed.

- Think of this like a "*network timeout*" for actual sync data.
- **Example:** `zone_sync_timeout 100ms;`

Sample Example

You have 3 NGINX Plus nodes in a cluster. One acts as the **sync server**, others as clients. You want **fast global rate limiting sync** and can tolerate a bit of extra memory/ network usage.

All clients use:

```
stream {
    resolver 10.8.8.8 valid=1s;
    server {
        listen 9000;

        zone_sync;
        zone_sync_server example-zonesync.nginx.com:9000 resolve;

        zone_sync_buffers                  512 4k;
        zone_sync_connect_retry_interval 100ms;
        zone_sync_connect_timeout          100ms;
        zone_sync_interval                 100ms;
        zone_sync_timeout                  100ms;
    }
}
```

***Figure 12.8**: Sample Example*

HTTP Traffic to Upstream Servers

When Nginx acts as a reverse proxy, it typically sits between external clients and your internal "*upstream*" servers—such as application servers or microservices. While HTTPS can protect data in transit between a client's browser and Nginx, the traffic between Nginx and upstream servers is often left unencrypted. If those servers are not located on a fully trusted network, there is a risk of eavesdropping or man-in-the-middle attacks.

Configuring TLS (SSL) to Upstream Servers

1. **Server Certificates:** Each upstream server needs its own TLS certificate. Depending on your environment, you might use self-signed certs or a private Certificate Authority (CA).
   You can also create your own internal CA with an OpenSSL library and generate the certificate. The server certificate together with a private key should be placed on each upstream server.

2. **Certificate Validation:** Nginx can verify the upstream certificate against a trusted CA bundle. If the certificate is invalid or expired, Nginx closes the connection rather than sending data unprotected.

3. **Server Name Indication (SNI):** If multiple HTTPS services run on the same IP address, Nginx can include the requested hostname in the TLS handshake (using `proxy_ssl_server_name on;`), ensuring the correct certificate is used by your upstream.

Let us first look into some important directives that will be used in the next session.

- **`proxy_ssl_certificate`**

Syntax	`proxy_ssl_certificate file;`
Default	–
Context	`http, server, location`
Example	`proxy_ssl_certificate  /etc/nginx/client.pem;`

Table 12.11: *proxy_ssl_certificate*

This directive specifies the cert *file* and its path with the certificate in the PEM format used for authentication to a proxied HTTPS server.

- **`proxy_ssl_certificate_key`**

Syntax	`proxy_ssl_certificate_key file;`
Default	–
Context	`http, server, location`
Example	`proxy_ssl_certificate_key  /etc/nginx/client.key;`

Table 12.12: *proxy_ssl_certificate_key*

This directive specifies the key *file* with the secret key in the PEM format used for authentication to a proxied HTTPS server.

- **`proxy_ssl_trusted_certificate`**

Syntax	`proxy_ssl_trusted_certificate file;`
Default	–
Context	`http, server, location`
Example	`proxy_ssl_trusted_certificate /etc/nginx/trusted_ca_cert.crt;`

Table 12.13: *proxy_ssl_trusted_certificate*

Specifies a *file* with trusted CA certificates in the PEM format used to verify the certificate of the proxied HTTPS server.

- **`proxy_ssl_verify`**

Syntax	`proxy_ssl_verify on | off;`
Default	`proxy_ssl_verify off;`
Context	`http, server, location`

Table 12.14: *proxy_ssl_verify*

This directive enables or disables verification of the proxied HTTPS server certificate.

- **`proxy_ssl_session_reuse`**

Syntax	`proxy_ssl_session_reuse on | off;`
Default	`proxy_ssl_session_reuse on;`
Context	`http, server, location`

Table 12.15: *proxy_ssl_session_reuse*

This directive determines whether SSL sessions can be reused when working with the proxied server. If the errors "**`SSL3_GET_FINISHED:digest check failed`**" appear in the logs, try disabling session reuse.

- **`proxy_ssl_protocols`**

Syntax	`proxy_ssl_protocols [SSLv2] [SSLv3] [TLSv1] [TLSv1.1] [TLSv1.2] [TLSv1.3];`
Default	`proxy_ssl_protocols TLSv1.2 TLSv1.3;`
Context	`http, server, location`

Table 12.16: *proxy_ssl_protocols*

This directive enables the specified protocols for requests to a proxied HTTPS server.

- **`proxy_ssl_ciphers`**

Syntax	`proxy_ssl_ciphers ciphers;`
Default	`proxy_ssl_ciphers DEFAULT;`
Context	`http, server, location`

Table 12.17: *proxy_ssl_ciphers*

This directive specifies the enabled ciphers for requests to a proxied HTTPS server. The ciphers are specified in the format understood by the OpenSSL library.

```
http {
    #upstream block
    upstream backend.example.com {
        server backend1.example.com:443;
        server backend2.example.com:443;
    }

    server {
        listen      80;
        server_name www.example.com;

        location /upstream {
            proxy_pass                      https://backend.example.com;
            proxy_ssl_certificate           /etc/nginx/client.pem;
            proxy_ssl_certificate_key       /etc/nginx/client.key;
            proxy_ssl_protocols             TLSv1 TLSv1.1 TLSv1.2;
            proxy_ssl_ciphers               HIGH:!aNULL:!MD5;
            proxy_ssl_trusted_certificate /etc/nginx/trusted_ca_cert.crt;

            proxy_ssl_verify        on;
            proxy_ssl_verify_depth  2;
            proxy_ssl_session_reuse on;
        }
    }

    server {
        listen      443 ssl;
        server_name backend1.example.com;

        ssl_certificate        /etc/ssl/certs/server.crt;
        ssl_certificate_key    /etc/ssl/certs/server.key;
        ssl_client_certificate /etc/ssl/certs/ca.crt;
        ssl_verify_client      optional;

        location /yourapp {
            proxy_pass https://url_to_app.com;
        #...
        }
}
```

Figure 12.9: *Example Configuration*

Securing TCP Traffic to Upstream Servers

When NGINX handles TCP-based protocols (for example, database connections, mail services, or custom TCP applications), you may still want an encrypted channel between NGINX and the upstream servers. This ensures end-to-end protection of data–not just between the client and NGINX, but also through to the final destination server.

NGINX Stream Module

For TCP (and UDP) encryption, you typically use the "**stream**" context in Nginx, rather than the "**http**" context (discussed in previous chapters):

```
stream {

    upstream backend {
        server backend1.example.com:12345;
        server backend2.example.com:12345;
        server backend3.example.com:12345;
    }

    server {
        listen      12345;
        proxy_pass  backend;
        proxy_ssl   on;

        proxy_ssl_certificate         /etc/ssl/certs/backend.crt;
        proxy_ssl_certificate_key     /etc/ssl/certs/backend.key;
        proxy_ssl_protocols           TLSv1 TLSv1.1 TLSv1.2;
        proxy_ssl_ciphers             HIGH:!aNULL:!MD5;
        proxy_ssl_trusted_certificate /etc/ssl/certs/trusted_ca_cert.crt;

        proxy_ssl_verify        on;
        proxy_ssl_verify_depth  2;
        proxy_ssl_session_reuse on;
    }
}
```

Figure 12.10: *Example Configuration*

Difference between ssl_certificate and proxy_ssl_certificate

When Nginx terminates SSL/TLS connections for clients (for example, on port 443), you use **ssl_certificate** (and **ssl_certificate_key**) in the server block. This certificate/key pair is what clients see when they connect via HTTPS.

proxy_ssl_certificate (along with **proxy_ssl_certificate_key**) is used upstream, when Nginx itself makes a secure (HTTPS) connection to another server. In other words, if Nginx is proxying traffic to an upstream server over TLS, and that upstream requires client certificates, then **proxy_ssl_certificate** is the certificate Nginx presents to that upstream server.

Here is the difference in a nutshell:

- **`ssl_certificate`**:
  - Placed in the server block to handle inbound connections from clients.
  - Identifies your server to the client.
- **`proxy_ssl_certificate`**:
  - Configured in proxy settings (e.g., location or upstream block) for outbound TLS connections to an upstream.
  - Identifies Nginx as a client to the upstream server.

Conclusion

Rate limiting is a critical feature that ensures our web applications remain robust, responsive, and secure under heavy traffic conditions. By carefully controlling the rate at which requests are processed, we can prevent overload, reduce the risk of denial-of-service attacks, and maintain an optimal user experience. As we have seen, Nginx offers flexible directives that let us fine-tune these limits to match our specific traffic patterns and resource constraints. Ultimately, effective rate limiting not only protects our infrastructure but also enhances our overall system reliability, making it an indispensable tool in our web server arsenal.

Index

M

N